Sean M_____,

May the Universe
come alive through
the pages of this
book

_____ _____

REPLICATING SPACE THEORY

SILVIO GONZALEZ

WESTBOW
PRESS®
A DIVISION OF THOMAS NELSON
& ZONDERVAN

WestBow Press books may be ordered through booksellers or by contacting:

WestBow Press
A Division of Thomas Nelson & Zondervan
1663 Liberty Drive
Bloomington, IN 47403
www.westbowpress.com
844-714-3454

All Scripture quotations are taken from the King James Version.

ISBN: 978-1-6642-5804-4 (sc)
ISBN: 978-1-6642-5803-7 (hc)
ISBN: 978-1-6642-5805-1 (e)

Library of Congress Control Number: 2022903016

Print information available on the last page.

WestBow Press rev. date: 3/16/2022

DEDICATION

I have been blessed with the greatest family in the universe.

Mom and Dad

My memories of you are as a sweet fragrance, wish you were here to see this book go to print.

Sister

Love you very much, promise this one will not give you a headache. I will include a bottle of aspirin along with the book.

To my children Lisi, Mr. David and Nano

You are the crown jewels of my life.

May God bless you, your children, and your generations to come.

ACKNOWLEDGMENTS

There are many people who have been instrumental in bringing this book to life. First, I would like to thank my publisher, Westbow Press for their attention to detail and their professionalism. I can't thank the readers of my first work enough. Their many questions served as a guide to choose the topics covered in this book. Lastly, I can't say enough about the care and expertise my friend and editor, Jeff Sterling, has poured into this book. Believe me when I say that without his grammatical and spelling expertise, this would be a very hard book to read.

CONTENTS

FOREWORD

Allow me to introduce the author, Silvio Gonzalez. I've been close friends with Silvio for 30 years but learned of his research and discovery of the cause of gravity, plus the 'nature of the universe' only recently. The Silvio I know works with mechanics, thermodynamics, modern farming and survival prepping. His interests are wide and seem to revolve around large hands-on projects. He's a people-person, with great love of God and family. So, I was surprised to learn why he was seriously delving into the mysteries and mechanics of the makeup of the universe.

I've been visiting Silvio's farm for years, and we staged scientific research projects in renewable energy. But lately we had been building and testing an electronic brain that would connect all aspects of his diesel-powered irrigation system to his telephone. Silvio had been talking to me about the universe for a couple of years when I was surprised to learn that he was writing a book.

Silvio encountered an understanding of the method that the universe employs to grow. He has extrapolated that to explain the mechanism for the growth of space, how that kind of growth causes gravity, how that kind of growth affects the speed of time, and how that kind of growth affects the size of the universe.

He doesn't need much conventional science to do it. After all, since the 1687 release of Newton's Laws of Motion and Gravity, astronomers and physicists haven't discovered much that can be proven about the birth and growth of the universe. There are theories and speculation, but "if they really knew what they were doing, they wouldn't call it research, would they?" (Attributed to Albert Einstein). Really, it's difficult to believe the old ideas once you've studied what Silvio has learned!

Until recently, my understanding of the make-up of the universe was probably similar to your own. We see the logic of Newton's Laws of Motion and Gravity, and we appreciate that Einstein discovered the relationship between matter and energy, and the speed-of-light stuff. We learn from television or YouTube about empty space, that Black Holes are out there, and that there are some discrepancies in the theories of the actual first billionth of a second of Creation. Add in the Big Bang theory, that the universe is expanding, and we're up to speed.

But Silvio Gonzalez is up to something totally new here. Silvio is describing creation differently, starting from its emergence. He proposes the theory of 'Replicating Space'. Replicating Space Theory explains exactly how and why the universe is expanding, and surprisingly, from where it is growing. Delving deeper in his second book, he applies Replicating Space Theory to all of the phenomena with which astronomers and physicists occupy themselves.

I think you will agree after reading this book that it's a bit of a shock to walk around possessing a better understanding of the origin of gravity than an academic astrophysicist. But don't worry. They'll catch up …. in a few decades.

Jeffrey Sterling

INTRODUCTION

Once again, I find myself in front of my computer, typing away with the goal of bringing to life a second book. Looking back, I don't remember ever thinking "I will write a book one day". Having written the first book, completing it and having seen it published, I was sure it would be my one and only book. After all, "There are three things each person should do during his life: plant a tree, have a child and write a book" (the great Cuban poet Jose Marti.)

Why are we here? This second book owes its existence to three things. Many of the readers of my first book, Let There Be Light, have asked me to further explain several of the concepts. Additionally, I have been encouraged by some, to write a second book. And lastly, I have completed new ideas based on those original concepts.

It is my hope that you have read my first work. Most of what you are about to read, either expands, clarifies or builds on the concepts introduced previously. You could say that this is what is missing from the story. I have real issues with my memory. I have read my own book three times to date, and have enjoyed all three readings, as if they were my first. It is evident that there was much I had thought about, but never wrote.

For the benefit of the reader who has not read my first book, let me give you a condensed introduction to yours truly. I'm but a simple farmer. My family was forced to flee into exile when I was just 11 years old. We left our native country of Cuba with the clothes on our backs and one extra set in a small suitcase. We arrived in our new country in 1971. Our new country has been one of the greatest blessings God has seen fit to bestow on our family. I will be eternally grateful for the opportunity to live in "the land of the free and the home of the brave".

I was always inquisitive, having the ability to question my elders to the point of being reprimanded for so many questions. If a man knows what has happened, he is a learned man. The goal of learning should go beyond memorizing information. Knowing why and how things happen is, in my opinion, more important than merely memorizing what happened.

We are born with an insatiable mind. Who has not seen a child pepper his parents with "why this", "what is that", "what does it do" or 'why does that look like that"? Unfortunately, after being told enough times to be quiet and to stop asking questions, most of us stop asking why. I suspect that, in most cases, children are asked to be quiet because they are exposing their elder's ignorance. I challenge all of you to never discourage a child from asking questions. If you do not know the answer, then show him how to find the answer, and you will have taught both him and you. Remember, non among us is all knowing, ignorance is universal.

At a very tender age, after making a little toy, I remember asking myself, "I built this, but who built all that?", referring to the world, of course. The universe is a great adventure. Never miss an opportunity to learn, wonder, dream and explore.

Our brain could well be the most wondrous and complex thing in the physical world. I dare to say that there are no two persons who have existed who are wired the same as anyone else. I learned with my own children that each one of them came prewired, and the best I could do was to tweak what they already possessed. I was once told by a good friend, Jeff Sterling, after admiring the qualities of a piece of Teflon, "It took 4 billion people to make that". I asked, "What do you mean?", and he responded, "It was developed only after we had enough different minds to contribute to its development". I say this because there are many who may not be interested in the content of this book. Not everyone is interested in the universe, per say. Being wired differently, not all of us share the same interests. As for me, it is just as important to know 'the why' of the universe as to know 'the why 'of me.

I repeat what I affirmed in my first book as to the yeast of these books. I do not claim these concepts as the product of my own understanding. I do not think it is possible for man to ever truly know the how and why of the universe. After all, in the absence of an observer, only he who did the deed can say how the deed was done. I have merely expanded on what I believe was given to me by our Creator. As you are about to learn, if you do not already know, we live in a universe of unimaginable size and wonder. We have been given, not ringside seats, but center of ring seats. No matter where or when you exist in creation, you will have a view from its center. The universe is the ultimate treasure hunt. As individuals, or collectively, we will never see and learn all there is.

So sit back once more in your easy chair, grab a cup of coffee or a tall glass of tea or lemonade, and enjoy a wild ride. This old farmer will take you on a guided tour of the true 'greatest show'. No, this show is not on Earth. The ring center seats are on Earth, but the venue is the universe.

CHAPTER 1

Universe: Did Science Get It Right?

F ULL DISCLOSURE. I have no formal training in any of the sciences. I'm a self-taught man. I do have a field and it is planted with tropical fruits. I'm but a simple farmer. Please note that what I state as the current scientific consensus is only my opinion. I try to find and distill, as best I can, an accurate and true consensus. If you have never tried getting an accurate picture of what science holds as true, I can tell you it is a fool's errand. You are faced with often needlessly complicated, vague and at times disingenuous statements, found on the websites of even the most prestigious universities. I think it goes to the very core of one of mankind's greatest ills, our inability to accept that what we believe could be wrong. To sum it up into one word: pride. Even when you think that a particular concept is indisputable, you find a statement or a paper from a well-known scientist that sends you screaming back to the beginning of the search for that elusive consensus. A word to the wise, once you do find consensus, please be aware that it could be partially or totally wrong. While it is true that in the multitude of counsel there is wisdom, if all the multitude is telling you the same thing, they are either all right or all wrong. The consensus issue is so much of a problem that scientists will agree with the statement, "We may never get to agree on anything to be 100 percent correct". Don't laugh, but even on this point, they don't all agree. This covers science.

As for the new concepts* I'm going to give you, they are my own, and in most cases, they are radically different, and never before heard, at least by me. Several readers of my first book expressed the need for citations. I need the reader to be aware that, regarding most of the concepts I will give you, there are no possible citations. They are not covered in any other book or published paper of which I'm aware. Great effort has been spent on making sure that the reader is made aware of the scientific consensus. It is entirely possible that you may find a concept which I claim as my own, that is well known and accepted as science. In those cases, it is due to the writer being ignorant of what science has claimed as fact. But please realize that if you find such conflict, it is legitimate ignorance on my part. Furthermore, it is a fact that I came to believe that concept because of my development of Replicating Space Theory*. Under Replicating Space Theory, space grows through regeneration. It does not simply expand by stretching. This spatial growth is the bedrock from which all the concepts in this book emanate.

Given the fact that the world is full of people and most people are full of ideas, we can conclude that most ideas are wrong. Or perhaps most people never make their ideas known. This could mean that Einstein was not the first to unravel relativity, but perhaps the first to be brave enough to write it for the world to see. I subscribe to the former. I think we generate a large volume of ideas on a daily basis that are plain wrong. How can we know that anything we come up with is right? Well, it helps to have someone to bounce your ideas off and get an opinion. But here I have a problem. These concepts are so radical that I know of no one with whom I can bounce these ideas. I'm sure that there is no shortage of capable men and women who can easily understand everything within this, and my first book. I just don't personally know any. I have no equipment to test any of these concepts. So here is what I have done. I have searched for the mysteries humanity still has. I have tried to answer any that remotely fit within the realm of these concepts. I have also tried to think of every possible problem in these concepts. So far, I found nothing that replicating space cannot answer. The universe no longer puzzles me. Things that distressed and puzzled me are a delight to see now. Does this mean that the universe has lost its sense of wonder for me? Absolutely not. A great wonder you do not understand pales in comparison to one you comprehend. Do I know the mysteries of the universe? How could I claim to know all the mysteries of the universe if I do not know what I ignore? One thing I can say. Those things that I know, I can say that I now know. Not that they exist, but why they exist, or at the very least, how they function. As a clarification, I, in no way want to minimize the great achievement of the dedicated men and women in science. We live in a world today of great convenience and incredible abundance, all derived from an incredible advance in the sciences. Case in point, this book itself is only possible because of the word processor and the advances in printing. Gone are the years of having to sell the value of your book to a publisher. Now through the advent of self-publishing, the publisher no longer keeps inventory, but prints on demand. This way, no large investment is needed upfront, making it possible for even simple farmers like me to publish their book.

Let us begin by giving you my condensed version of the scientific consensus of how the universe came to be. Please try to work with me. I'm trying to condense 13.8 billion years and countless thousands of scientific books and papers into one paragraph. If you want the full version of the chronology, do an internet search for 'chronology of the universe'. Hope you are a fast reader. You will get about 100 million hits. We will only be covering the current universe and inflation.

We begin with a singularity about the size of an electron. In this minute speck, all of the energy of the universe resides. For reasons unknown, that speck starts expanding. The initial expansion is of a magnitude so great, that it expands faster than light speed. Please understand that the term "the big bang" was actually a name given by an opponent of the theory, and it stuck. I have not found a single credible article or paper in which it is referred to as an explosion. Time and space begin at a point in this process, thought by science to be at the split millisecond when this expansion begins. Somewhere along the early timeline, matter is made by a process not yet fully known. Within this shrouded period, the inflationary epoch slows or stops. Why or how is unknown. We cannot see into this early period. Even though our space-borne telescopes can peer into the distant past, the first 370 thousand years or so, are opaque. The condensed soup, within this period, did not allow light, if it existed yet, to emanate from within. Within 200-500 million years, stars and galaxies start forming. At just 400 million years after the beginning, we see our first galaxy, GN-z11. From the location of GN-z11, all the way back to our vantage point, we see a universe populated by trillions of galaxies. For reasons unknown, matter is evenly spread out over an ever-expanding space. The even distribution of matter is said to be to an accuracy of 0.01%.

I don't know if what I consider logic and common sense is actually illogic and foolishness. I think we are all blind to our own biases and ignorance. For this reason, I will put before you my observations of what I see wrong with the picture that science paints for us. You can make up your own mind.

Let's start at the beginning. Where did the energy come from? How could energy, a physical, tangible thing, materialize into the nothingness* before the beginning? Please don't tell me it was the remnant of a previous collapsed universe. I hope none of you subscribe to that belief. Yes, belief. There is no proof, whatsoever, of such an event. Even if we entertain such a wild notion, it begs the question of where that other universe came from? What mechanism, prior to the existence of anything, caused the exact amount of energy to be introduced? Why exact? If we are to accept the current theory of the universe, the amount of energy had to be exact. Just a little more and the universe would never have coalesced. Just a little less, and the universe would have collapsed upon itself, or so we are told. At the point at which the placement of this exact amount of energy happens, time still did not exist. How can any process begin and progress without time? What would coerce such a massive speck of energy to start expanding when all of our observations, in the physical world, show the opposite? In the physical world, a concentration of mass only wants one thing: to stay together. Just take a look at a black hole. Once expansion begins at such an incredible rate, what puts on the brakes? How can there be fully formed galaxies within 400 million years of the beginning? Once matter formed, some of it collected and made galaxies. But why not just one giant galaxy? What neutralized gravity to allow matter to spread so evenly in the universe? If all matter was created early in the beginning, how can it be distributed so evenly? Why are the oldest galaxies smaller, when they had all the matter in the universe close and available, with which to build themselves? How can that same time and space expand for so long without rupturing? There are a total of 10 issues in this list of concerns. These, along with others, will be answered in the rest of the chapters.

With the introduction of self-replicating space in the next chapter and subsequent chapters, many of the great conundrums of modern physics and cosmology will melt away. Where is all the missing energy? Is dark matter and dark energy real, or is something else causing the effects on matter? Why the inflationary epoch? What caused it? If it is over, what effect did it have? If not over, what effect is it now having on the universe? What makes matter and how? Why the discrepancy in the different measurements of the expansion of the universe? What is really the cause of gravity? What is the cause of inertia and momentum? What explains action and reaction in propulsion? Why is spacetime relative? Why have we not succumbed to the Big Freeze, the Big Crunch, or the Big Rip?

CHAPTER 2

The Key, or Rosetta Stone

I T IS OF utmost importance that you understand the key or Rosetta stone. Just as its name implies, it is the key to opening the door to understanding the rest of the concepts. I will explain it in as many ways as I can imagine. Here is the key to understanding how this universe is even possible. I believe that space is not merely stretching. Space is growing. The true God particle resides in every point within created space. I have named it the Fountain Of God*. Its physical size is equal to that point in space that we theorize was present in the beginning of the universe. It is believed to be so small that it is called a singularity. You will learn that I do not believe in the existence of a singularity. But I would like to give you an idea of the size of the self-replicating energy quanta particle. This entity makes up everything within the universe. Let's get a glimpse of the micro world. Just how small is an atom? An atom, compared to an apple, is like an apple compared to Earth.

It is believed that there are more atoms in a glass of water than glasses of water in all the oceans. Let that soak through your mind. Have you understood it? I know some of you did not believe me and searched the net. Now that you have all accepted the statement, get ready - the other shoe is about to drop. As you will read later, Ernest Rutherford proved that matter is 99 percent empty. So, one percent of a glass full of solid atoms has more atoms than glasses of water in all of the oceans. But wait: this is not a bipedal. This animal has more than two shoes. Here is the next shoe to drop. An atom is incredibly large compared to the particles that make them up. The atom (meaning 'unable to cut') was proposed by Greek philosopher Democritus in 400 BC. It was not until the 1800's that physicist J.J. Thomson proposed a model for the atom. Thomson's discovery of the electron proved the existence of the atom.

The atom, however, was proven not to be elementary or irreducible since it was found to contain electrons, protons and neutrons. But the electron is the only particle considered elementary out of those three. The protons and neutrons are made up of quarks. These quarks are in the same league with the electrons. As it now stands, quarks and electrons are the elementary particles in an atom. They come in at around a billionth of a billionth of a centimeter. Is this the end? Are quarks and electrons the actual elementary particles: the smallest building blocks of matter? Not really. There are many other elementary particles. There are also a great number of non-elementary particles. There are so many that they are too numerous to list here. For a time, it was joked that the Nobel Prize winner should be the scientist who went a full year without the discovery of a new particle. If you want to learn more, look up the standard model.

If I seem a bit dismissive as far as particles are concerned, you are right. I think it is possible that we are making new particles in labs: particles which do not exist, nor have ever existed. No, I'm not insane. Remember, the universe is all energy. By rearranging that energy, I don't think there is a limit to how many particles can be created. However, I think the Fountain Of God particle, or energy quanta, is the only elementary particle. I believe it is actually the one and only fundamental building block. There are currently many different known fields in physics, they are made up of individual particles. These fields are the construct or matrix where the physical manifests itself. I equate them to my field where my trees grow and give fruit. But all these fields are, in my opinion, overlaid onto the elementary field of spacetime. The closest thing to God's Fountain would be the graviton. If this entity was real and responsible for gravity, it would also be a field. The name Graviton does not do it justice, since it restricts its identification to gravity.

As you are learning in this book, the Fountain Of God makes up everything we see. If I'm correct, the Fountain Of God is the first and only elementary entity. I do not accept that any of the current known fields can be considered elementary. I think there is nothing elementary outside of the quanta particle I have called God's Fountain. I have concluded that all that is in existence in this physical universe, is made of this energy quanta. It is the one and only true God particle or quanta. It is irreducible and indivisible. Its primary manifestation is spacetime. The emergence of spacetime is a direct result of the emergence of physical reality from the replication and movement of this entity. It is indivisible/irreducible being composed of nothing but energy. It replicates in 3d, creating spacetime at the speed of light.

These tiny quanta particles, or more likely, self-replicating energy fountains, are doing today what one single specimen began doing 13.8 billion years ago. It is duplicating itself, emerging from a place yet unknown to us. It seems logical to me that it emerges out of its predecessor. Once the first Fountain of God emerged, all of the ingredients of the universe were present within it. They are responsible for what we have called Quantum Fluctuations. I think these fluctuations keep temperature in spacetime. The nature of the growth of space gives spacetime a constant infusion of energy to keep the universe from the Big Freeze, The Big Crunch or The Big Rip. I believe, as unfathomable as it sounds, that this God Particle has the ability to duplicate itself with no further energy input required.

It replicates by making an exact copy of itself. Being irreducible, it cannot merely divide. It makes an exact copy of itself. Within the realm in which this particle exists, the nature of spacetime and the laws of physics are still a great unknown. You can dismiss the previous statement as just ignorance on my part, but you would be wrong. At the quantum level, our accepted normal gives way to abnormal. Our intuitive reasoning is useless: our logic and common-sense melt away right before our eyes.

There have been few days darker for science and for our country than October 21, 1993, when Congress cancelled the superconducting super collider. The SSC, for short, may have been able to peer into the occurrences in the mysterious realm of the smallest of the small. This monstrous machine would have been housed in a tunnel 87.1 kilometers long. Its energy would have been 20 tev per proton. Compare that to the current record holder, the European Large Hadron Collider. Its tunnel is 27 km, with 6.5 tev per proton. There is always the possibility that even the largest SSC we could ever build would not give us the answers. As I understand it, we accelerate known particles to smash them head-on at close-to-light speeds. But how can we ever hope to accelerate that which amounts to the smallest thing in the universe?

I have now come to believe that this God Particle, this self-replicating packet of energy, is physical reality itself. I believe that within the observable universe, relativity maintains physical reality's cohesion. In those regions outside of the reach of information, physical reality is maintained through quantum entanglement. Even if we could identify this God particle, we could never accelerate it to smash it. It would be as if we were fish and we tried to accelerate water from within water. Water for a fish is its medium. It cannot separate water from water. Its lab would be full of the medium. No testing is possible. It's funny but when I picture a universe full of this energy field, it looks like a fluid. This fluid, made of energy, would have waves just like the ocean. For us, testing replicating space is even more complicated than a fish testing water. You see, it is self-replicating, and already moving away from itself at light speed. And, it is smashing into itself at light speed. This interaction is key to a functioning universe. The best that we can dream of doing is to accelerate a particle to light speed. But, you see, that is already happening in this universe. To test replicating space, it would need to be propelled beyond light speed. But how can you separate spacetime from itself in order to crash them together?

There is an obvious question a lot of you must be asking, so let's get an answer. What is the shape of the Fountain of God quanta particle? At this point, we have all the shapes we can imagine as possible shapes for this energy fountain. Stop right here and pick your shape.... Many of you have probably already decided on a shape that is frequently on the news. To you it's a string. Others have envisioned the elementary building block of creation as a circle or loop. Then of course some prefer more creative shapes like diamond shape, squares or perhaps even an Icosahedron. I know that a small group of you have settled on the great disnub dirhombidodecahedron. I fell in love with this shape myself. If I was a younger man, then that is the shape I would assign to the Fountain Of God quanta particle. Being too old to allow romanticism to rule over logic, I cannot agree with this choice. The allure of the great disnub dirhombidodecahedron is that we can envision this shape replicating itself from every one of the prongs. I'm afraid that I only see one possible shape for the Fountain of God. It is definitely a sphere. Here is why I believe it must be a sphere. Any shape other than a sphere would not give us a seamless smooth Arrow Of Time. In the case of a string, it is long and narrow. Clearly, there would be inconsistencies in any timeline created by a string. A loop can be reshaped, and it is flat, which is two-dimensional thinking. These dimensionally caused issues would plague all other irregular shapes. Including the others mentioned: diamond, square, icosahedron, and let's not forget the stunning great disnub dirhombidodecahedron. A sphere of solid energy* cannot be divided nor compressed any further. I cannot stress enough how important this is. This is the one and only elementary particle. Its shape and size are the pattern that everything else is made from. A sphere will also give us a smooth replication into any area, regardless of demanded flow. This shape, then, would give us what we see in our observation: a smooth and seamless Arrow Of Time, even when transitioning due to a time dilation. Spacetime is not a wall. Spacetime is a four-dimensional fabric. At any given point, locality can demand a change in flow. It is also imperative that each point in space have the capacity to give you the ability to move in any direction you chose. Only a sphere can, in my opinion, give you such an ability. If I was forced to pick a descriptive name for spacetime, it would not be an easy task. When dealing with something so foreign, our language is just not up to the task (especially with my language skills). Here comes my best effort. Spacetime can be best described as a reticulating energy fabric.

The Fountains Of God cannot be flexible, reducible, dividable nor compressible. They create a field which is a matrix of spacetime itself. The Fountains are space. The flow is time. Space and time emanate, as the Fountains replicate. Time, however, does not flow past the locality from where it emerged. If it did, then the flow of time would be unilateral, and by consequence, reversible. Time only washes over you locally. If time flowed with space, then it would be cumulative. When an observer looks at you over great distances, he does not really see your past. He is not witnessing what is occurring. He is witnessing a reflection of that which already occurred. His existence may or may not be in your future. By the time he sees your reflection, you may no longer exist. Spacetime emanates from every point. As you travel, or more accurately, flow with space, the faster you travel the less spacetime can emanate from you. Theoretically, if you travel at light speed, then time stops for you. This is because you do not spend enough time in one place for time to wash, not over you, but, more accurately, out of you. Yes, you understood it right. Do not think of time moving with space, and washing over you like a river. Space moves as a river, while time emanates from within you as a spring. Wow! A fountain.

Perhaps you remember my wild speculation about lightning, in my first book. I proposed the idea that lightning was actually an area of super low pressure in spacetime: that the tremendous amount of energy passing through the atmosphere was parting spacetime. The collapse or reunification of a column of spacetime vacuum makes thunder. There is another bread crumb that leads us to a possible solution of the mystery that is thunder and lightning. As a farmer, I know that lightning gives rain its nitrogen content. Does lightning fix nitrogen to the rain merely by the huge electric discharge? Or can it be possible that the collapsing wave fronts of spacetime energy fix the nitrogen to the rain? The Haber process uses 12,000 psi and 800°F to convert nitrogen ($N2$) into ammonia, to manufacture fertilizer and explosives. This is how I think lightning fixes nitrogen to the rain. I think the electric discharge of a lightning bolt supplies the heat. A space analogous to an elongated black hole is created and the collapsing wavefronts of space time supply the pressure to fix nitrogen compounds to the rain.

By now, the learned ones are ready to throw this book out the window. But, if you fellow-farmers and lay people will allow me, then I will clarify something for them. This is not a return of the steady state model. I do not subscribe to an eternal or infinite universe. But I do believe that both theories have part of the truth, but neither are all true. Out of the two, the Big Bang is closest to reality. But as is often the case with divorce, neither side is completely right nor completely wrong. There was a beginning and an inflationary epoch, but the entire energy of the universe was not present in the beginning. I do not accept that you can start with a fixed energy value and end up with a stable, expanding relative universe.

How can I prove that this self-replicating entity exists? Let's pull out all the stops and bring every possible argument to bear. If we fail here, the entire book has failed. I lack a particle accelerator and state-of-the-art scientific test equipment. Fortunately, both you and I possess the greatest tool man will ever have. It is the human brain. The brain, which we could call 'hardware' is perhaps only outmatched by our 'operating system'. Have you heard of artificial intelligence? Well, the operating system that runs our brain is much more than AI. We are SA (self-aware). Our operating system creates or manifests a separate and distinct entity for each of us. We see ourselves as unique in the universe, and we are right. There are many things we physically possess which are unique, just to us as individuals. We will discuss them all before I write the last page in this book. For now, I want to highlight your brain, because that is what I will use to bring this concept home to you. I will use those things that you already know, and have observed firsthand, to make this concept come alive.

Why am I sure that spacetime is the cause of gravity, and that it is replicating? It is common sense, once you really know what you know. Here are the known facts. We know for a fact that speed affects time, regardless of direction. Gravity affects time. Gravity is a 'push' toward Earth. The energy of spacetime rushing in toward Earth is pushing you to the surface. Gravity increases closer to its source. We know that time slows closest to a gravitational source. Is the picture clear to you? What? Don't you have a mental sharpie? Can't you connect the dots? If you accelerate through spacetime, then time slows. If spacetime accelerates through you, like in a gravitational field, then time slows. It can't be any other way, due to relativity. The evidence leads you to a sole conclusion: the medium is replicating from every point in space. If the medium, that is, spacetime, were merely expanding from a central point, then time and gravity would vary with direction. For example: if you're familiar with the Space-Time-Twin-Paradox, the twin who leaves Earth on a fast spaceship returns to find that he has aged less than his brother who remained on Earth. The astronaut brother traveled at high speed into space and returned to Earth, and yet his clock was slower. This would not be possible if spacetime flowed unidirectionally. If spacetime flowed unidirectionally, then a person standing on a planetary body, facing the inflow of spacetime, would feel gravity while the person on the opposite side of the planet would feel negative gravity. But it's not. It's omnidirectional.

Our observation of the universe also confirms replication. Our telescopes see the universe as a sphere. We see the same distance outwardly in every direction. Light must be traveling from us and to us equally in all directions. Spacetime accelerates into a gravity well through acceleration of replication. This, however, is highly localized in light of the vast distances in the universe. How localized? Well, Isaac Newton taught us that every time the distance doubles between two bodies, the gravitational force is diminished by a factor of 4. So, as you get further from Earth, gravity diminishes. The other thing that diminishes is the time dilation. Why? It's simply because spacetime is no longer accelerating toward the gravity well. As spacetime is left to its own normal effects, equal emergence of spacetime from each central point in space creates the fastest clock. For most readers, the last sentence went under the radar. Some understood it but are rejecting its true meaning. Yes, you understood it correctly, I believe that replicating spacetime makes, and by consequence controls, the speed of the passage of time. But we have no time to discuss time in this chapter. Time will be revealed in due time in Chapter 7: What Is Time? As tempting as it may be for you to skip to chapter 7, please stay the course. Great time and mental treasure have been spent by this old farmer to lay out the concepts in proper order. Each chapter builds your ability to comprehend the next chapter.

Gravity is caused by differences in the flow of spacetime. This, however, brings us to the realization that gravity is energy. If gravity is a flow of energy, then gravity has mass. There we go again. Each time I assign an attribute to anything physical I must remind you that everything in the universe is energy. There is nothing but energy. Matter has an obvious mass because it is compressed energy. Why wouldn't gravity, a concentration of energy in motion, have mass? We, on Earth, live under a sea of energy in the form of gasses. These gasses are held to the surface by the power exerted by a constant inrushing sea of energy. This concentrated flow exhibits a force proportional to its flowrate. What in the universe does this mean? How does this affect the reality of universal cohesion? How does this energy fabric contribute to the expansion, acceleration and cohesion of the universe? If spacetime energy had no mass, then the acceleration would have been never-ending. You may ask, "Why can't it continue to accelerate outward?" You must factor in expansion through replication from every point in space. The expansion is cumulative over distance. This fact is not exclusive to replicating space. If space was merely stretching, this acceleration would also hold true. Under a given expansion rate, bodies must move in proportion to their distance. An object twice as far must be moving twice as fast. After expanding for billions of light-years, what would the speed be? This, however, is self-limiting through spatial pressure*. There came a time when the mass of the cumulative spacetime already in existence could no longer be pushed any faster. This, I believe, coincided with the emergence of light, time and physical reality itself.

All that exists physically not only exists within spacetime, but it's made up of the same energy in varying forms of density. It should be clear; space does replicate and grow from every point at the speed of light in every direction. It was possible, in the beginning, to maintain such a speed. However, as the universe grew, it reached the point where the outward growth could not continue accelerating. This created the spatial pressure that allowed light to become visible, and by consequence, created time. Spacetime still replicates and travels outwardly from every location at the speed of light. There is good reason why it does not expand the universe cumulatively at the speed of light, from every point. Upon clashing with itself, the created pressure can only propel the expansion of spacetime at the current rate of 44 miles per second per mega parsec.

I do not accept that all the energy required for the universe could have been present in that tiny speck in the beginning. If we did not have it there in the beginning, I see only two possibilities. Either it has been gradually added as the universe has grown, or the speck in the beginning did not house all the energy yet had the capacity to replicate itself without any further energy needed. I must confess I'm torn between both choices. Science has already proven beyond a doubt the existence of quantum fluctuations in a vacuum. I believe the energy seen is not the Fountain Of God. But it is the result of this Fountain in the act of creating spacetime. Incredible! It is the appearance of energy in a vacuum, not out of thin air, but seemingly out of nothing. We can claim that the evidence of quantum fluctuations supports either possibility. Since both choices would produce the same results, as far as spacetime is concerned, let me pick one. The winner is an energy entity with the ability to replicate itself without any energy added: self-duplicating energy. How it gets done, while important and interesting, is not a deal breaker. This energy entity is of a size which, I believe, we will never have the detection equipment to observe. It is the sole ingredient of the physical universe, including spacetime and reality itself.

The Fountain of God is the ingredient or building block of all the physical universe, including spacetime and physical reality itself. I can sense the visceral reaction from some of you. First, among the more learned, you could be wondering if I have ever heard of thermodynamics. Adding energy into a closed system is a no-no. Well, here I would like to make you aware of a little-known fact.

Science already accepts that space stretches, creating new, never before seen space. This space that somehow materializes comes with the same level of energy as found in the rest of space. They even have worked out how much energy is contained per given volume of space. Don't ask me how they rationalize new space coming into existence by stretching without diminishing the energy in the medium being stretched. These are not ignorant people. They can recite all the laws of nature. Why, then, don't they see their folly? It is a proven fact that all of space contains a base level of energy. Are you ready for the only explanation that I have found in which science explains this?

Science says that the law of conservation of energy is observed, considering that newly created space has the same level of energy as the rest. This is an observation I have seen in human nature. Depending upon your bias, you filter that which is before you. How else could an intelligent scientist claim that the total energy has not changed, merely because the energy level is the same per given volume of space? So, the total amount of energy is the same even if space doubles? And this, because the level is unchanged per volume? There is nothing to see here, it is what it is. Get over it. Let us insert an analogy to highlight this absurd belief. Let's say you had 5-hundred-dollar bills in your hands. I came and gave you 5 more-hundred-dollar bills. Now you have double the amount of hundred-dollar bills. Not only do you have double the amount of bills but double the amount of value. What would you say if I told you that since they are of the same denomination you still have the same amounts? That's right, you would be happy that you doubled your money, but you would know that I'm a few cards short of a full deck.

You readers are amazing. Some of you have realized that there is a white elephant in the room dressed in a checkered polyester suit with roller skates and dancing to jazz. According to science, then, the universe is not a closed system. According to science, new space emerges, or as they say, stretches from existing space, without breaking the law of conservation of energy! If that is their belief, then why can't the universe simply start from this same basis, expanding outward from one single replicating fountain? After all, according to science, thermal dynamics does not apply. I really think those scientists would like to add a caveat to the law of conservation of energy. It would read "this law does not apply to created space". Perhaps, it has already been added and we commoners did not get the memo. The amazing thing in this whole energy issue is this: spacetime does not merely stretch, it replicates. The effect, which science has already documented, is exactly what we would expect. If you replicate or copy something exactly, it will all be uniform. What a convenient turn of events! Science cannot credibly argue that replicating space violates the Law Of Conservation Of Energy. How could they, when they have already said it does not apply?

Let's begin with the large body of evidence to support replicating spacetime. Here, I would like to start with a little cosmic relief. In my old country, we have a reputation of being a bit vociferous, dogmatic and self-assured. My first evidence is 'it must be right because I tell you so". I have a feeling this first argument, other than getting a few smiles and perhaps a chuckle or two, will not sway anyone.

Let's continue. Let's play we are aliens. Let's make believe we just arrived in this universe from an alternate universe. We are a very ancient, advanced race, but our mode of transportation is limited to our consciousness, not our physical bodies. We can see energy directly, unlike Terrans, who only see the effects of energy. Upon our arrival, we see replicating space as an intertwined energy field or fabric. We record all we observe but we cannot experience gravity, motion, or the physical forces at work. We take our findings back to our universe and we convene a panel of our best minds. The major question to answer is "what effect does this energy fabric have on the inhabitants who physically live in this newfound universe?" It is speculated that since the energy field is replicating from every point in space, radiating and replicating in 3 dimensions, that, there was a beginning from a single point. Then, having concluded that there had been a beginning, we move on to the question of how this field affects the creatures. The observations prove that matter, a name given to entities made up of condensed or compressed energy, creates a time dilation. We observe that the energy fabric, which we have called spacetime, is diminishing in flow as it replicates from within matter. We come to realize that the reason why the Terrans stay on the surface of the ball of condensed energy we have called a planet, is that the inflow of energy is greater than the outflow. It is obvious that this difference in flow creates an acceleration causing the Terrans to be pushed onto the surface of the planet. We also decide that the inward acceleration maintains the atmosphere that these primitive creatures need to survive. It is obvious that those areas filled with a dense energy, which they call liquid water, derive their properties from this same acceleration in the spacetime fabric. We observe that the large satellite, which orbits this planet, affects the planet's acceleration of energy, and makes the water rise and fall in its banks. The meeting is adjourned for one of our days.

After a day, we reconvene to put the finishing touches on our report. The report concludes: "this newfound universe is radically different from our own. It had a beginning as a tiny speck of energy, that we have named a 'Fountain'. This energy multiplies at great speed and volume, as is evident from the dense cloudy rim region, seen at the edge of their universe. After a period of rapid expansion, the tremendous volume of energy could no longer maintain such a rapid doubling rate. Slowed by the mass of its energy, it created space, and time, which together make spacetime. This spacetime fabric, along with its flow characteristics, is responsible for gravity, the expansion rate of space, orbits, and all other movements seen within this universe. It is the finding of this panel that this universe, along with its beautiful inhabitants, is a great wonder of wonders." There you have it. An advanced alien race just agreed with me. Convinced yet? Some are not. Let's move on.

Do you agree that things which act in the same identical, predictable way are most likely caused by the same thing? Let's talk about gravity, centrifugal force and inertia. I contend that they are all the product of the same thing. An acceleration of spacetime.

Gravity. Spacetime does not only replicate in open space. It also replicates within matter. It is a proven fact that there is nothing solid. Look up Ernest Rutherford. He discovered that matter was not solid, but was, in layman's terms, 99 percent empty. He was so affected by his finding that when he awoke the next morning, he feared getting off the bed. Why he thought his bed was any more solid than the floor is anybody's guess. It makes total sense, if matter is not solid, spacetime also resides within it. There is a simple experiment that illustrates this perfectly. Take a drinking glass. Fill it completely with rocks. Is it full? Take fine sand and start putting sand in as you gently bounce the glass. When no more sand fits, is it full? No. You can add a lot of water to that full glass, so is it full? No. You can add 4% of the water volume as alcohol. Is it full? No. If this was a pressure vessel, you could pressurize it. I remind you that gas is matter. You might think that the vessel is now full, but you would be wrong. Science has proven that it is still 99 percent empty. The rocks, sand, and water cannot be compressed further, but they, themselves, are not really solid. They may seem solid, but they are mostly empty. The space between all of the nuclear components is empty.

At this time, you may be asking "Matter is not solid. So what?" There is a good reason why I would spend time trying to convince you that matter is not truly solid. Let me ask you a very revealing question. Wait. How can a question be revealing? When you are asked a question, you answer it, right? Well, when you formulate an answer, you do so from your own knowledge and beliefs. At that point, if the answer is in line with the questioner's belief, the argument is settled. Here is the question. What would happen to gravity if the Earth's matter was truly solid? Bingo! Gravity would literally go through the roof. This causes the difference in weight which we see in different items.

Who can argue, per given volume, that lead is not heavier than foam? Weight is gravity. A lead weight experiences the same weight, or 'push' toward Earth, as the planet experiences toward the lead weight. Now we should all realize why non-solid matter is so important in making for a life-sustaining universe. If a human being was materialized on the surface of a truly solid planet, what would happen? Let's think it through. The first thing we can imagine is that we would smear onto the planet's surface like a liquid. We would smear like a liquid, but in reality, at this point, we would be very solid. Yes, indeed, we would be compressed into a much more dense state of matter (more dense energy). All of our descriptive characteristics would vanish. We would, I believe, be transformed into an imaginary state which we have named 'solid energy'. Some of you are thinking, "What would happen to time?" Sorry, that is not for this chapter. Do not despair. It is covered in later chapters.

Back to porous matter. Matter does not warp or change space in any way shape or form. Matter does, however, warp or change time. This notion of warped space is truly Einstein's biggest blunder. I'm glad you are reading this and not hearing it in a lecture. Things like shoes, cell phones, tablets and even dentures would be flying toward me. I know that in science, disagreeing with Einstein is tantamount to touching the third rail. Let me make it very clear. Yes, I disagree with Einstein. I believe that the idea of warped space is a blunder. Warped space does not explain gravity. A time dilation explains gravity. Forget all those demonstrations you have seen, using bowling balls and trampolines. Never mind those illustrations of our planet warping the fabric of spacetime. All of those have one fallacy in common. They depict space as two dimensional. Space is three dimensional. But it is even more complicated than that. Space is not complete without time. Spacetime includes three dimensions of space and the one dimension of time. Spacetime, then, is four dimensional. Why would we reduce our demonstration of gravity to just two dimensions? Because as beings within spacetime, we cannot manipulate our medium. We, therefore, use gravity's two-dimensional effects to try to show a four-dimensional occurrence.

I have blasphemed the god of physics. I think a well-explained defense is in order. Why do I tell you that warped space is nonsensical? Here it goes. We have no way to prove that space can be warped. Gravity in no way warps space. There is no discernible difference in distances or characteristics of space. One mile of space close to Earth's surface is 5280 feet long, exactly the same as a mile in intergalactic space. Please quiet down and allow me to explain my point. I know for you learned ones; it is hard to hear a mere farmer dismiss Albert Einstein's assertion that gravity is created by warped space. I should remind you that he, himself, admitted to his biggest blunder. If you admit to your biggest blunder, then you are admitting to having committed more than one. We can, then, speculate whether the one he named was indeed his biggest. It's been a century since Einstein asserted that warped space gives us gravity. Mind you, in this century, man has advanced more than in all of his previous history. You would think that we should know, by now, what causes gravity. But in reality, no one has proven what makes gravity. We can detect no difference in the dimensions of space anywhere in the universe. We do detect a difference in the dimension of time. Space is set in stone. Time is set in bubblegum. We can, therefore, conclude that since space is fixed and time is relative, that time variation is the cause of gravity. So, a new phrase is in order to replace the space-warping nonsense. Matter tells time how to dilate; dilated time tells spacetime how to flow; and flow governs how matter moves. In no way do I challenge any of the observations or math behind the idea of warped space. I'm just telling you that warped space is not possible. Since there is no space warping, then something else must be responsible for our observation.

Before we leave Einstein's biggest blunder behind us, let me tell you what he, himself, said about it. The blunder was the addition of the cosmological constant to his field equations. He used the Greek letter λ (lambda). He used this constant to insert an expansive force in his field equations to balance the inward force of gravity. His goal was to balance both inward and outward forces to enable his equations to show a static universe. This static view of the universe was the consensus for much of the 20th century. Please do not expect that I will be explaining Einstein's field equations. I have no advanced math skills. I have truly tried to learn advanced math. But not having the memory needed and having to know the why before I can learn anything, I have failed and accepted defeat. I do not believe math is needed to realize that this was not Einstein's biggest blunder. Today, more than 100 years later, this old farmer is telling you that this was not his biggest blunder. This was one of his biggest insights. Without knowing it, Einstein inserted an expansive force in his equation that is a shoo-in for the outward force in replicating space theory. A small note to you naysayers who do not believe Einstein really confessed to his biggest blunder: I have read a few of the million results you get if you search the net. I have no doubt he said it. This proves again his incredible intellect, as well as his capacity to be wrong. He said he was wrong, when he was right. This, of course, meant that he was wrong, in his opinion of his opinion.

If matter were truly solid, then no spacetime could emerge from within it. If you stop the emergence of spacetime from any location, then that location has no time. If you stop time, you create a super low pressure in space. Since everything travels with space, then nothing can travel away from an area with no time. If space cannot replicate, then time cannot flow. The growth of space creates time. Therefore, the arrow of time cannot be reversed. If you reverse time, you immediately arrive at a time with no spacetime replication. This means you have arrived at a 'time with no time'*. How exciting! A lot of you get it. For those who do not get it, here is how time is dilated by matter. I hope everyone has accepted that matter is mostly empty. If you still think matter is solid, please put the book down. Do not waste any more of your time. You would be better served to use your time to attend a flat-Earther convention. OK, let the rest of us continue. Let's take Earth as an example. Earth is composed of matter. Matter is mostly empty but it is definitely partly solid. Spacetime has the ability to replicate and emerge from within the Earth. However, the spacetime that is in space is expanding at a different rate than the spacetime that is within matter.

Spacetime cannot emerge out of Earth in straight lines. Spacetime therefore emerges out of Earth in a zigzag* pattern. As spacetime zigzags out of Earth, it dilates time. It's simple. Anything zigzagging takes longer to get to the finish line than anything running in a straight line. This time dilation means that spacetime must accelerate into Earth. This acceleration creates the push we call gravity. This topic was covered in great detail in my first book, in Chapter 4 'Time Dilation and Terminal Velocity'. If you have any doubt on the concepts in the last few paragraphs, you would be well served to read my first book.

Allow me to ask you a question. What weighs more? A pound of lead or a pound of cotton? A few said, "the pound of lead". No, a pound is a pound no matter what it is made out of. How about this? What occupies less space? A pound of lead or a pound of cotton? The lead, of course. OK, then what would dilate time more? A trillion-ton ball made of lead or a trillion-ton ball made of cotton? I suspect the lead. I doubt if the cotton ball would show any meaningful gravity or time dilation on its surface. What makes the difference? Density. Intuitively, we may think that the smaller ball would just concentrate gravity. But in actuality, it is the time dilation difference that influences gravity. A clarification: I believe that a trillion-ton ball of cotton in outer space will compress over time in response to the slight time dilation it creates. This, I believe, is a must. We see cotton as very fluffy, but it is a solid. If gasses coalesce into stars, then we can't expect less from solids. But obviously, it will never turn as dense as lead. The reason is obvious. Lead was made under extreme gravitational pressure. That is something a trillion pounds of cotton cannot do. Back to the matter at hand. Why does a dense material create more gravity? More mass in a smaller area impedes the flow of spacetime. The denser the material, the longer it takes spacetime to emerge out of it. This literally means time is slower within matter. Here is a very simple way to look at it. Space is energy, matter is concentrated energy. Matter, therefore, is synonymous with space, since they are both energies. Yes, indeed, matter is a concentration of energy, which would make it compressed spacetime energy. If spacetime has a set speed of light speed, then how long will it take to traverse matter? Longer than empty space. This means that spacetime will be slower coming out of matter than running into matter. In this case, the term 'slower' is not a term of speed. The more exact meaning would be 'less flow', not slow spacetime. Since spacetime takes longer to emerge out of matter per given time, you get less volume of spacetime flowing out of matter. Less volume or flow of spacetime is synonymous with a time dilation.

The same thing that makes our universal view spherical, makes heavenly bodies round. The duality of spacetime (covered in Chapter 15) in any one spot in the universe creates a circle. Since spacetime is omnidirectional in its flow, it will flow inward from every direction into a sphere. Indeed, it is responsible for making the sphere in the first place. We now see more clearly. The lead weight represents more time (if you crossed it as spacetime) than the ball of cotton. The cotton ball offers almost no resistance to spacetime flow. It's as if it wasn't there, and you were traveling through deep space. There is no gravity in deep space. As a result, spacetime is not under any acceleration. If no acceleration, then no gravity. In my first book "Let There Be Light", I go into the progression of spacetime as it travels through our planet. If for no other reason, you should read that book. It is amazing how gravity changes direction within our planet. These changes fuel the counter rotation of our core and many other vital processes.

Within the last two paragraphs is something so important that it requires us to expand upon it. Spacetime is energy. Matter is concentrated energy. The conclusion is that matter is concentrated space. If we were sitting in my living room, I would ask for a few minutes of silence. This is one of those times when the words cannot do the concept justice. I think it requires time to camp-out upon the statement. First, we need to erase all our previous learning and beliefs. Then, the following simple yet profound statement needs to soak into our minds. 'Spacetime and matter are made of the same thing: they only differ in density'. Once you have internalized this concept, the mystery of time dilation ends. If matter is concentrated space, then time within matter cannot be equal to time in space. Never mind how it works. It just can't be any other way. Here we will split up into two groups: those who have truly understood and accepted this profound concept, and those who have not. First, let me instruct those who are incredulous. Do not read further. Stay here until your mind opens to the possibility that matter is compressed energy. It is compressed spacetime energy. Don't worry this is a book. You will catch up to us. All of this plays out in our minds. You could say we are all in a place without time while we are reading. For the rest of us, let's go on to the next paragraph.

Great! We are all here. You see, I told you reading a book is a magical experience. All the readers are in now time. OK, let's forge ahead. I just intend to whet your appetite with the implication of time dilation caused by matter. The full story will be in Chapter 6: 'The Emergence of Spacetime' and in Chapter 7: 'What Is Time?' Spacetime is a flowing medium. The fixed half is space. The variable is time. If spacetime needs to flow through media of different density, then it must vary its time. If you factor in the duality of spacetime, then the problem of time dilation disappears. Think of spacetime flow as two opposing fronts of wind. Set up a wind tunnel with fans on each side. Power them up to the same flow rate. What happens? No wind should exit the tunnel. Reduce the flow from one of the fans, and 'Voila!' The stronger running fan will blow air past the weaker one. Wait! Stay with me. Someone has just said "Hey, if we increased the flow to a really high level, then we would turn the other fan backwards. That would reverse time, right?" But it's not yet time to deal with time reversal. Be patient. The rebellion has been crushed. Let's move on.

Since space emanates from everywhere in the universe, the space that emanates from matter is filtered by matter's density. The resulting suppressed flow creates a low pressure in spacetime. The spacetime in the vicinity of said matter responds to the low pressure. Flow increases into the low-pressure area proportional to distance. This acceleration of flow creates the push we have labeled gravity.

It has been amazing for me to realize that the essence of our entire universe is energy. Matter is energy, information is energy, time is energy, and spacetime is energy. It's all energy. Perhaps nothing is more incredible than the fact that we are energy. We are living, intelligent and self-aware (SA) energy. Our bodies are composed of the compressed complex heavy elements made within stars. Yes, we are made of star dust. Pick an observation point outside your body. Look into yourself. What do you see? That's right! You see an arrangement of matter in a cohesive, functioning form, contemplating that it is matter (composed of energy) which came from stardust. Intelligent and self-aware (SA) star-compressed energy analyzing and contemplating energy. How mind-boggling and awe inspiring is that?

Gravity is limited by distance. The current consensus is that every item in the universe pulls on every other item. Nonsense. Let's dismember this statement. First, no exception is made for bodies outside the limit of the information barrier. If we do not see a body how can the body, feel us? Gravity has been proven to travel at light speed. So, right off the bat, gravity is limited to the objects sharing the same spacetime. If we can't see it with a reasonable time delay, we can't feel it. Please consider this: the furthest things we see are billions of light years away. They are further in distance than in time. By the time we have received their light, and by default gravity, where are they? The belief that space is warped by mass also gives us this fallacy. Logically, if space was really warped by mass, then this would have to be true. Any change to one area would have to affect the whole. One effect reaching the whole of the universe is not relativistic, not to mention that everything is in motion. Good luck with that modeling. Imagine two moving objects attracting each other billions of light years away.

This belief of ever-present or gravity-without-end is Newtonian. This is in no way possible. Gravity, in my opinion, is limited by spatial pressure to within its vicinity. Spatial pressure is analogous to atmospheric pressure, but it refers to energy, not gasses. Remember, gasses are matter, which, of course, is energy. We have 14 psi of air pressure at sea level. This is because gravity pushes those gasses toward Earth's surface. As spacetime replicates, it creates a similar pressure effect in space.

Here is an example to prove spatial pressure to you. Look up the Pioneer anomaly. The Pioneer 10 and 11 spacecraft are among the furthest manmade objects from Earth. They are showing an unexplained loss of speed. This anomaly was said to have been solved by blaming a slowdown of the craft on anisotropic radiation pressure. Heat loss from the spacecraft, coming from the power source. Only, that is not possible, because the power source is dying, and the anomaly is ongoing. There is a second occurrence that points to this spatial pressure. In all of our astronomical observations we have rarely seen interstellar visitors. I don't mean intelligence. I mean heavenly bodies. The only one that comes to mind is Oumuamua. It is believed that we only get one of these visitors per year.

"Wait just a minute, Mr. Farmer. Let me see if I understood you right. Are you claiming that this spatial pressure is caused by replicating space? Being that it is a type of pressure, will it cause a drag on any object traveling in space? You need to reevaluate your position. How can you say that nothing travels through space, and now you are telling us there is drag associated with travel through space?" Yes. I could not have phrased it better, myself. Spacetime does facilitate easy travel of anything at sub-light speeds. But there is a drag associated with traveling in this medium. It comes from the pressure created by replicating space in every point in space. This would mean that, eventually, everything in the universe would lose its so-called momentum, and only travel outward with replicating space. Read carefully. In hopes of minimizing confusion, this is the only place in this book that I will cover this occurrence. You are indeed traveling in a carrier wave of new space but this wave travels through existing space. It is existing space that sports this spatial pressure. You are traveling with space, through space. The fact that you travel with newly created space makes it correct to say that you travel with space. The reason I can only give two examples, to prove this drag in space, is that the universe is a very big place, and we are very limited as to our ability to travel. In a universe of such richness of heavenly bodies, without this travel-limiting spatial pressure, the universe would be like a huge arena full of bumper cars. You may also want to factor in, that with each impact, untold numbers of fragments would join in the mayhem. I think we have just stumbled upon a dynamic duo. Has anyone seen this dynamic duo yet? Yes, indeed, within our solar system we have the vacuum cleaners that are Jupiter, and Saturn. And who can forget the Sun? He is our big brother. The Sun creates, by far, the most powerful gravity well in our solar system. There is very little which comes near it that can escape its gravity. Then, of course, we have a two-step system. The Sun, Jupiter and Saturn do the cleanup job in our vicinity, while spatial pressure cleans up the universe.

In regard to gravity, it could be argued that infinity is in the last gram of push, but if no result can come from such a push, then is gravity present? Over great distances measured in parsecs, would the other gravity wells not cancel each other? Here is the elegant, simple and more-likely possibility. Gravity is limited to a given area governed by distance, influencing gravity wells, and spatial pressure. For instance, how far is the Earth's gravity felt between the Earth and the Moon? Is there not a point where both gravity wells balance out? If you get closer to the Moon beyond that equilibrium point, will you not be pushed to the Moon? If beyond that equilibrium point on Earth's side, would Earth's gravity not be what you experience? There cannot be everlasting or ever reaching gravity. Spacetime limits everything to within the information barrier. In other words, when two objects are separated by great distances, they are also separated by a lot of time. This time separation impedes gravity. Keep in mind that both objects are moving in relation to one another. The great time and distances isolate one from the other. Furthermore, the interaction of competing gravity wells cancels out gravity effects. There is one more insurmountable obstacle. Gravity is not a pull. Rather, gravity is a push. In other words, you need to reach behind the item before you can exert a push toward you. How in this universe can you reach beyond an item that is beyond the information horizon? Finally, at a given distance, a weak but ever-present spatial pressure ensures that gravity is neutralized.

"Eureka!" I heard some of you say. "Does the interaction of spacetime expanding within matter create, within the atomic structure, the same order in orbits we see in the universe?" I believe this to be the case. Here is my reason for such a wild idea. We accept that if all energy in the universe equalized, there would be no further movement. This condition is called the Big Freeze. The universe would die because the absence of heat or movement of energy would stop all processes in the universe. This seems reasonable to me. But if this idea works in the large scale of the universe, does it not also apply to the atomic level? If you have no movement of energy at the atomic level, would it not permeate all of the universe? I believe that the answer is absolutely 'Yes'. The only way to have a functioning universe is to continually add energy, causing expansion. I have not read enough in this field to know if science knows exactly what keeps the atomic structures orbiting, mimicking solar systems. If there is any doubt how it happens, this should answer those questions. A constant emergence of spacetime from within these structures would keep them in a constant orbit without collapsing on themselves. Just as a film of oil under pressure between the moving parts in your car engine keep the parts suspended without making metal to metal contact.

I sense that some have understood the full meaning and importance of spacetime replication at the atomic level. The switch has flipped. It is not that power comes from without. Power from within keeps the universe functioning. Conduction, convection and radiation are all movements of energy facilitated by replicating space. Let's just take a star as a test subject. If there was no replication, then light and heat would not travel. A star would intensify its heat buildup until it would blow up. But even blowing up is facilitated by spacetime moving through replication. I imagine it would just sit there, increasing its runaway nuclear reaction. It would burn up very quickly, never giving any heat or light. But wait. Can nuclear reaction take place without replicating space? If spacetime was to stop replicating, then all movement would collapse, or at least stop. This means that time would stop. The effect would not be localized. It would spread through the entire universe. I think all orbits, at the atomic level would stop. Yes, learned ones. I hear your objections. The atomic structure does not really orbit. It is more like a cloud. Well, guess what? You are mistaken. That cloud you see is actually a blurry picture. It has to do with exposure rates. What happens when you take a picture of something moving fast? It seems fuzzy or out of focus. Both, your test equipment and your mind, are too slow. Don't despair. I promise I will make this clear, before the end of the book.

Here's another mystery, at least to me, that is solved with the concept of replicating space. Have you ever thought, "How is it that we can pressurize things?" Why would a pressure vessel increase in pressure if there was nothing in it? One might think that applying pressure into a pressure vessel might cause it to leak into that which might be called 'subspace'. So how is it that we can pressurize a tank? Within our atmosphere, the answer is easy, even if wrong. In the Earth's atmosphere, we are pushing into a space that is already full of gases. Placing any further matter in an enclosed space would have to increase the pressure. Here we throw a monkey wrench in your thinking. How is it possible to pressurize a cabin, within a spaceship, in the vacuum of space? What in the world are we pushing on? Why does it create an even pressure outward from the center, in all directions? I know, some are sure that the outer walls of any container are what allow us to pressurize everything. The thought is logical. But that would be definitive if we were in a steady state universe. We are not. We are living in an expanding universe. How do you incorporate the expanding space, along with its quantum fluctuations? I guarantee you that the fluctuations are present in a vacuum. But they are also present in every other state found within the universe. Basically, when we pressurize anything, we are putting matter (dense energy) into an enclosed location. This location is already full of energy. It is not as dense as matter, but definitely present and expanding. In other words, the walls seal a space in the macro world, while spacetime seals the micro world. Not only does it seal the escape of energy, but it pushes on it as it emerges. Spacetime energy becomes the inner wall, if you will. Think of it this way. If you were to place a steel ball into the center of a pressure vessel, it would act as an inner wall of the pressure vessel. The same can be said of spacetime. It creates a barrier past which no energy can enter. Any attempt to increase energy content, whether gas, solid, or liquid, will be met by a proportional pressure increase created by replicating space. Can we compress gases into solids? Yes. It's done all the time by stars. We just do not have the capacity to duplicate a star's pressure and temperature. I believe that spacetime is everywhere, emanating

33

at light speed in every direction, giving you this ability to pressurize that cabin.

Someone has a valid question. "If it is true that spacetime maintains the pressure in a pressurized vessel, why is it stable if spacetime keeps replicating?" Great question. Spacetime replication does not increase pressure by adding energy to the pressure vessel. The spacetime, emanating from within the vessel, flows right out of the outer containment wall, with very little effort. What spacetime does is to create a leak-proof environment or inner wall. This inner wall pushes back with the exact same pressure exerted on it. Is that not what the outer wall does as well?

Just as on Earth, where we have 14.7 psi at sea level. In all of created space, there is a spatial pressure. As you increase matter within a given area, you start accelerating into outrushing spacetime. Think about it. You are trying to fill the space through which spacetime is traveling. This backpressure is analogous to the gravity that we feel on Earth's surface. Interesting. We just found another manifestation of gravity. I know some of you think it's not gravity. This is a push, not a pull. Sorry to have to correct you. Gravity is a push. Actually, there are no pulls in the universe. Whether within Earth's atmosphere, or in space, the result is the same. Within a confined space, if you increase matter content, then you are pushing against the outrushing spacetime. The more matter you push into a finite space, the more you increase spacetime's outward push. Why then, do you get no pressure increase when adding a piece of furniture into a room? Actually, you do, but since you are not adding matter into a sealed area, you are just moving it around. Pressure is only brief. "I got you there, Farmer", I heard a reader say. "By your logic, if I add matter to the Earth, the atmospheric pressure will increase?" Yes, it will. The link here between cause and effect is not as clear. But, the greater a planet's mass, the greater is its gravity. The more gravity, the higher the pressure exerted on its gasses. We are told that there is nothing in a vacuum. If that were truly the case, we could not pressurize a volume which has nothing in it. In other words, something with nothing in it, by my logic, is nothing. If an area has nothing, how can we say it is itself something? In order to exist, a given area of space must be permeated with something.

Let's imagine a conversation between a child and his father. "Dad, what is in the space between things on Earth?" "Son, the air is full of gasses. That's what we breathe. The wind moving the branches on those trees are gasses you can't see, in movement." "I understand that Dad, but what is in space between the planets?" "Son, there is nothing in the vacuum of space." "But Dad, if there is nothing, how come I can see it? "No, Son, we can't see empty space." "Yes, we can, Dad. I see that between the Moon and the Earth there is space." "Yes Son, you see space, but that space doesn't have anything in it." "But Dad, if it has nothing in it, it has no purpose. Why don't the Sun and Moon just get together?" "Son, be quiet and finish your dinner." I could sense the uneasiness you readers would feel as I wrote each question. Especially you dads. Children have the ability to corner the best of us with their questions. Do you see this imaginary child's logic? Why would space even exist if there is no purpose? What keeps it from deflating or imploding on itself? What powers its expansion? Please stop referring to space as empty. I would like to think that I have kept a little of that child wonder within me. I have a question for you learned grownups. If space is empty, explain to me why we think there can be waves or ripples in space? Explain to me how it is possible for a wave to travel through empty space, if there is no medium present? Oh please, learned ones, tell me how space can be warped to make gravity. No, I don't believe it warps. But you do. How can something, namely matter, warp nothing and form something. To put it mathematically: Gravity = matter/zero. Space is not empty! It is filled by spacetime. Spacetime is the energy fabric that is, itself, the construct, the medium, the plexus or the matrix that allows for the physical existence.

Let's take a stroll through history to see how man has dealt with space. This history is a condensed consensus of internet information. I do not quote any single link because my hope is that this book will outlive those links, and possibly the net itself. Allow me to go off topic for a moment. Most people, today, believe that they will leave behind themselves a lot of information for posterity. They think that all of their online information will be their legacy, forever. In reality, the Stone Age civilizations left more records of their achievements than we will. All you have in your computer can vanish with a hard drive crash, or the theft of the computer. Everything you have in the cloud is a solar flare or EMP away from vanishing. Are not all of your devices and accounts password protected? If you died today, who could access them? Most families no longer have picture albums. Those fancy frame displays can die, even from a power failure. Do you want to leave something for posterity? Write a diary, print your pictures, and make an album. At the very least, back up your files in CD or DVD. This media should not be lost in solar flare or EMP. Here's a good idea: write a book. Some of my most treasured possessions are old books

Let's get back to our topic: Space. Aristotle is credited with saying "nature abhors a vacuum" This stood for over 1000 years. Since no one could produce a vacuum, it was thought that it could not exist. Well, in 1643, Evangelista Torricelli proved the creation of a vacuum, and by default, created the barometer. He took a long tube, sealed on one end, and filled it with mercury. He then sealed the other end with a finger. He immersed the open end in a receptacle full of mercury and removed his finger. The mercury flowed down until it balanced out with atmospheric pressure. The top of the tube showed empty space. He is quoted as saying "We live at the bottom of an ocean of air". With one experiment, he had invented the barometer, weighed the atmospheric pressure, and proved that a vacuum was real. Or was it? A while later Blaise Pascal would experiment with Torricelli's invention. Taking it up a tall building, he realized that the air thins out as you go higher. This, of course, meant that in outer space we had nothingness. Or did it? Further experiments showed that if you place an alarm clock in a vacuum you could not hear it ring. But to their surprise, you could see through the glass as it performed the ringing action, silently. Again, we reasoned, there was something in a vacuum if light could travel through it. We see the alarm clock on Earth in a vacuum, and we see light from space. They must be the same medium. In the eighteen hundred, we again believed space was not empty. It was full of luminiferous ether. Or was it? In 1887, the experiment carried out by Michelson and Morley showed that there was no such ether. Or was there?

Less than a century later, science is sure of quantum fluctuations. What are they? Scientists claim a quantum fluctuation is energy appearing from nothing and quickly disappearing. Please, Mr. Scientist, say "energy appearing out of an unknown place". After all, science is the study of the physical world. Nothing, by definition, is not physical. As a man of science, you cannot say that something came from nothing. After all, nothing does not exist. Whatever their reasoning, as it stands now, science no longer says that what they call empty space is empty. Well, at least they are on the right path. Enter this old farmer who tells you there is nothing empty in the universe. It is full of the energy fabric known as spacetime. I actually believe that spacetime, although unseen, is more real than what we see. Spacetime is reality itself. All that exists physically, exists within spacetime. It fills every place in the universe. This energy fabric is replicating itself. Quantum fluctuations are but one of the byproducts of this replication process.

As my editor and I were getting ready for the final proof-read of this book, prior to sending it to the publisher, a momentous announcement was made. Do a search for "Department of Energy's muon g-2 experiment" (1,580,000 results as of today 5/10/21 2:14am). Science is prying open the floodgate to the knowledge of "the Fountain Of God". At the end of this Chapter, you will read the following: "Wouldn't replicating space have been accepted, if proposed along with Newton's laws, or Einstein's theory of relativity? Of course, they would have. Being layered on top of the currently accepted theories, and being in opposition to parts of the status quo, I have no hope of seeing any of it accepted in my lifetime". Well, that was a year ago. I now believe I have a chance (if I'm granted 10 more years of life) to see Replicating Space Theory and the Fountain Of God proven as scientific fact. We could see final analyses of this experiment much sooner, if quantum computers can be used to sort through the huge datasets in these experiments. The biggest question still remains: can we ever see the Fountain Of God, directly? I believe not. If you noticed, the above-mentioned experiment is using muons to probe a vacuum. This tells us that we can infer that there is energy within that vacuum, by how our muons act. But we cannot see or measure what is in that vacuum, directly. I think the Fountain Of God is immeasurable. If there is an entity in the universe which we have not seen, or of whose existence we are unaware, then that entity can be indescribable, by our experience. One thing I believe is indisputable: that there is nothing smaller, or more elementary, in physical space. Due to its size, and the fact that it is the medium in which we exist, I think we will never be able to test it directly. The news of this unbelievable development is bitter-sweet. If it had come to my attention sooner, I may have been able to explore my concepts further. But I also realize that a preliminary report of something this complicated could have contaminated my understanding of the concepts I have proposed and developed in this book. I will, therefore, make no further efforts to read any more than the few paragraphs I have already read on this subject. Of course, I will follow these developments closely, after my book has been published. In the light of this new information, it is tempting to go back and filter what I have already written. The reality is that nothing has changed. This new information is intimately related to that which I have already written. But I can't say it directly contradicts any of the concepts in this book. To the contrary, it supports them. For these reasons, I have chosen not to use this new information to make any changes to this book. All that pertains to these tremendously, world-changing developments, is found only within this one long paragraph. I shall just limit myself to tell you this. Science has proven one of the pillars of replicating space theory, as written in this book, that EMPTY SPACE IS NOT EMPTY.

There is another monumental discovery (proposed hypothesis) like the one above that is also decades old, but I just became aware of it on 7/20/2021. This is even more shocking to me. Upon reading it I sent a note to my good friend and Editor Jeff Sterling saying the following. "If we do not hurry up and get this book to the publisher it will be old news by the time it is published". The theory I'm talking about is Loop Quantum Gravity. This concept states (and I paraphrase) that gravity is made up of particles that have been called quanta. These particles make up space and time. They can be thought of as the pixels that make reality. What we perceive as space is actually an accumulation of quanta, while time is actually the evolution of these same quanta. These quanta make up the threads of spacetime fabric. This concept is said to make time travel impossible because time does not loop back into itself. That is too close for comfort! If the proponents of Loop Quantum Gravity would add the word 'replicating' to 'quanta', and replace 'evolution' with 'flow', then they would be well on their way toward understanding Replicating Space Theory.

I hope you have accepted that matter is not solid, and that the fabric of space, known as spacetime, resides within it. Spacetime is energy. Being energy, it permeates every nook and cranny in the universe. Now things start making sense. It is a proven fact that time is slower at Earth's surface than it is above its surface. Now remember, relativity also proves that the faster you go in any direction, the slower goes your clock. The closer you are to Earth's surface, the less spacetime flows out of Earth, and the more spacetime accelerates into

Earth from above. Even if we could somehow hold Earth completely stationary, getting rid of orbits and rotation, we on Earth would be moving with space. Wait. How could that be? If Earth is stationary and we are stationary, how can we, in essence, be accelerating with space? There is an acceleration of spacetime into Earth due to a decrease of spacetime coming out of Earth. This acceleration creates the push you feel toward Earth and gives you a slower clock. It matters not whether you accelerate through spacetime, or spacetime accelerates through you. The result is the same: gravity. Contrarily, under the current understanding, space is warped by Earth's mass. If you view the artistic drawings of how space warps into Earth, you begin to get a picture. It should be noted that a snapshot would be Newtonian, whereas a movie would mimic relativity. All you need to do is to view that picture as either relative or as a movie. Then would you see spacetime as it swirls and rushes into Earth. The lines that do not go into the Earth are redirected or lensed.

It is a great feeling to have confirmation of what I have written. I was not aware that Einstein had predicted Earth dragging spacetime as it spins and moves throughout space. He called it frame-dragging. Do a net search for "gravity probe b experiment". I don't know how I had missed this, until now, on the eve of publishing this book. This, in scientific terms, is ancient history. Probe A was launched in 1976, and probe b was launched in 2004. The results were announced in 2011. Bottom line: that which I call the swirling effect, caused by replicating space near a rotating body, Einstein had called "frame-dragging". The probe-b experiment confirmed this effect. I can't stress enough the importance of having confirmation of an effect that I perceived as an obvious consequence of replicating space. I covered this concept in my first book. In 'Let There Be Light', it was mentioned 5 times, including twice on page 36.

Let's get a bit into lensing. If you have ever seen gravitational lensing depicted, then keep reading. If you have never seen an explanation of how gravitational lensing works, you need to see it.

Do a net search for 'gravitational lensing'. You will notice that in some of the cases they depict the light that is heading directly into the obstructing body, getting lensed. This is complete nonsense. If this were true observers would only see the lensed items. We would not see the items doing the lensing. If you go a bit deeper, even the lensed item would not be visible, for it would be lensed around us by the mass of the Earth. We would actually see nothing at all in the cosmos, from our vantage point on Earth. Lensing is not caused by warped space. First, let me say that space does not warp, compress or stretch in any shape or fashion. One mile distance, close to Earth, is one mile distance in intergalactic space. Warped space is 2-dimensional thinking. It came as an explanation for an occurrence that was not understood. What we see as warped space is actually warped or stretched time. It is the time dilation, created by mass that causes an illusion of warped space.

If you change time, and space is left intact, you form a low pressure in spacetime. Let's say we look out, and we see a large galaxy in our telescope. This galaxy seems to show an image or halo of another galaxy that is behind it. What is going on? The galaxy directly in front of us should block all of the light from the one behind it. But instead, we see the light from the further galaxy, as a halo. It's like you are looking at someone in front of you and seeing the person behind him. In the case of the two galaxies, the light from the furthest galaxy, headed directly into the closer galaxy, does indeed disappear. If we were to move to one side, we would see the galaxy in front of us as closer, and the one behind it, by its side, but further away. Light travels, not through space, but with space, in straight lines. As it gets near the gravity field, it seems to start bending or lensing. Why? Because the time dilation caused by the mass is causing spacetime to accelerate into the obstructing body. The light shining directly into it will be lost to us. The light that was traveling near would also redirect to impact the obstructing body. The light that was traveling further away gets redirected inward toward the body. Then, it continues toward us, as the tugging gravity or rushing spacetime aligns its path with our vantage point.

Let me give you an example to drive this home. This will illustrate that there is no warping. Here, flow is causing lensing. A few years ago, I sailed from Nassau, in the Bahamas, to Fort Lauderdale, Florida. It was not a pleasant experience, even though the wind was directly in our back. We had a four mile per hour wind. For those who have never sailed, anything less than 6 mph wind is not worth sailing. We had no choice but to motor all the way. To make matters worse, we were in the Gulf Stream, with a north current of 4 mph. Most are not familiar with just how powerful the Gulf Stream is. According to NOAA, the Gulf Stream transports four billion cubic feet of water per second. This means that the Gulf Stream transports more water than all of the world's rivers combined. Navigating in this moving medium is challenging. Even though we were headed west, to Fort Lauderdale, we had to continually steer southwest toward the Florida Keys. We were steering and motoring to the Florida Keys but heading toward Fort Lauderdale. Why? Because we were traveling in a medium which was moving. Thankfully, we had a steering wheel to compensate for the Gulfstream's redirection. Light has no such compensating steering wheel. If caught in a stream of spacetime, light will keep traveling in a straight line. This is exactly what happens with lensing. In other words, light is headed straight. The spacetime that is flowing into the closer galaxy, lenses the light toward us. Please forget about warping space. That is an illusion caused by the flow of space. Nothing travels through space. Everything travels with space.

In this book, the word 'light' appears almost 600 times. I think it is fitting that what makes the universe visible should play such a role in this work. Most of us take light for granted. All it takes to value light, is to find yourself in a place with no light. Have you ever found yourself trying to find the key to your front door, in complete darkness? If you have a large set of keys like I, it is humbling. I think it is fitting that light would give us clarity in Replicating Space Theory. Light is a constant. Light is also said to have no mass. Yet, we know that we can propel a spacecraft with a light sail. If light has no mass, then what pushes a solar sail? The solar sail reflects light and receives a transfer of momentum from the photons of light. The force is very slight, and that explains why solar sails are always depicted as huge. But wait, if there is a transfer of momentum to the sail, then why is the light reflected from the sail? Furthermore, why does it reflect in a different direction, with no loss of speed? I see no possible explanation in current science. However, the transfer of momentum to the sail fits like a glove in Replicating Space Theory. Again, I remind you that nothing travels through space: everything travels with space. Light, being very close to massless, is propelled by spacetime. We could believe that light is initially propelled through space by the push that a photon receives, from the release of energy, as an electron moves to a lower level. Let's say that sets it in motion. But why does it move at a constant rate? Why, after hitting a solar sail, did it change direction, while keeping the same speed, even after it transferred its momentum? Have you connected the dots? Light is propelled by replicating spacetime. It will always remain constant, because it runs with the medium. It runs with the medium because its tiny mass allows it to fit between the duality of spacetime. Therefore, light is propelled by spacetime. Being at the equilibrium point of spacetime, it sees no time.

The learned ones must have thrown the book out the window. Perhaps they have been daydreaming. They have not yet realized that there seems to be an Achilles heel to spacetime flow being the cause of gravity. Let me help you. I contend that spacetime is an energy fabric. This energy is accelerating into Earth because of a low pressure, if you will, caused by Earth's matter. OK, if that is the case, then there is an obvious question. Where is the energy? Earth's mass is not increasing. So, where is the massive amount of energy going? Here is the answer to the perceived Achilles heel. This seemingly missing energy is, itself, proof of replicating spacetime. We do, indeed, receive a great deal of energy constantly, 24/7. I would say that without this energy, Earth would be a dead planet right now. Without the ability to make the math calculations, I'm going to go out on a limb and give you a guestimate. The Department of Energy estimates that in approximately one and one-half hours, the sun gives Earth enough energy to power everything on Earth for one year. This is a lot of energy. I think this is very little, when we compare it to the constant energy rushing into Earth as spacetime. So where does it go? It is used to keep the core counter rotating, keeping the magnetic field active. We also get all the geothermal heat, as well as the volcanic activity and the movement of Earths plates.

Why is geologic activity important? You may remember, I'm a farmer. When we go to plant a field, we plow or till the soil. There are several good reasons for plowing the soil. For one, plowing kills all the weeds growing in the soil. It softens up the soil for the young roots of whatever we plant. Perhaps more important, it brings nutrients up and mixes them on the soil surface where the plants can get to them. This same process, on a huge scale, is done by Earth's geological processes. The movement of our plates, and the lava flows, bring nutrients from deep within Earth. If we had no geological activity, the Earth's soil would be infertile at this stage of Earth's history. The movement of the plates, the volcanic activity, along with erosion, wind, and rain, perpetually replenish nutrients for our farmlands.

Some have said that the heat in our planet is residual, and from the decay of uranium. Residual ran out long ago. As far as the radioactive decay, this too is caused by the emergence of spacetime within a dense material. Uranium is 1.6 times denser than lead. A gallon of milk is 8 pounds; a gallon of uranium is 150 pounds. That is an astronomical difference! Currently, it is believed that the competition between the electrostatic repulsion versus the strong nuclear attraction, is responsible for the instability. I think that replicating space is the tipping force that makes elements beyond lead unstable. Elements less dense than lead do not offer as much resistance to the outflow of spacetime. Beyond lead density, the outward force of spacetime aids in the dismantling of those heavy elements. Does that mean uranium will decay until it becomes lead? Yes. To my surprise, uranium-238, for instance, decays to become lead-206.

There is one more mind-blowing piece of evidence found in the interaction of uranium with replicating space. Do a search for uranium in a cloud chamber. Did you see the emergence of the particles, straight out like an explosion? You are witnessing spacetime dismantling uranium. Notice the straight trajectory of the particles. Imagine this in 3d, in every minute speck of space. That is the perfect picture of replicating spacetime.

I don't know about you, but there is a nagging question that I just can't shake, regarding uranium. If it cannot survive in normal space, just how and where was it created? Well, I just had to find out. To my surprise it correlates perfectly with all the new concepts in this book. We do not have absolute proof of where and how the uranium found on Earth, was made. But we are fairly certain that this heavy element, along with others, like gold and platinum, are produced in stars. More exactly, they are made by the demise of stars. The immense pressures created by supernovae and collisions of neutron stars are the best suspects. The neutron stars seem to be a shoe in. The material of a neutron star is calculated to weigh 5 billion metric tons (11,023,113,100,000 pounds) not per gallon, but per teaspoon. Unimaginable orders of magnitude heavier than uranium. Remember, uranium weighs in at 150 pounds per gallon. At 768 teaspoons per gallon that would make neutronium weigh-in at 4 quadrillion metric tons (4 followed by 15 zeros) per gallon. Back in 2017, humanity was witness to a collision of two neutron stars. If you do a net search, you will see that the evidence seems conclusive. The collision of these stars produced great amounts of heavy metals, including uranium. I have proven (at least to my satisfaction) that the energy running into Earth is not a problem; it's the opposite. Rather than this energy being a problem for the concept of replicating space, it's actually one of its biggest proofs.

Just in case any of you think that it would be great to make neutronium paperweights, don't do it. Neutronium, apart from its host environment, would be much more unstable than uranium. If you could remove one teaspoon from a neutron star and materialize it on Earth, we would be no more. Without the immense gravitational pressure of its host star, the resulting explosion would, I imagine, vaporize Earth. Does anyone see anything wrong with this picture? If matter was the only thing at work in warping space, why would a teaspoon of neutronium not warp space enough to keep itself stable? Easy. The inflow of spacetime rushing into the small amount of neutronium is no match for replicating space. The outward pressure within the material is much greater than the inward pressure created by such a small volume. Think this through. If gravity was indeed warped space, then how much warping would be done by such a dense small object? The resulting depression or warping would encapsulate the teaspoon of material in a pocket of spacetime. On the other hand, replicating spacetime would create from within this teaspoon of material an outward force unlike anything ever seen by humanity. The resulting explosion would send this dense material expanding at close to light speed. When it was all said and done, the explosion would have created untold amounts of new space. Wait what? Yes, if you release all of that energy, it's converted from dense neutronium to light spacetime energy. It is, after all, energy. For some, explosions have been demystified. "So that is why things explode? It is concentrated energy, reverting to spacetime energy? Does this also mean that the explosive force is another manifestation of gravity?" Give that group a Doctorate, on explosives.

Centrifugal force. Centrifugal force is also an acceleration, but in this case, the item, moving in a circle, is actually accelerating toward the center of rotation. This means that it is encountering a greater flow outward than inward. Hence, the gravity is pushing the item out, away from the center of rotation. When the rotating body is suddenly released, it is no longer accelerating inward, and the gravity that was felt, immediately disappears. Forget centripetal force being the only real force. Both are real. They are both wings of the same bird. For those of you who are not familiar with 'centripetal force', let's bring you up to speed. If you are twirling a ball attached to a string, the force you feel on the string, pulling outward, is the centrifugal force. The force felt by the ball, tugging inward, is the centripetal force.

If you are not yet convinced that both gravity and centrifugal force are caused by the same thing, then research artificial gravity. This is thought to be the answer to the detrimental effects on the human body when in space for prolonged periods. The concept is simple: rotate a cylinder in space, at the right speed, and you will create in its inner rim the same thing we have on Earth: gravity.

In conclusion, there was no Big Bang, and yes there was a Big Bang. What? Yes, I meant what I wrote. The Big Bang suggests an explosion, and there was one, but there was none. How can something be true and false at the same time? Allow me to explain. We think of an explosion as a concentrated amount of energy exploding outward, releasing its stored energy. What is seen is manifested the same, but for a different reason. The rate of expansion was, indeed, at a speed that dwarfs any explosion witnessed by man. However, I believe the expansion was not due to a release of stored energy, but as a result of a growth process. We are sitting 13.8 billion years from the beginning. We look back through the prism of an expanding universe. To us, it seems like a classic explosion, but was it really? From our perspective, it looks like an explosion. From the perspective of the origin, it looks like a growth process. Does our frame of reference affect our perception of the magnitude of this explosive beginning? Definitely! Our point of reference is governed by relativity. A turtle taking one step per year on Earth would be seen as a speed demon by someone close to a massive black hole. Furthermore, as spacetime doubles, time halves. Please don't blow a gasket. Common sense must tell you, that if you are going to travel double the distance (at the same rate) then it will take you twice the amount of time. Get in your car on a freeway at 60 miles per hour. How long did it take you to go one mile? One minute. How long will it take you to go double the distance? 2 minutes, how about double again, to four miles? 4 minutes? The more astute among you are on to the error in my analogy. Every time space, or in this case distance, doubles, time also doubles. Why then, did I tell you that time is halved? It's simply that, in space, we are not dealing with a moving object. It is space that is growing or stretching. Again, get back in your car, but this time park it. Now, it's the road that is stretching. In this case the opposite is happening, so time must be cut in half each time the distance doubles. Once the road has doubled in distance, it would take you double the time to transverse it. Hence, your time is worth half of what it was before. So, if you double space, then time halves. If this relativity was not observed, then we could not have a seamless spacetime continuum. Therefore, what we see as an explosion now, was a growth process back in the beginning.

Have you ever noticed that the Sun is hottest at noon? Can we conclude that the Sun's temperature changes over the day? Or, could you say, it's closer to us at noon? Not at all. At noon, the layer of atmosphere, between us and the Sun, is at its thinnest. When the Sun is closer to sunset or sunrise, there is more atmosphere between us and the Sun. This filters and absorbs the Sun's rays and heat. Spacetime creates the same paradox, as we look back in time. Replicating space, finally, gives us an answer to so many conundrums in cosmology.

I think most of you have already realized that it could not have been a Big Bang or an explosion. The evidence, within matter and the universe at large, does not support an explosive beginning. There is no logical conclusion outside of a growth process. I think the Rosetta Stone is plain for all to see. We have approached this topic from many different angles. The current theories on beginning, growth, and the eventual end of the universe, are ludicrous. Space only makes sense if it replicates. Each new point in space also replicates. This growth process makes time, space and matter.

One among us believes that he has evidence against replicating space. I would rather not close this chapter before all concerns against RST are put to rest. All right, let's have it. "If RST is correct, then there must be a great void in the universe. This must be the case, because according to replicating space theory, space creation began before matter came into existence." Well, first, congratulations are in order. You have really understood RST. The void, whose existence you have so expertly deduced, does indeed exist. But this is not the chapter to discuss it. You will have to wait until Chapter 5: Matter Creation, Is It Ongoing?

I have no doubt as to the validity of replicating spacetime. I do, however, fear that I will probably die without ever witnessing any acceptance of this concept. Wouldn't replicating space have been accepted, if proposed along with Newton's laws, or Einstein's theory of relativity? Of course, it would have been. Being layered on top of the currently accepted theories, and being in opposition to parts of the status quo, I have no hope of seeing any of it accepted in my lifetime. I hold this belief for many reasons. Among these, science, once having developed a consensus, is slow to consider another alternative. It is also no easy matter to examine something that is an integral part of your own existence. Lastly, the scale is so miniscule, that it is quite impossible to detect this 'true God particle' or' energy quanta' using our present technology. To put it in perspective, it is like trying to see the furthest of galaxies, using reading glasses. I hope you have fully understood replicating space. With the understanding of this concept comes the ability to understand many things. The following chapters will explain the mysteries of the universe in the light of the fountain of God.

CHAPTER 3

Expansion Rate Made Simple

L ET'S START BY explaining the current consensus on universal expansion, and why I do not believe it. It is believed that the universe merely expands existing space. It is expanding at the rate of about 44.7 miles per second per megaparsec (one megaparsec equals 3.26 million light-years). You should know that this rate is currently in a state of flux. In our endeavor to shave our margin of error, we have, instead, come up with rates which put in doubt the current expansion rate. So, if you needed an example to understand why it is so hard to find a true scientific consensus, here you have it. The expansion rate was discovered by Edwin Hubble. That's why it was coined the Hubble Constant. His original calculation equated to 303.18 miles per second per megaparsec. Let's compare the original Hubble Constant with the current, soon to be dethroned number. The current rate is 44.7 miles per second per megaparsec. That means we have lost about 85 percent off of the original calculation.

Back to our universe. How can our universe be expanding space for billions of years? I see no other example of anything physical, which can be expanded indefinitely, without a catastrophic failure. I encourage you to do a search, in any search engine, on how a rubber band works, or how a spring works, or how a balloon stretches. The reason why all of those items stretch, and are elastic, is due to the electromagnetic force. But who has not seen a rubber band or a spring snap? Who has not seen a balloon pop? You see, as soon as you overstretch any material, it will separate or fail.

The expansion rate of the universe, the Hubble constant, is the rate at which the universe expands, per given unit of size, called a megaparsec. A megaparsec is 3.26 million light-years (light travels 5,869,713,600,000 miles per year). The best estimate of the current expansion rate of the universe is 44.7 miles per second per megaparsec. Again, that seems to be the current consensus. There is a lot of discussion and opinion, about whether this is correct. I remind you about the 'scientific consensus': the only thing known for sure, when dealing with a scientific consensus, is that nothing is for sure.

There are several pertinent questions that any inquisitive person should ask about the expansion rate. Has it always been the same? If not constant, is it speeding up or slowing down? Is it the same in the observable universe, as in the rest of the universe? What causes it? In my mind, there are a few questions which displace all of the others. How can we ever hope to have a meaningful handle on the expansion rate, if we only see a small part of the universe? Perhaps more importantly, how can we use the speed of light to affix the expansion rate, if clearly, the fastest thing is not light, but spacetime itself?

Why would I conclude that space is the fastest thing in the universe? Well, Replicating Space Theory demands it. According to RST, nothing travels through space: everything travels with space. This means that, under normal speeds, light travels with space. In situations where space travels unidirectionally, at high volumes, light can only travel in the same direction. This is the case at the event horizon of black holes. This is not the only proof we have of space being the fastest thing in the universe. As space expands, galaxies that are not gravitationally bound to us move away from us. The further they are from us, the faster they are moving away. We know for a fact that the farthest galaxies are moving away from us faster than the speed of light. The third and last proof I will give you is given to us by light itself. When we see light from distant galaxies, we see that the light has redshifted. This redshift shows us that light has been outrun by stretching space.

Let's take it in a linear fashion to see if we can all understand, both learned ones, and we common folks. Light starts shining, after the universe is completed, with a period of unbelievable expansion, called the inflationary epoch. At this point, we can start the clock for the visible universe. We are now 13.8 billion years from the beginning. (That is 'age'). When we look out, in any direction, we see back in time to about 13.4 billion years ago. This does not mean that we are seeing a distance of 13.4 billion light-years, because during the time in which that light is travelling back toward us, the universe keeps expanding. Keep up now. There is a disconnect between time and distance. The very medium itself, spacetime, is growing. If space did not stretch, then the distance and the time would be exact: one year of time would be one-light-year of distance. Space is, indeed, stretching, and this makes all the difference. What we see as 13.4 billion years, could not be merely 13.4 billion light-years away, because even as light travelled back to us, space stretched. So, what we see at 13.4 billion years in the past, is much further away than 13.4 billion light-years away, by now.

Even harder to understand, is that when we finally see the light, we are not actually looking at what those stars were doing 13.4 billion years ago. We are actually looking at what happened a much shorter time ago, close to us. As a matter of fact, we could be looking at light being emitted close to the place we will someday occupy. Yes, the light we see, emitted 13.4 billion years in the past, was emitted a shorter time ago, from our future former backyard. Why are some of you refusing to read further? Are you so bewildered that you are evaluating my sanity? Allow me to walk you through the implications of the 'future former backyard' comment. We can all agree that light speed is a constant. Furthermore, we should also agree that redshift* accurately predicts the time that light has traveled. So, the light we have seen from the furthest galaxy tells us that it was emitted 13.4 billion years in the past. At that time the universe was very small compared to what it is today. This light was emitted close to our relative location. But Earth was not in existence, yet. That makes it our backyard, or front yard, depending on how you look at it. That takes care of future, because the light was emitted where, one day, we would be. Now, let's deal with the 'former'. It is former because, by the time we materialized, that old galaxy had gone past our point in space, by billions of light-years.

Welcome to relativity. All this time, you thought that time was written in stone. Well, time is written in a medium that is more pliable than bubble gum. Wait just a minute! That means that we don't see the present. Never, ever have you seen the present. Even what we touch, is the past. Yes, the tip of your finger may be part of your body, but it is the brain that is aware. The information from whatever you touch is old news by the time it reaches your brain. It is a matter of fact, that your eyes give you a report sooner than your touch. If you put a hand on an extremely hot object, by the time your brain gets the signal, your hand is already burned. Why can't we live in the present? Because the present would have to be everywhere at once. Spacetime could not be relative. Everyone would have to be aware of everything. In other words, it would be a static Newtonian universe. Our physical universe only functions if time and space are tied at the hip and are relative.

There is an obvious question related to this emergence of time. Is time a fixed entity under a constant frame of reference? I believe time

Silvio Gonzalez

is not fixed. Don't be confused into thinking that I'm referring to a challenge to relativity. What I mean is that time is not a fixed entity throughout time. Even if you are in a place which sees no change in acceleration, and is absent of influences of gravity wells, I believe that time changes over time. Time is changed by an increase in spatial pressure that is created by an ever-growing universe. This occurrence further complicates the search for the elusive expansion rate of the universe. I will not take that rabbit trail. If you wish, go ahead and think through how slowing time affects the expansion rate.

Let's take it back out to space. The Sunlight we see on Earth was emitted from the Sun's surface about eight minutes ago. If the Sun stops shining at 1pm, then we still see the Sun shining till 1:08 pm. Side note: the light in the Sun starts near its center. The light we see currently being emitted by the Sun took at least 150 thousand years to emerge from the center of our star. Science says it gets absorbed and re-emitted many times, on its way out. But you who have understood replicating spacetime, know better. Time dilation, created by matter, slows the flow of spacetime. This reduces the flow out of matter, as compared to flow in empty space. Hypothetically, we would not realize that the Sun had stopped producing light, until it stopped reaching us from its surface. At that time, we would know that the last light was emitted from the Sun's surface, 8 minutes ago. If this is the case with the Sun, which is the closest star to us, then what is the implication for a star 13.4 billion years in the past? They could all be gone, and we would not know it, until the light stopped shining, or more precisely, stopped reaching us. This really makes the phrase "seeing is believing" one of the most foolish phrases a person can utter. To utter such a phrase would be to make an utter moron of oneself.

OK, this chapter's name is Expansion Rate Made Simple. So far, we have not delivered. Let me cut to the chase and tell you how replicating space makes child's play of finding the current expansion rate. After I had fully understood the universe in light of replicating space, I said to myself: "Self, the visible universe is a sphere governed by light speed. Can't we calculate the expansion rate without all this costly equipment and these complicated methods"? The answer, of course, is yes. But, I did not answer myself. You see, talking to yourself is OK, but if you answer yourself, then you are just deranged. Here is the math. Let's use math to confirm the current expansion rate of 44.7 miles per second per megaparsec.

Hurray! I heard the learned ones say, "Finally, we'll see proof". To the rest of us, words are all we need. To the mathematicians among us, math proves it is real. Let's see if we can bridge the great divide, with a math bridge that we can all understand. According to this new concept of replicating spacetime, the speed of replication is light speed. We are dealing with light speed in every direction. We don't see space in all directions at once. Being linear creatures, we only look to outer space in one direction at a time. Expansion rate, therefore, is the expansion rate along a straight line. Draw a line across the center of a circle that symbolizes the diameter of the universe. We can envision spacetime stretching along the entire length of that line at 'the expansion rate'. According to replicating space theory, the total perceived expansion rate is governed by light speed. We perceive spacetime as growing, at twice the speed of light, along that line we drew through the center of the universe. Space therefore is growing across its entire diameter at 44.7 miles per second per megaparsec, made possible by the growth at its outer diameter. This gives us a total expansion of light speed times two. Light speed is 186,282 miles per second. Twice light speed is 372,564 miles per second. So, we have 372,564 miles extra space every second. When we look toward the edge of the universe, we see 13,800,000,000 years in a radius, giving us a diameter of 27,600,000,000. If we divide this total of 27,600,000,000 by the number of light-years in a megaparsec, (3,261,640), then we see that the universe is 8,462 megaparsecs in diameter. Recapping, we know that we have a universe that is 8,462 megaparsecs in diameter. We also know we have a total expansion of

372,564 extra miles per second. Now, let us divide the extra-miles-per-second by the size of the universe in parsecs. 372,564 / 8462 = 44 extra miles per second per megaparsec. Our math, therefore, shows that we have an expansion rate of 44 miles per second per megaparsec of space. We are off by 0.7 miles per second. This puts us within 1.56 percent of the currently accepted rate of 44.7 miles per second per megaparsec. Considering that NASA rates their best estimate at plus or minus 3 percent, we are spot on! Here is the best equation this old farmer can envision. E=2C/D. where E is the expansion rate per megaparsec, 2C is light speed times 2, and D is the diameter of the universe in megaparsecs.

Amazing, is it not? With a pencil and a piece of paper we can do that which has taken science many decades, not to mention instruments worth many billions of dollars. I suppose that some of the more learned ones have already seen a chink in my math. You see, I set the visible universe at a distance equal to the age of the universe in each direction. It is true that when we look out, we look back in time, to almost the total 13.8 billion years of the universe's history, in each direction. But time does not equate to distance, when looking into space. The medium is expanding. The true observable universe is said to be 93 billion light-years in diameter or 46.5 billion in radius. Let's go in small steps. Let's take galaxy GN-z11, as an example. We see it 13.4 billion years in the past. In regard to distance, the light we see now was emitted very close to where we are now. GN-z11 is no longer where it was when it emitted the light we see now. Neither is it presently located from where its light appears to emanate. It is actually much further away. The final question is "Does it exist at all?" The answer is: "We don't know." We can only be sure it existed 13.4 billion years ago, because its light is just now getting back to us from that time. But, at any second, we could see a chomping ball, like the one in the video game, appear and gobble it up.

"Wait just a minute", I heard one of the learned ones say. "Don't you get current news in South Florida? Have you not heard that the universe is speeding up?" Yes, I assure you, we do get current news, even in the farm fields of South Florida. But either the scientist got it wrong, or more likely, the people writing the news did not understand the scientist. Wait. Please don't blow a gasket. I can explain. Why do you think we just concluded that the universe is speeding up? What has changed in the last few years in our observation of the universe? Yes, our ability to look further into the vastness of space. Do you remember what happens when you look far into space? That is right. The further we look into space, the further back in time we see. So it is, that in the past, the universe expanded faster. The growth of the universe is measured by light and information. Both of these travel at light speed. If light speed is a constant, then there has always been a constant expansion, equal to twice the speed of light. I'm no mathematician, but it is quite obvious that if you divide a set number of apples amongst a group of children, the fewer children, the more apples each gets. The present moment is emanating from our center of mass. In other words, right here, with us.

Faster expansion rate is, indeed, in the past. You may be tempted to say that it is only now, with our present technology, that we can compare the very distant past with the present. You would be right that we have recently acquired the ability to peer further into the distant past. I agree with you, but it is only recently that astronomers have come up with this 'faster expanding universe in the past' concept. We were not really in the dark ages. We could already peer into the distant past. If, up until recently, we were unable to see this speed increase with the distances nearest to us, then how can we trust the distant data from the end of the universe? We should also not forget that time is not the same throughout time. This, along with different time zones and the great distances, makes this idea of an ever-increasing expansion rate not believable. The further back we apply our formulas and theories, the more room there is for error.

I have looked at the evidence given by science to prove that the universe is speeding up. I believe it to be factual and reliable to the extent that we, in our ignorance, can create data. But the bottom line is this: All that is available to us is light and information. These sources of knowledge are viewed through the prism of our relative clock, the limitations of our vantage point and our biases. This is a great handicap. Light and information are extremely limited. They are each limited by the speed of light and by our vantage point. This means that we can only see what our vantage point and our time zone allow us to see. We see a miniscule amount of the total content of the universe. We are governed by a relative clock. This clock is a product of the gravity field we are under, and the speed of our planet as it spins and travels with space. Imagine if we found a way to communicate with one thousand intelligent extraterrestrial races. Each would be living on a planet of different mass. Each of us would have a different clock and, due to rotation and orbits, our years would all be different. Whose clock would we use as the valid time? How old would we say the universe is, when our calendars and clocks don't match? Given that all planets are traveling in different directions and speeds, which direction would we choose in order to observe standard candles (an astronomical standard of measurement)? It would be logical to use the same direction for all observers. Here we would create a serious problem, depending on the direction each observer is moving, their data would be skewed. The frequency of redshift seen by an observer is affected by whether they are moving in the direction of the observation or away from it. We will never be able to determine, from within this relative universe, whether time has been constant throughout time. Time is relative. It is governed by time zones, which are in turn dictated by speed and gravity fields. These are great handicaps. Even in the case of a constant frame of reference, I have no doubt that time has changed over time. Recapping: science says that spatial expansion is speeding up. Even if the information used to prove that spatial expansion is increasing is 100% correct, it is not indisputable, as it relates to expansion.

Through the years, telescopes have improved. In the last few decades, technologies have exploded into most areas. Our ability to observe the cosmos has been one of those fields which have experienced tremendous advances. The Hubble space telescope alone has been a tremendous leap forward. Is it any wonder that, as time multiplies our tech, we see further back in time? But, if you see further into the past, then how can you say the universe is speeding up? Well, the only conclusion is that the past expansion was faster than the present. At this point, we should take note of the cosmic distance ladder (also known as the extragalactic distance ladder). This ladder is one of the ways we measure distance in the universe. We shall not go down that ladder together. If you want to, you can search for either ladder on the net. Be ready, each rung gets further from us, and more complicated to follow. I'm sure we had the expansion rate right, for the distances closest to us. As soon as we became accurate using the distance ladder, we arrived at an accurate rate, in space close to us. It takes no great imagination to believe that the closer a distance is to us, the easier it is to measure that distance. Since we started our measurements with the closest to us, we proceeded from recent to further in the past. So, if we are told that the universe is speeding up, then it's the past, not the present, which they are talking about. I don't think anyone would argue that the universe has never expanded faster than inflation in the beginning. We believe that, in the beginning, the universe expanded faster than light speed. I believe it has been slowing down ever since. This belief is born from the logical conclusion of replicating space theory.

Here's the full story. I believe that this increase in the expansion rate, in the past, will mean a slowdown in the future. So, the Hubble constant is constant through space but not through time. If you were to make a graph of the rate through time, it would curve through time, and the curve would be less pronounced in the future. Very far in the future, it would seem like a straight line. But why? The reason is simple. It is a curve based on time. I believe that every time space doubles, the expansion rate halves. Once you get, let's say to 1 mile per second per megaparsec, it would seem to be a straight line. What happens when space doubles again? That's right! It would expand half a mile per second per megaparsec. Someone has just refused to read forward unless we answer an obvious question. "In this scenario, won't you get to zero expansion rate very quickly, or at least eventually?" Not at all. There is no limit as to how many times you can split that last mile. Let me show you how. One becomes half, then quarter, then eighth, then sixteenth, thirty second, sixty fourth and so on. Given that each time the expansion rate halves, the universe must double. Do you get the picture? There is infinity between one and zero in both the expansion rate and in the size of the universe. The infinity argument is indeed powerful. But this animal has two legs, so here is where the other shoe drops. Why must we divide space into megaparsecs? Why not gigaparsecs? Then, don't forget tera, peta, exa, zetta, and so on. We could also expand time instead of space. The expansion rate is miles per second per megaparsec. Why not miles per trillion years? How about inches per trillion years. You get the idea. There is more than one way to skin a cat, as President R. Reagan use to say.

What accounts for the math? How can we use distance and time in the equation, even if not comparable, and still come to the right answer? It's quite simple, really. If you are using the speed of light to check the expansion rate, then is it any surprise that you would come up with a rate explained by the speed of light? So, what was the expansion rate when the universe was half the age it is today? Easy, it was twice what it is today. What will the expansion rate be when the universe is twice the age it is today? Half of what it is today. The biggest question is, why is it so? It's not hard to understand. If you double anything, then you have twice as much as you had before. Replicating space has a constant amount of energy. As it emerges, each time space doubles, the expansion rate halves. "But wait," you say, "does it not also mean that there is double the amount of energy?

Shouldn't this fact keep the rate the same?" No, the inner space, or more accurately, the newer time, is under greater backpressure force. To maintain the same expansion rate, the speed would have to double. The speed of light, if it really is constant, will give us an ever-diminishing expansion rate. The big question is, "are we measuring actual physical expansion, or a mirage made out of light?"

I think most would say that we have thoroughly whipped this dead horse. But I have it in me to whip it one more time. I seriously doubt that the scientists who claimed they found the expansion rate is speeding up, sampled enough data. The shear amount of work needed would discourage the hardiest among us. What do I mean? Earth is not stationary. Earth spins on its axis with a speed, at the equator, of about 1,000 miles per hour. It rotates around the Sun at 67,000 miles per hour. The entire solar system rotates around the center of our galaxy at 514,495 mph. Our galaxy is part of a local group. This entire group of galaxies is moving at about 1,000,000 mph toward the constellation Hydra. One must wonder, if we had the proper vantage point, would we then see our galaxy in rotation around a central point in the universe? What would be that speed of rotation? Why does the speed of Earth, our platform from which we make our observations, matter? Because, depending on whether you are traveling toward a light source or away from it, the light characteristics change. There is, then, the question of the direction toward which the observations of the standard candles were viewed? Was it in the direction of travel, or at a 90-degree angle? How many comparable angles were used? I would imagine the best approach is in single degree angles, encompassing 360-degree arcs around the globe. This, of course, would be a massive undertaking. I was unable to find an answer, but I suspect it was done from directly opposite sides of the planet, in only one plane. There is one last thing I would like to point out. Get ready. This is a brain teaser, or is it a brain twister? When we look into deep space, we are looking at the past. The data used to determine that the expansion is speeding up, is of the very far past. Consider for a moment, as we receive the light from the past, through what medium did that image travel? Is it traveling from past to present or from present to past? As each moment goes by, the universe gets older. As the universe gets older, we see more of it. That new space we see is younger space. As our view recedes from us, isn't it receding into the future? As that image travels back to us, isn't the redshift an effect of travel through younger space? Yes. Indeed. That which we observe is the past. The effects of travel on that image from the past, are the consequence of travel through a chronology of younger to older space. In conclusion, even if science is right and the past is seen to be slower than the present, it is not the effects of the past they are seeing, but of the future. Remember, we are not really witnessing the past, but rather, its reflection. The effects of its travel are from younger space than what we occupy. When we look into outer space, we are looking at a mirror image. This mirror image turns time inside out.

I really think we are like a dog chasing his tail. This search for the exact expansion rate is a fool's errand. I challenge you to find a single current scientist who believes we know the exact size of the universe. It is elementary. To truly know the real expansion rate, you need three things: total size of the universe; how long it has existed; and a vantage point outside of the effects of time dilations. Out of the three, we are only somewhat confident of our estimate of the age. I will not open this Pandora's Box but will make you aware, in case you want to open it. A major factor in determining age is the expansion rate. That's right. The age determines expansion rate and the expansion rate determines age. Good luck with that circular conundrum.

We will never know the true size of our universe. As far as our measure of time is concerned, this is a real problem. Can the age, or the expansion rate, seem the same to us, looking out from Earth, as to someone close to the black hole, at the center of our galaxy? How about someone on the inside of that black hole, just beyond the event horizon? It is believed that beyond the event horizon, time stops, or at least, slows to almost a standstill. Looking out from that black hole at the center of the galaxy, an observer would say that the vastness of space expanded within a few seconds. Should we throw up our hands and stop learning? By no means, but it is delusional to think that we have a handle on the true expansion rate. I want to believe that scientists privately laugh at the notion of knowing the exact expansion rate. One thing is for sure. I have never read any news or science article where this reality was ever mentioned. All I have read, is that they are earnestly trying to come up with an exact expansion rate.

There is a small group of you who still have a problem with my 'take' on expansion. Some have pointed out "how can the expansion be at light speed at the edge, if we see the farthest galaxies moving away at greater than light speed?" Well, there is a logical, albeit difficult, explanation. When you talk about the light speed barrier, it is always between two points within a spatial common point. They must share the same time. In other words, they must be in the same spacetime. Two items, very far away from each other, no longer share the same time. This causes us to see far away galaxies moving faster than light. It is so, because they do so in a different time. In reality, once you factor-in time, they are moving well below light speed. If we see a galaxy in our neighborhood, it will always be moving away at a fraction of light speed. It is true that, if moving at the same speed, the two would share the same clock. But those clocks, or time zones, are only valid at the locality they occur. Once you look through great distances, what you see is the past of that other time zone. What you see is both the past and spacetime as they have traveled and stretched, together. It seems to you, that you and the other galaxy are in the same time. But your clock is the local clock. Meanwhile, the other galaxy is on their local clock, plus all the time we have gained due to the distance. From a vantage point, there is a difference in time between images of galaxies very far away from each other. I still sense confusion in my readership. Let me try one more angle. Let's say you stared at a galaxy through a telescope for one second. How much time is that on your clock? Right, one second. But how much time of that far away galaxy have you witnessed? It could only be the same one second if you were watching up close in real time. But due to the distance, you see it in the past. But a past that has stretched. So, suppose you spent one second, but it equaled 15 seconds of time for those in the other galaxy. This was due to the stretching of spacetime. Their perceived movement would be 15 times more than their actual local movement. You really need to try and accept that everything in the universe is its own reference point. The only way you can use a point of reference, other than yourself, is if you are on the surface of a heavenly body. A body that is only gravitationally bound to another body in space, is not an accurate reference point. Orbits and rotation make everything in the universe useless as a reference point. Of course, the worst case is a body that is not gravitationally bound and not under the same time. I know some of you still have questions about stretched time, but this is as far as I can go into time, at this time. Don't despair, time will be explained properly. Be patient. Most of the book is still ahead of you.

If a galaxy is gravitationally bound to us, it will not be moving away. It can even be moving toward us. Andromeda is actually moving toward us, on a collision course. Do not sell your savings bonds, yet. It will be 4.5 billion years before we collide. Even then, chances are that there will be few, if any collisions. Galaxies look closely knit but there are huge spaces between stars. It is very likely that some are still stuck. Let's do away with all of the confusion. Science has proven, time and again, that nothing with detectable mass travels faster than light. Since this is a proven fact, let's use it. If the universe has, as I believe, an edge, how fast is it expanding? Well, if you were in a galaxy located very close to the edge, how fast would the surrounding galaxies move, in relation to yours? Correct, nothing around you could move faster than light speed. But wait just a minute. If this is true, then how and where will the light speed expansion manifest itself? Great question! The newly created universe would manifest itself as it emerged from a 'time with no time' into linear time. At that point, any item within that new spacetime will move away from you at the usual sub-light speeds. For the learned ones, it is the frontier between linear time and the quantum world. The creation of matter will be at light speed, as it emerges out of a 'time with no time'. But the light speed barrier is not broken because this is new space coming into being. It is not existing space bound by time to the observer. Hence, it is as I stated before, the frontier between linear time and the quantum world.

A very small group has realized the Achilles heel of our figures on expansion rates. According to what I'm telling you, nothing travels faster than light at the edge of the universe. But the universe itself is growing at light speed or faster than light. So how does it not violate the light speed barrier? Because the appearance of space and matter, indeed, is, at least, at light speed. But the other side is the nothingness where space will soon expand. But without a local point of reference, you can't say the light speed barrier has been broken. You see, you can only measure time after an item has materialized. From that point forth, it will move away from everything else in its vicinity at sub-light speed. Now, if you ask how fast the edge is growing, in relation to yourself, then yes, things are appearing at faster than light speed. But movement does not start until things appear. I think most of you have understood. To the ones who have not, don't despair. The next few chapters clarify this further.

Here I need to write a correction to my first work. I thought it logical that, as space expands, we would lose sight of galaxies. It is said that when the universe goes past the 19-billion-year age, we will start losing galaxies. Science believes that light from anything beyond the 19-billion-year age could never reach us. This is consistent with their belief that all matter in the universe was created in the beginning. This, however, gives us untenable consequences. It means that all but a few of the galaxies that currently exist began in the beginning of the universe. If this were the case, then we would see all of the galaxies, since what we see is time, not distance. They would also look the same, since they formed at about the same time. This would also mean that, at one time early on, they were all very close to each other. That is ridiculous. If all galaxies were present at the beginning, it was then one solid galaxy. I would like to ask you the following. How can we see galaxies receding from us, at greater than light speed? The light is continuous, as is the expansion of the universe. It is true that matter is being propelled away from us, with space. But light is being propelled to us by the same expanding space.

I would like to point to the raisin bread analogy, where the universe is like a raisin bread in the oven. As it gets larger, the raisins get farther apart. If it were true, then in the beginning, the dough contained so many raisins per volume, that they were touching each other. But at no time is there ever a point where there is no dough between each raisin. In space, the dough, or medium, stretches in both directions. I no longer believe we will ever lose sight of anything we currently see. Why? Because, once you see something, unless light stops shining, it is like a rubber band reaching back to us. If the light can stretch to a point that it would no longer be visible or detectable, then that is another story. In all I have read, I've never found a limit at which light becomes undetectable. We will continually see new things as time goes by. All the while, never losing what we already see. We will, however, never see the universe in its entirety. As the universe ages, the light-borne expansion will slow. No matter how old the universe gets, we will retain what we see, and just keep increasing our view. "How can a finite number be infinite", you ask? You already read how. The answer is simple. Just answer me how many fractions of a mile in one mile? That's right, there is no limit to the number of pieces you can divvy up a mile. Keep in mind, each time you cut it in half, the universe would have doubled. Let's use the smallest scientific length, the Planck. How many Planck lengths are in a mile? There are 1,609,344 millimeters in a mile. There are 61,87

9,273,540,000,000,000,000,000,000,000 Planck per millimeter. This would give us virtually infinite expansion.

Perhaps a simpler way to think of this expansion business is not from space, but from time. If space expanded at a constant rate, then it would double in size at a set time. This would mean that each time space doubled, the next doubling would take equal the time.

I hope there is no doubt in your mind that time and space are tied at the hip. If you have no problem with this scientific belief, then you can leap with me into wonderland. Are we changing merely space when the universe expands? If traveling through space, at great speeds, slows time, then what happens if you have more space through which to travel? The new space cannot be ruled by the same time. It seems perfectly logical to me, that if you have doubled the space, then you have halved the time. As is often the way when looking at something in the duality of spacetime, it can be equal opposites. You have half the time and double the time at the same time. Let me see if I can untangle part of the knot that I just put our brains into. I can't undo it all in this chapter. It would be easy to tell you which chapter to go to. But, great effort has been expended by a man without a memory (yours truly) to arrange these topics in order. I promise that this knot in your brain will disappear by the time you finish this book.

What happens if you get into a very fast ship and speed away? This will take you out of phase, if you will, with your starting point. Under a set speed, you are flowing with space. Under an acceleration, you are traveling through time. This time travel sets you at a spatial time zone* that has a slower clock than your starting point. Why? Because less of the time that is emanating from your original location can wash over you. Please note your original location, while accelerating, is in constant change. Your place of origin becomes where you were a split second ago. As soon as you are under an acceleration, time starts changing its progression for you, in relation to all other objects at different speeds. In other words, at a constant speed, you are at a given time zone. Under an acceleration, your time zone is changing continually.

Some of you are feeling betrayed. That pretzel knot in your brain has gotten worse, not better. Therefore, I have told you that as space doubles, time halves. It is the result of relativity. As space expands, can time remain the same? Not at all. If space and time are indeed tied at the hip, then any change in one must change the other. In this way, all of space can be covered by the same time. This is also why I do not believe there are alternate universes. All of creation is within this bubble universe, within the sea of eternity. Science is certain, however, that expansion has changed over time. I concur. Expansion changes over time. Where we part is when they claim it is speeding up. It is actually slowing down. It was never any faster than in the inflationary epoch. I believe it has slowed down ever since. This means that if we think of time, rather than space, it is much simpler. As any portion of space doubles, it takes longer to double again. Light speed, being a constant, means that the rate of expansion of space over time must diminish. By using time, rather than space, we solve the expansion limit. How long is too long for space to double? Infinity. I hope you were able to follow me, and make the switch. If you did, the expansion conundrum should have disappeared from your mind.

I just know there are a few of you who are very aggravated. You are probably screaming at the book by now. "Mr. Farmer, how can we see to the end, or actually to the beginning, without seeing the whole?" Let me bring everyone up to speed, then, to tackle this conundrum. When we look through a telescope, the farther you look, the further back in time you see. The furthest object we have seen is 13.4 billion years in the past. This should scream out to you the following question. If we see all the way back to the beginning, then why don't we see all of the universe? Take a sip of your iced tea. Put on your best thinking cap. Are you ready? Let's go. We see all there was, within light's ability to get back to us. The oldest galaxies are at the rim of the visible universe. But what we see is not reality, but light. So where will the younger galaxies be seen? Well, if we see the older ones at the rim of the universe, they will always stay at that rim.

Eventually, the younger galaxies must come into view within our current view of the universe. Yes, you understood the statement. They will pop into view between those older galaxies, at the rim, and us. I say 'pop', in a relative way. To us, it would appear like a galaxy is forming. It is a gradual process, regulated by time. From our point of view, we really can't deduce a true chronology, nor order of appearance. We can be sure, however, that those which we see at the rim, are the oldest. 'Oldest' refers to the first galaxies that formed. The younger galaxies came after them. Here is a weird implication of this paradox. At this very second, we can see galaxies in the distant past which are not within our field of view. They are hidden behind galaxies which came after them. Wait, just a minute. How can we see them? Well, the galaxy could have emitted its light before it went past the point in time where the newer galaxy would one day be. Simply, the older galaxies have been emitting their light long enough for their light to reach us. They started emitting when they were closer to our present location, while the younger galaxies formed further away from us, a shorter time ago, and their light has not had time to reach us.

There is another possibility. The light was emitted beyond the location of the newer galaxy. But that light, which we now see, went past the location before those newer galaxies materialized. We see all that time allows us to see, but we cannot ever see all of space. The passage of time will manifest more of the preexisting space. But we will never see all there is, at any given time. You must remember that the light getting back to us runs back at light speed. But the distance between us and the beginning is light speed plus the distance that space has grown. You must also remember the current belief is that the content of galaxies changes over time, but that they were all made at the same time. That is not possible. If all galaxies shared the same age, then they would all be the same. The evidence shows us that the galaxies farthest from us are smaller and have less iron in their stars. We do see stars of different age, within individual galaxies. That is normal since stars die and new ones are born over time. But think this through. If galaxies all started simultaneously, they would all be the same size and share the same make up. Now if the process was gradual, then the first stars would show a small iron content, since iron is made in stars and is propagated by the death of stars. Furthermore, if all matter came into existence in the beginning, then the first galaxies would be huge. The evidence is the opposite.

Congratulations. Some of you have fully understood the nature of time and space. You are now basking in the knowledge of spacetime. This concept was coined by Einstein's former mathematics professor, Hermann Minkowski. This entity called spacetime combines the three dimensions of space with the one dimension of time. In a manner of speaking, we will lose sight of the first older galaxies but only because those that came after them will one day block their light. Hold on now, breathe slowly. I have just told you that we see the elder first and the younger last. More troubling is that we see the further first and the nearer last.

How can you possibly see the furthest before the nearest? It's not as strange as it sounds. It is caused by The Arrow of Time. This Arrow demands that you see the eldest first and the youngest last. Given that, when you look out toward space, you are looking back in time. You see the eldest before the youngest. As with any concept, there are always people who do not believe it is true. In the unlikely event that you do not believe in The Arrow of Time, then answer this. How can you deny The Arrow of Time if what you do today builds on top of what you did yesterday? I hope that convinced you. Did you not see your eldest child first and your youngest last? This is a perfect illustration of the universe. First, the way a child grows, by basically splitting cells to copy them. I'm no biologist, but it would make sense that, as a cell splits, it is half the size it was before. But I have a question for you. What would happen if the cell was irreducible? Yes, what if the cell was already the smallest thing in the universe? The only logical answer is, that when it splits in two, they are both identical. Not just identical in makeup, but in size. This is the case with the replicating energy of spacetime. It is the smallest anything can be in the universe. When it splits, it must be identical in size. In the case of a child, it is using existing matter to create something new, just like heavenly bodies. As a matter of fact, a child's growth rate is greater. It takes a person about 22 Earth years to get to full size. It took the universe 13.8 billion years to get to its current, mature size.

To compare your child with the universe, think of this. You saw your first child grow up, but just like the universe, there was a period of time shrouded from view. He was not yet ready to be gazed at. Once he popped out into view, it was amazing. But he was not very organized, or defined. All his basic components were there, but they needed time to mature. One last thing: you parents were there from 'the beginning'. You saw all of his stages. But, from the perspective of a man who didn't meet your son until he was four, he did not see that first child pop into view. If you have another, then what? Well, if he is a good friend, he might be there on day one, when your new baby comes into view. This describes the beginning, and the progress of the universe perfectly.

I fear many may still have a mental block. Not to worry, you are experiencing a mental block for good reason. The reality is that, in our observation of spacetime, we actually see young and old, at the same time. It's as if we are looking right through matter. Well, more accurately, it's as if we are looking through the space where the matter will be, one day. The odd thing is that our vision is limited by light speed. Even with this limitation, you need to factor in the following concept. Nothing travels through space - everything travels with space. It is true that galaxies, very far away, are moving from us at faster-than-light speeds. But we still see them, right? The reason is that spacetime is expanding in all directions. The galaxies may be moving away from us, at faster than light speed, but spacetime is also expanding toward us, bringing light back to us, at faster than light speed. You must understand that the duality of spacetime causes light to flow with space, at faster than light speed. Think this through. As light travels with space, it does so at light speed. But, from the time it begins its travel, it is doing so at light speed, plus the speed of expansion. Here, I must remind you that this is not the same as two objects. All objects travel well below light speed. So, light outstrips light speed from the first second it departs. By contrast, objects traveling at sub-light speeds take a lot of time to get to an accumulated speed beyond light speed. What accumulates to give objects greater-than-light-speed? It is the sub-light travel speed of the object, plus the growth of space due to expansion. Please understand, this does not mean we are breaking the light speed barrier. We are talking about faster-than-light, between two far objects, so far from each other, so as not to be in the same spacetime. We can only see some of the galaxies, namely the older ones. The younger galaxies, we can't see yet. The younger ones are too far from us for their light to reach us yet. This proves my belief, which is that we will never lose sight of anything we currently see. Our view of the universe will only grow with time.

Let's clear the air and get everyone up to speed. Let's say, for a moment, we lived in a universe that was static. It was not expanding. Everything was of the same age. Since it all materialized simultaneously, we see it all. Nothing new would ever come into view. But our real universe is not static. We live in a relative universe. The speed of light is the fastest thing that can provide us with information. So, the furthest we can see is the beginning of the universe. But what we see are objects which emitted their light so close to us, that when you factor in expansion, their light has had enough time to get back to us. Newer objects came into being further away from our location in spacetime, and their light has not made it back to us, yet. Make no mistake. Presently, everything that exists is closer to us than those things we see 13.4 billion light-years away from us. Physically, they exist, and they are definitely in the proper order, as are those we see at the edge of the universe. The reason why we can't see them, is that the news of their existence, has not had time to reach us yet. I know we must have lost a group of readers. Here is the wall they hit. How can the older galaxies flow past the newer galaxies, without a collision? Earlier, I explained that the newer galaxies already exist, and that the older galaxies must flow past their location, before the newer can become visible. What keeps them from colliding? It's that what we see reflects what has already happened. Don't you see? They occupy the same space, but in different time.

I am amazed to read luminaries in cosmology claiming that everything was present in the beginning. They envision a singularity. According to them, this entity had within it, all of the energy in the universe. But that can only be true if the universe was static. The fact that the universe expands, making new space, blows this concept out of the water. What is amazing to me is that the great men of science, with no understanding of replicating space, have deduced that everything started from a single spec. They are absolutely correct that the potential of the universe was contained in the very first Fountain Of God. Here is their biggest blunder, in this concept. Everything never resided in one place at one time. The universe is not static nor Newtonian. The universe is Einsteinian, or to be more exact, relativistic. Potentially, all that will ever physically be, was indeed present in the beginning. But, that singularity, which these luminaries speak of, is all around us, right now. If you could isolate one of God's Fountains, and materialize it within nothingness, it would create a whole new universe. You see, the universe is composed of nothing but energy. The energy is this replicating spacetime, which I have been drilling into you. Once you internalize this concept of the replicating fountain, everything else is easy to understand.

I see all the comments, associated with the expansion, as one-sided. They always say that the universe is expanding away from us.

One-sided thinking, of course, is what drives this 'disappearing view' of things we now see. No one ever mentions that light is expanding toward us. Space is expanding by replicating from every point to every point. "There he goes, right off the deep end", I heard a reader say. "Does he not know that almost every galaxy is moving away from us? This is proof positive that nothing moves back to us." Please stop and allow me to explain your error. No matter where you are, you see everything moving away. But in space, every point is its own reference point. What seems to you to be moving away, is moving in the direction of every other item, in that direction. That's because it is the medium that is growing. The information is brought back to you on replicating and expanding spacetime.

I hope you have understood that nothing travels through space. It travels with space. We look out into the universe with our telescopes, only to see the past. What we see is a hologram of what things were, all the way back to 13.8 billion years ago. This hologram will grow with age, at the speed of light. It is governed by the relativity of space. A disconnect exists between time and distance. Think of this hologram as a revealing shadow. Instead of a normal shadow, which blocks light, this is a shadow of information. As time progresses, the shadow obscuring the future, gives way. The light returning to us, reveals what had already come into existence. Please give up this notion, ingrained in all of us, about a real expansion rate. The closest thing you can equate to an expansion rate is an interest rate. Imagine the reaction of an economist who devoted his life's work to finding "the exact interest rate through time". He would be the laughingstock of the world. Everyone knows that interest rates change through the years. In this case, the expansion rate is just like that. It appears to be the same rate, through space, at any given point, but not throughout time.

Most of you will be shocked by what I'm about to tell you. Electricity travels through a wire slower than the pace of a turtle. "Well, there he goes, again. This time he has really flipped!" someone said. "I turn on a light, but no matter how far away the light is from the switch, the light turns on immediately. So that means the electrons flow from the switch to the bulb at light speed right"? No, not at all. Think of it this way. Fill a twenty-foot-long pipe with water, with a riser on each end, and make them level. By the way, if you didn't know, this is the easiest way to find two level points, at a distance from each other. Water in a pipe will find its level, no matter how far the ends are from each other. Back to our pipe. Let's say, you set up a 20-foot pipe on a table. You install a one-foot riser on each end. Now you fill the pipe to the brim and level both risers. You now have both ends full of water, as well as the pipe. Put a funnel on one side. Pour in a pint of water in the funnel. How much water will overflow out the other end? That's right. One pint. Is it the same water you poured in the opposite side? Of course not. The water you poured in, displaced the water coming out the other side. How much water would you have to add before the first pint flowed out of the other end? If the apparatus took one gallon to fill, and it took you one second to pour the pint, then it would take eight seconds of constant pouring, before the first ounce of water you poured came out the other end.

This is what you see in electricity. A good conductor, such as copper, is already full of electrons. When you push electrons through the wire, they displace the same number of electrons out through the other side. But a copper wire has a lot of capacity. It's like a big fat pipe. So, it actually takes a long time for the electrons to flow through, to the other side. You see, the flow starts from the end of a wire at light speed (less loss by resistance) but electron flow speed (known as drift velocity) is quite low. The speed of energy, within an energy universe, is the speed of the medium. Being the speed of the medium, which is spacetime, light speed is also the speed of information. What does this have to do with expansion? Here is how drift velocity comes to aid us in understanding expansion. Pretend that the tube with water was attached to the beginning of the universe, and to our planet. If the tube was elastic, it would stretch with the expanding universe. Light, since the beginning of time, has been loading into the pipe for billions of years. But the pipe has gotten longer and thinner. As we investigate that light, what do you see? Just like the pipe carrying water, you would never see what just now came into the pipe. You only see the light that has had time enough to travel the vast distance to you. The color has redshifted, and the amount of light has dwindled, over the eons. That is why we need such huge telescopes, to see billions of years in the past. I hope this was useful to illustrate expansion.

I would like to make you aware of yet another mystery in cosmology, solved by replicating space. How can light from stars 13.4 billion years in the past be seen by us? Common sense would tell us that light at that distance would be so dim and so redshifted as to be undetectable. When we factor in relativity, caused by replicating spacetime, we see the answer clearly. It is true that light from distant galaxies require powerful telescopes to see it. Furthermore, we must make composite pictures to coalesce that light into a discernible photograph. But both these facts are not caused by dim light. It is not dim photons, but fewer photons that gives us the difficulties we encounter when observing light from far away. Here, I must remind you, that light travels with space in its equilibrium point. This equilibrium being one of time. These photons travel to us in the boundary of the duality of spacetime. This means that they are not in linear time. They are in a time, with no time. So, they never get old, tired or dim. Now, remember what I have taught you about spacetime. It travels in straight lines. Each photon emitted by a light source, travels in a straight line, on its own heading. As photons travel away from the source, there are fewer and fewer of them per given area of space. This is normal light, not a focused laser beam. Over large distances, fewer photons are available to strike the lens of our telescopes. Therefore, we need larger and larger telescopes to look ever further into outer space. Every photon we collect is as it was when it left its source. But why? Because it is the same age as when it left the source. It has never been subjected to The Arrow Of Time. It travels in the boundary of time.

Some of you are still lost. You can't rap your head around the conundrum of this expansion of time and space, and what we see. Let me make my last attempt. Forget that the universe is in a constant state of flux. Let me make it easier for your mind to grasp what is happening. Let's imagine that our telescopes could take only one quick photograph of the universe, every 10 years. This allows you to ignore an expanding, dynamic, relative universe. What would you see in each photo? Why a photo? Because a photo is Newtonian, while a movie is Einsteinian or relativistic. In each photo, we would see clear back to the beginning. This, of course, is only possible with our current technology. The difference is that each time we take a photo, we must add another 10 years to the universe's age. This, when you factor in expansion, is a lot more than 10 light-years of space. Our photo would show us 10 light-years of the universe, plus the cumulative expansion. Would you see more stuff in each successive photo? Of course, you would. Each new photo would show 10 years' plus of new stuff. We could not say for certain how much of it is new. Why is it so hard to pick out the new stuff? We don't yet know, nor have we cataloged everything we currently see. But I'd bet my future dentures, that each new picture would have new stuff in it. Your mental block comes from two mental glitches. First, your brain thinks that you are looking at the present. And second, your brain assumes that since you see back to the start you are seeing all there is. Neither is possible. You are seeing the past. The past as it existed 13.8 billion years ago. You only see a small portion of the whole, due to light-speed causing a barrier of information. What you see is not real. None of what you see is where you see it.

Imagine that you asked a friend to walk away from you. You will always see his back, a reflection of where he has been. His light takes time to travel back to you. In such a short distance, it's a very little time period, but there is a difference. You can never see all he has traveled, or what is on the other side of him. The universe is much larger than what we see. As light returns to us, we see more and more. But, due to expansion, the growth is not seen at one end or at the other. It is seen within our field of view. This field of view is solely dependent on light speed. It has nothing to do with the actual size of the universe.

Get ready. You are about to get a nugget of information which belongs in the explanation pages to Einstein's theory of relativity. Recapping: spacetime emanates from every point in space. This makes every point in space its own reference point. But don't think of spacetime as static. It is in motion, because it is replicating. So, at any speed below the speed of light, you are flowing with space. If, you are traveling at a constant rate of speed, space sees you at a standstill. Why, because at that speed, or what I have called spatial time zone, spacetime is emanating at light speed. That is, light speed from your frame of reference. In other words, you see light as a constant, but your clock varies with anyone else who is at a different speed. Why would your clock slow down as you go faster? It's due to spacetime washing less over you, than someone at lower speeds. Here's the key to unlocking the reason why light speed is the same for every frame of reference. It's because light speed is the speed of the self-replicating medium. Understand this, and you will know the why of relativity, which, to the best of my knowledge, eluded Einstein and modern science.

I will close Chapter 3 by declaring that our estimates of the expansion rate are completely and utterly worthless, and without merit. As far as it relates to the actual expansion, the universe is not governed by light-speed. Light speed does not govern, nor reflect the actual existence or expansion of the physical universe. Light speed merely governs the transfer of information. The news of how far the universe has expanded, has not reached us yet. No doubt, what is visible is further than where we see it. How much bigger is the universe, than the part we observe? There is no consensus on the estimates. Some believe it could be as much as 250 thousand times bigger.

The current observable universe is estimated at 93 billion light-years across. Multiply 250 thousand times 93 billion. The answer will be in light-years. Multiply the light-years times the miles in one light-year (5,869,713,600,000). You do the math. I think that the number you get from this exercise pales in comparison to reality. I would not be surprised if the final number of miles you end up with, is actually the number of megaparsecs, not miles. We can only imagine that the universe is bigger than what we observe. There is no way to know, since it can't be observed. Both the beginning and the end are surrounded by a nonphysical eternity. There is nothing physical before the beginning and nothing physical at the end. I have no doubt that the cited expansion numbers are all wrong. They are the result of the limitations of light. If there was a time where space expanded at more than light speed, then your basic unit or yardstick is wrong. We have come to the end of this chapter. It has left me with a headache and I'm hungry. In conclusion: universal expansion rate? "HUMBUG". The rest of the story of the universal expansion rate is waiting for you in the next chapter.

CHAPTER 4

The Inflationary Epoch

B E AWARE THAT I'm not going to give you a chronology of the universe. If you want to know the details, do an internet search. In any search engine, write the query 'chronology of the universe'. I hope you like to read. You will get about 100 million hits. My main focus is in the inflationary epoch, and the current universe. First, let us explain the inflationary epoch, for those who are not familiar with the term. This was a period of rapid expansion of the universe. It went from the size of a dot to a bit larger than a grapefruit, or something perhaps 62 trillion miles long. Please understand that there is no consensus on this, either, but it is well accepted. The reason for this rapid expansion is currently unknown by science. You need to understand this is very complex, like almost every topic we deal with in this book. A single topic can fill a book, by itself. I personally find any topic covered ad nauseam, just that: nauseous.

So, let's accept the condensed snippet description and concentrate on how and why.

I believe there was/is an inflationary epoch. If we are to believe that space does not merely stretch, but that it replicates, then inflation is a must. Let's use 'impersonating thinking'* (IT). I wish I could get every one of my readers to understand, and use, impersonating thinking. Allow me to explain. I started using IT, for short, when I started my self-taught discovery in electricity. I found that by impersonating, or imagining myself, as electricity, I could follow a circuit best. I already knew electricity followed the path of least resistance, and it would not flow into a dead-end circuit (and yes, it can be lured into a capacitor). In replicating space, I want you to imagine that you are that very first dot, at the beginning of the universe. Your desire is to make as many copies of yourself as you can, as quickly as possible. Unopposed, you start expanding outward, replicating at what speed? Beyond ludicrous speed! The speed of this expansion would be like comparing the speed of light with a turtle, stepping once every trillion years.

Are you ready to become the dot? Here we go. We are a dot. We start expanding in 3 dimensions, as one becomes many, in a circle around the first. We do not divide and grow like a cell. The processes are similar, except that each dot replicates identically, in every way, including size. It then spreads, deploying in straight lines, away from its progenitor. The process is repeated continually, by all of these entities, creating an energy fabric. The size of this particle, or energy quanta is indivisible. Everything in the universe is composed of this basic entity. Once it replicates, each of the new ones, as well as the old one, continue to replicate. Are you 'getting the feel' of the doubling effect? Each new dot repeats the replicating cycle, along with all of the previous dots. How long did it take to create 62 trillion miles of space? Milliseconds? Billionth of a second, one googolplex of a second? Actually, if someone claims to know how long the inflation took, ask them to show you the Swiss stopwatch they used to time it. This watch must have measured time, before time existed. More importantly, what method did they use to observe a process that happened 13.8 billion years ago? I should also mention this process was, and is, invisible to us. But there is a more serious problem with this picture. At some point, this runaway expansion slowed down. We know this, because as we look back in time, there are about 380 thousand light-years into which we can't see. This period was under such a high expansion rate, that we did not even get light from it. I don't accept that inflation lasted a tiny fraction of a second, as science believes. I think it lasted through the opaque period. There is an even better reason why I don't accept this time estimate. I believe that when inflation was occurring, time did not yet exist. This was a period of universal existence, where critical mass had not yet been reached. The spherical fruit, representing the universe, was composed only of its pit, if you will. As you will learn, I believe that time started after this center pit had become the outer peel. So, what applied the brakes to this inflation? We are not there yet; we first need time.

Allow me to tell you a fairytale story I heard many years ago. Its origin and veracity are unknown to me. I think it will help you understand the power of doubling anything. Once upon a time, there was a very smart man who invented, among other things, the game of chess. He presented it as a gift to his king. Upon being given the game and its rules, the king was very impressed with his gift and the generosity of his subject. He told the inventor I appreciate such a wonderful gift and would like to be kind to you. Tell me your needs. I will meet them. The man, being among other things a mathematician, told the king, my needs are modest. Please put a single grain of wheat in the first square on the board and double it in each subsequent square. Do this, Oh King, until you have reached the reward that a merciful king is able to bestow on this humble subject. If the king is able, have this done until the 64th square is reached. It is said that doubling one grain of wheat 64 times, is more wheat than humanity has harvested. Total number of grains: 18,446,744,073,709,551,615. My math tells me that at 9,333 grains of wheat per pound this would equal 1,976,507,454,592,258 pounds or 896,528,701,402 metric tons. According to the USDA, the world production of wheat in 2019 was 732,000,000 metric tons. That would mean 1,224 years' worth of production at 2019 levels. Given that wheat production has increased throughout humanity's history, this is indeed more wheat than we have harvested. I don't know if this is accurate, but I do know that it would be a lot of wheat.

A bit of trivia. Did you know that the unit of weight originated using grains of wheat or barley? A 16-ounce pound (avoirdupois pound) is 7000 grains. A grain being the weight of a barleycorn which is equal to 1 1/3 grains of wheat. The unit, carat, is also seed based. One carat is the weight of one carob seed, equal to the weight of four wheat grains, or three barleycorns.

Keep in mind that each time space replicates, one dot, becomes many. Think of this process happening, with each dot, all the while, expanding out at a rate much faster than light speed. This, I believe, is the space we can't see into. The first 380,000 years. Here is the white elephant in the room. What was the expansion rate in that inflationary period? We think it was faster than light. What amount of space is covered in that 380,000-year opaque period? We don't know. It will always remain hidden from us. This opaque period can easily be confused with the 4 to 5 hundred-million-year mark, when the universe finally became conducive to star light.

Why can't we see past a certain point, to the very beginning? Science says that early on, the universe was dense, and so hot, that not only did light not yet exist, but it couldn't have traveled through such a dense soup, of whatever was there. I do not share that belief completely. I think there was no light, nor matter, nor time as we know it, because the universe had not yet reached critical mass.

As expansion began, there was no control or back pressure at all. Spacetime was unfettered in its expansion. As a result, each time that space doubled in volume, so did its speed. The outer rim could keep doubling its speed, but the inner body could no longer sustain the ever-doubling rate of expansion. As more space was made, the volume of energy could no longer be pushed ever faster. A frontier developed, where the hyper speed of the inrushing spacetime clashed with the lower speed of the inner body of the universe. I have called this process the Spatial Hammer*. I would like to introduce this new term to you. I named the process 'spatial hammer', after the water hammer effect observed in plumbing. It is, basically, a compressive shock of a substance, by means of a clash, or a sudden stop, as it encounters a barrier. In the case of space, the resulting compression of energy creates matter, be it basic gases, but matter just the same. As matter is created, it is spread evenly, and gravity coalesces matter in concentrated areas. It may not seem to us, sitting within a galaxy, that matter is evenly distributed in the universe. But when you look at the big picture, matter is said to be distributed equally, throughout the visible universe, to an accuracy of 0.01%. If matter had not been made all at once, as science believes, but was, instead, created as space replicated, then that would explain its even distribution. For you learned ones, this solves the flatness problem. This continuous generation of matter explains why we have seen galaxies at the edge of the beginning. To date, the youngest and furthest one seen is GN-z11. Youngest, because it's the closest we have seen to the beginning of time, and furthest because we see it at 13.4 billion light years. The actual, or proper distance from us, right now, taking expansion into account, should be several times the distance seen now. Of course, that is, if it still exists. Remember, we are talking about the observable universe. Beyond what we see, no one has a clue.

I believe that the creation of matter, once it began, has never stopped. Yes, you read right. Don't back up to read it again. Matter is still being made. You will find the full story in the next chapter.

CHAPTER 5

Matter Creation, is it Ongoing?

SCIENCE BELIEVES THAT the creation of matter occurred within that beginning, within that opaque inflationary epoch. The expanding universe then spread matter, evenly, to an accuracy of 0.01%. Here, I think, we need to cut through the misinformation, and the pride that would create such a statement. Firstly, how could we say for sure that matter was made only in the beginning, if all that we now see, does not cover that beginning? The mechanism that created matter, is, and will probably always be, out of our reach to study. We do know that matter is simply compressed, or dense energy. Here, again, I can imagine many readers arguing that matter is not compressed energy. Look, you can give it all the names and explanations you like, but, at the end of the day, it can only be one thing. Energy. Why am I certain that it is compressed energy? Because energy is all there is in the universe. Matter is a lot of energy, occupying a small volume. What else could it be, other than compressed energy? So, all that is needed, is energy for the raw material, and more energy to compact, compress or somehow coalesce that raw material, into the finished product.

How can we conceive that compressed energy makes up all we see? All gasses, liquids and solids are made from this compressed energy. It is not hard to imagine. Do a net search of photos of snowflakes. When you are able to recover from the shock caused by their beauty, you will notice the following. They radiate from the center, splitting in ever-propagating rays. This is a portrayal of regenerating spacetime. The other thing you will realize, is that no two are the same. They do seem to fall into families, but just like human families, no two members are the same. This is a great way to imagine the endless possibilities, for the creation of differing shapes, using such small pixels (the atom). Here I must remind you that according to RST, the atom is not the elementary particle or quanta that makes up all we see. Atoms are, indeed, the final building block of what is visible to us. However, if you could magnify your gaze to the last possible setting, you would see the Fountain Of God quanta particle. It is the elementary entity of which all else is made. Most of you are familiar with graphic manipulating programs on the computer. Well, those computer programs can illustrate how compressed energy can make up everything we see. Open any picture or graphic on any one of those programs. Now, zoom in to the highest setting available. Voila! You see individual pixels. Keep in mind that these pixels are monstrous compared to atoms. Now, imagine how many ways we can combine atoms. There is virtually no limit as to how we can combine atoms to make matter. With their minute size, you can make any texture or appearance you want. Have you ever seen a mote of dust? You have but some of you don't know you have. A mote is that dust particle revealed by a beam of light. Well, those motes of dust are a million atoms wide. The closest we can get to see this tiny pixel (the atom), is with an electron microscope.

Particularly, a transmission electron microscope. Do a net search for TEM pictures. They are really interesting.

We need to resolve how matter was created, before we can find out whether the process is still ongoing. Let us travel in our minds to the beginning of the universe. I think I have made it clear that the universe could not have begun with all its energy from the start. It is illogical to believe that a speck can house all of the contents of the universe. More troubling is that physics would not allow it. There is no way in which so much energy, in such a small area, would ever expand. Well, it looks like you are wrong, I'm not the one with the most vivid imagination. Science holds that title. Faced with such an illogical obstacle, science used its boundless imagination. Here, science conjures up a convenient creation. A singularity. A singularity is a point in spacetime where matter is infinitely dense. Don't worry about trying to fit that into your thoughts. It's not rational. It's like the cartoons where the character looks into a tepee, and it's infinitely large inside, yet he can rap his body around the outside.

OK, let's give science the benefit of the doubt. Let's say a singularity existed. If it did, then it obviously had to transition from that state and start expanding. At the moment it started expanding, it was no longer a singularity. Yet, it must still contain all of the energy of the universe. If it ever managed to expand, it would form one big single galaxy. If it somehow formed multiple galaxies, then it would make those first galaxies huge, and those galaxies which came later would drop in size as the universe got bigger. Yet, what we see is the opposite. The first galaxies are smaller. This is no small matter. In a universe so evenly distributed, such a regional aberration is not to be taken lightly. Consider that even without the benefit of communication, the universe is evenly distributed. The distribution of matter is said to be consistent to an accuracy of 0.01%. Let's bring this home for everyone. Who among us has not done some painting? Let's say you need 5 gallons of paint to paint your house. You go to your paint supplier and choose the paint. Problem. They only have gallon sized containers. They make the color in each can, by adding the right amount of each color to the base paint. You get home, and not being a professional, you start with one can and paint the contents of each individual can. When the walls dry, the full extent of the disaster is seen. There was a small difference with each can. The colors were off a bit. The house is painted with 5 shades of the same color. Why did this happen? There was no communication between the contents of each can. Had you been a professional, you would have emptied all 5 gallons into a pail and mixed all of them together.

the universe has been making galaxies for billions of years. Yet, the universe is distributed, evenly, close to perfection. All this, without the ability to communicate with the various parts. The great distances insure that the information cannot travel between its areas. How is it so even? More importantly, it looks the same in all directions. But wait, why is the beginning different from the rest? It's simple. Matter did not appear all at once, in the beginning. The process started gradually and ramped up quickly to a uniform state.

If all matter was not formed in the beginning, then how did it get here? By applying replicating space to the problem, the solution is both simple and obvious. The creation of matter started from the center, and as it expanded, it formed the outer rim of the universe. It is, as you will learn later, doing the same that it did since the beginning. In this Rim of Creation, there is no limit to the speed of space-energy, for there is no time. Within this region, without the constraints of time, the outer flow clashes with the inward flow. The difference between the two, makes the Spatial Hammer. The density of this Creation Rim diminishes and dissipates into the nothingness of the outer border. This dissipating energy has a silver lining. One of the greatest mysteries in Big Bang cosmology is the creation of matter. It has been accepted that matter has an evil twin. His name is antimatter. If matter and antimatter come in contact with each other, they annihilate each other. If, as science believes, they were created in equal quantities, then, we should not be here. But how about, if, as a byproduct of creation, antimatter was expelled into the void outside of creation? There, it would cease to exist, leaving matter to be dominant in creation. This unbalanced universe brings us stability. Together with antimatter, we can imagine that magnetic monopoles and exotic particles are also purged in the same manner. We can then give RST credit for providing us with the solution to the exotic relics problem.

At the end of Chapter 2, a reader raised an issue with RST, pertaining to the topic of this chapter, the creation of matter. The issue is this: if RST is correct, then why don't we have an area in the center of the universe devoid of matter. I tell you that the center of the universe is now its rim. Logically, if the universe started from a center, then that center has no matter. The Spatial Hammer did not start making matter until the inflation stopped. This means there should be a great void somewhere in space. This void should be empty space. Well, there is such a thing. Do a net search for "supervoid in the universe". This monstrous void is about 1.8 billion light years across and devoid of matter and dark matter. It's interesting that if matter is missing, then so would be dark matter. I have not found information on its shape. But you probably already know which shape I would assign this void. Of course, you do. I'd bet dollars to doughnuts; it is a sphere.

I just know the learned ones are hungering to wrap their hands around my neck. I can even imagine that some are thinking "if this ignorant farmer dares to write a book about things he has not formally studied, then I can write one too." Well, good for you. Go ahead and commit to the time, effort and expense to bring your book to life. But I caution you not to quit your day job. Remember the Pareto principle. The vast majority of all efforts end in failure, while success is concentrated in the few. Let me give you an angle on ignorance that you may ignore. The more you know, or learn, the more ignorant you are. This closely resembles the universe. As the sphere of the universe grows, so does our ignorance. Well, as our knowledge of any topic grows, we become aware of just how ignorant we are. Therefore, for the sake of humility, I must now claim I'm extremely knowledgeable on the topic of cosmology. If you insist, I'm very ignorant on the topic of the universe, I truly thank you for the compliment.

The evidence for a finite, expanding universe is very abundant. Here is something that is fairly easy to understand. As the universe expands, matter must be created, along with space. If matter is not continually created, then the edge of space would have to grow with nothing in it, as it expanded. In that case, there would be a very large ring around the edge of the universe, with nothing in it. That ring would appear to be a space between the edge and the first galaxies.

I would like to offer you a small piece of evidence that fully indorses the concept of the Spatial Hammer. Please look up 'Ralph Alpher and Robert Herman helium' on any search engine on the net. Yes, indeed, primordial nuclear synthesis is a well-accepted concept. The math and the concept is a 'given' in cosmology. It has been a great joy to see my concepts supported by previous discoveries. Perhaps, the greatest joy is to learn that science has known the evidence for a good while. We are not talking about learning a scientific fact, and then searching for an alternative explanation. It is the coming up with a concept first, and then imagining what would have to be true, if the concept is correct. Lo and behold! I have found that proof of most of the concepts in these, my two books, are supported by known science discoveries. In the case of Ralph Alpher and Robert Herman, they were puzzled that the abundance of helium could not be explained by the stars. We believe helium is 25 percent of all matter in the universe. There is no way that the stars could have made that much helium. Alpher and Herman's answer to how helium could have preceded the stars, was that the helium was made, in the beginning, by the universe. The only difference between their findings, and my concept of the Spatial Hammer, is that I believe that the process of making helium is still ongoing. Both of these men believed it happened very quickly, in a short time, in the beginning. In a manner of speaking, we are all three right. It happened in the beginning. The only thing they got wrong, is that they assign a set period of time to that beginning. I don't think time existed or exists in the beginning. The absence of time means that a process that somehow starts, never ends.

With the advent of the Hubble Space Telescope, science has had to rethink many things. Let's get into one of those things. Prior to having the ability to peer into the very distant past, we thought that galaxies took longer to form. I don't mean the length of time they took to materialize. I mean the length of time it takes for them to show up, after the beginning. For instance, let's take galaxy GN-z11. This galaxy is believed to be 13.4 billion years old. We see this galaxy fully formed, 13.4 billion years in the past. But wait! A galaxy does not poof into existence. The image we see, is of a fully formed galaxy. We are seeing light from the stars that make up the galaxy. But how long did it take to form the stars that make up that galaxy? Then of course, there is the small matter of those stars coming together to form a galaxy. We can dig deeper, and ask how long it took for matter to become available, for stars to form in the first place? The formation of galaxies, so quickly after the beginning, has several implications. Firstly, expansion seems to be faster in the beginning. Clearly, we require space to house those early galaxies. If they formed in close proximity, they would have coalesced into one, or at the most, a few large galaxies. Secondly, these early galaxies are visibly smaller. This could only be the case if matter had become available gradually, and not, as science believes, created entirely in the beginning. Lastly, the fact that we see these galaxies farthest away, and that they are different, proves the following: the universe did not make all of its contents simultaneously. It had a beginning. This tells me, that if it had a measurable beginning, then it cannot be infinite. Anything infinite in space must be infinite in time. Have you forgotten space and time are inseparable?

Spacetime and matter only become possible and visible after light is emitted. Light, of course, denotes the existence of spacetime.

Spacetime becomes available at the critical spatial pressure at which light can exist, and travel with space. Prior to this point, light may exist, but it is invisible because space is faster than light. So, if space is expanding beyond light speed, then no light can flow out of that region (Light does not travel through space: light flows with space). It creates an event horizon, like a black hole. This raises a question. Why does a black hole not create matter? It is true that the event horizon and the opaque area of the Rim of Creation are both horizons. There is a difference between the two. In the Creation Rim, which is that part of the universe which is opaque to us, the flow of spacetime is many times more voluminous, than in a black hole. In both cases, all that's needed to keep light from emerging, is for spacetime to travel, just a bit faster than light speed.

The Spatial Hammer did not begin at full efficiency. It did not begin creating matter at full capacity. The uneven flow of spacetime had not yet reached critical mass. Once the system stabilized, the creation of matter was stable. This stable creation built an equally distributed universe.

Matter creation has never stopped. I don't mean new things, like planets and stars, made out of existing matter. I mean the actual material to make planets and stars. Why would I go out on a limb, to the end of the universe, so to speak, and make such a claim? Here are some of my observations. Once something starts, there must be something that stops it. If you fall off your feet, then you'll the ground, unless something stops you. If you throw an object, then it will never stop, unless acted upon by something. Even in my daily life on the farm, I found that if you don't want a dog to eat your eggs, then don't let him taste the first one. Once he does, you are both in for a rough time, unless you can break the habit. Back in my school days, I saw many bullies. They never stopped until they got a good taste of their own medicine.

Have you considered matter distribution? Matter is distributed so evenly, that it could not have been present in the beginning, while maintaining that even-distribution, throughout the expansion. Logically, we would expect that matter would be spread more densely, closer to the beginning. It is a great mystery how matter is so evenly spread, all the way back to the beginning. In all that I've read regarding this matter, I have found no credible answer to the distribution dilemma. Not only is matter distributed evenly, but galaxies are smaller in the beginning. This makes no sense, according to current Big Bang dogma. In that case, we would see massive galaxies, as soon as they started to appear. After all, the universe was very small in comparison to its current size. According to science, all the matter in the universe was present, in close proximity. Gravity should have attracted massive amounts of matter to form huge galaxies.

So, here again, replicating space comes to our rescue. In this early period, the creation of matter was weaker (as you have read and will read in the next pages). This would give us less available matter with which to make large galaxies. But, equally important, is the following question. Did spatial pressure begin with a set value, or did it build up gradually? I think the answer is obvious. It built up gradually. Differences in flow can only happen in a system, if there is some pressure. In the absence of pressure, no flow differential can exist. Flow is key to gravity. Within the Rim of Creation, there is no spatial pressure, so there is no gravity. If, as I believe, spatial pressure increased gradually, then so did gravity. Less available matter, and less gravity to bring it together, makes smaller galaxies. Voila!

Time is central to this universe. It is discussed throughout this book. Time is covered in greater detail in Chapters 6 and 7. But, here, I must take a short excursion into the emergence of time, as it relates to matter. I think everyone understands my concept of how space is made by the Spatial Hammer. I do know, however, that some of you do not accept that this is how matter is made. One possible objection might be, that a brief contact between two wave fronts of energy, can't possibly create matter. Here is where time comes into play. It's not only matter that is being made by the Spatial Hammer.

You must realize that this effect is happening at the frontier, between linear time and a 'time with no time'. It can be argued, with good success, that space, time and matter must all begin simultaneously. If you have matter and no space, where would you put it? If you had matter and space, when would you put it? I believe space, time and matter are created within the outer rim of the universe. Here are two key questions. How long does it take to make time? It takes no time to make time. How long does it take to make matter? Since it's made along with time, it takes no time. The same holds true for space. I believe that space, time, and matter emerge, in unison, from the outer rim, to become part of the universe.

Question related to this topic. How many of you have pondered, how it is that living things grow? At first glance, it seems that life creates matter. Let's take a tree, for instance. Who can deny that wood is solid matter? If you have any doubt, tap your head with a baseball bat. So, how does a tree make wood, and is it making solid matter? Well, it may surprise many of you to learn that trees make wood out of thin air. You have heard the evils of CO_2. Well, let me tell you the full story. Trees, and life in general, are actually the closest thing to a matter replicator. Unlike the Sci-fi replicators, trees do not convert energy to matter. Trees take CO_2 (gaseous matter) from the air. They take water and a dash of minerals from the ground, and with some power from the Sun, they make wood. So what percentage of the wood is CO_2? Wood is about 50% water and 50% CO_2. You may want to tell the guys demonstrating against CO_2, that without it, there would be no trees, no food, and no oxygen. If I could return to my youth, I would love to devote a part of my life to discovering how a tree makes wood. If we could duplicate that process, we would be able to make food and anything that we make out of wood. How great would it be to make a 50-pound mango for a family gathering? Imagine a replicator that could make anything of wood. Supply it the choice of wood, the plans for a piece of furniture or even a house and wake up the next day to a brand-new furnished home. Mind you, a house unlike any other, without nails, nor seams. A one-piece house grown overnight. Even the roofing material would be made like skin on a fruit, or the bark of a tree. All made from a few dollars' worth of minerals, a few hundred dollars of energy, some water, and a lot of thin air. Picture a tree house, I mean literally a house that is complete with rooms, decks, and railings, all made from a living tree. Of course, you could choose between a living tree house and a dead one. The living, complete with root system and leaves, versus an inert tree house, like we currently make out of harvested wood.

I've concluded that the answer to the 'issues' with the creation of matter, are all resolved by replicating space. Replicating space, incrementally producing matter, explains the early appearance and the even distribution of matter. The Spatial Hammer effect did not begin at the moment where the creation of matter was optimal. The process began from the minimal side. It is simply logical, that if you start from the minimal, you'll get less than if you start from the optimal point. Therefore, replicating space does not merely accommodate the early appearance of matter, and its modest beginning. Replicating space demands them both. Then how do we go from this modest beginning, relatively speaking, of course, to the average, or norm? Please, never forget, looking out into space, we are looking back in time. That which we see the furthest, is younger than the closest. It is, then, completely logical that the first galaxies we see in the past, would be smaller. Then, as we get closer to the present, where the Spatial Hammer is at full capacity, we see the norm emerge. We should also point out, that the Spatial Hammer is not capable of giving us solids. It gives us gasses. Those gases, then, are made into solids, by stars. Those stars use gasses, and energy in the form of gravity and heat, to create solid matter. Just as a tree creates wood from CO_2, stars create solids, such as metals, from gases.

To an old mechanic and farmer like me, this two-step process makes total sense. In mechanical repairs, compressed air is one of our greatest tools. We don't only use it to blow things clean. We run it through all kinds of tools that multiply our strength and speed in doing work. To compress this air, we routinely use a two-stage pump. The pump is composed of at least two cylinders. One will be larger than the other. The first cylinder will pull a large volume of air. This air is then injected into the second, smaller cylinder. That cylinder will further compress it into the holding tank. A single cylinder, or one stage compressor, is normally set at 125 psi. A two cylinder, two stage, compressor is set at 175 psi. If you needed a lot more pressure, you would just increase the number of stages. For those of you who scuba dive, look at the compressor used to fill scuba tanks. You will notice several cylinders in a row of ever decreasing size. This, of course, mimics the creation of matter. The Spatial Hammer produces gases by compressing energy. The stars take that compressed energy, compress it further, and make solids from gasses. Why does the Spatial Hammer not make solids directly? There is simply not enough pressure. The power of stars is another matter, altogether. You see, the Spatial Hammer relies on flow, in order to compress energy. Two colliding fronts of energy are limited in the amount of pressure they can exert. But in a spherical star, there is virtually no limit. A sphere, under equal gravity pressure from all sides, is limited in the pressure it can create, only by its mass. The bigger the star, the higher the pressure. The star is the final piece in the puzzle of the creation of matter. A star is obviously not possible, unless you have gasses: the two main gasses being helium and hydrogen. Spacetime is not dense enough to collect and to make stars, but gasses are.

I need to quote from my first book. I have tried my best to stay away from doing this. I see quoting oneself as tantamount to telling you "I told you so". It just rings badly. My enthusiasm, or should I say my surprise and delight, has caused me to quote myself. Some of you probably think that I call myself a farmer, and unlearned, to dazzle you with my scientific statements. Perhaps others think that it is a false modesty. After all, "modesty is the only sure bait when you angle for praise", Lord Chesterfield. But truly, I mean what I say, and I say what I mean. I may, however, at times, not say all I could.

Here is the quote from my first book, Let There Be Light, on page 80, in Chapter 6, Matter, Energy and Spacetime. "Matter. What is it? To me it is compressed or dense energy. What can compress energy to a point of becoming solid? Energy is all it takes to make matter as both an ingredient and a facilitator". Among the most joyous moments in the adventure of writing these books, is when the concepts are confirmed. No, it is not that anyone has confirmed any of what I have written. It is that, as I research different topics, I find the confirmation of what I had already written. And here, my quote above is confirmed. When you hear the words atom smasher or super conductor, super collider, or particle accelerator, what comes to mind? What do you think they learn by smashing particles? Well, to the unlearned, like to myself, it means that they smash particles to learn what is in them. But I was pleasantly surprised to learn, that is not what accelerators do. They accelerate particles to almost the speed of light, then they collide them head-on to make matter. Within the split second of the collision, the newly resulting particles are detected. The data is recorded, to find what new matter was made. They do not accelerate energy particles, as in the True God particle that makes up spacetime. They start with hydrogen gas, then split the electrons from the protons, and they smash these protons. The protons are the ingredient. The accelerator supplies the energy. The end product will be matter. So, energy in the form of protons, and energy in the form of acceleration, gives us matter. This should leave no doubt that matter was, indeed, created in the beginning, which is still continuing. The only difference is the location. The beginning started in the center. Now, it is the outer rim of the universe.

There is one more nugget we can extract from particle accelerators. We use protons to collide them and make different particles. Wait just a minute. That's like saying I'm going to smash two bananas together and expect to get a fruit cocktail out of it. Why do we get different particles from the same collision while using a single type of particle? Because it's all energy. The matter being forced to collide at high speeds is energy and the force causing the high-speed collision is also energy. So, what makes up everything? Energy. We who understand RST know that everything is energy, initially replicated by the Fountain of God.

I will conclude this chapter with the strongest and best argument, as to how and why matter is still being made. Here, relativity rears its ugly head, again. The outer rim of the universe is moving, at least, at the speed of light. Once we reach the speed of light, time is believed to be close to a standstill. The lack of the existence of time in the outer rim, means that there has been no deviation from its beginning, 13.8 billion years ago. Even more mind boggling is this thought. That outer rim, if traveling at greater than light speed, is actually losing time. Losing time? Yes, theoretically, regressing into the past. If you could travel through this outer rim, time would start running backwards, until you reached the moment of the beginning. There, all time, all movement and all reality would stop. You are back at the beginning. So, we could say, that the beginning keeps going on, because it is brand new. The beginning is no longer the center. The beginning exists at the edge of the universe. It is brand new, because no time has elapsed within its frame of reference. Even beyond this concept, it is brand new, and getting younger. It encompasses even the beginning of the Big Bang.

CHAPTER 6

The Emergence of Spacetime

I T IS WELL accepted by science, that spacetime began right at the beginning of the universe. This seems perfectly logical to me. Some of you already know what is coming. But I don't believe time began with the beginning of space. "Get a strait jacket", someone screamed. Someone else just swallowed his chewing gum. Yet, others have had enough, and they are throwing the book out the window. For you, brave ones who have stayed, let us reason through this most time sensitive of problems. Science is fairly certain, that the speed of light is a great barrier. It is believed that nothing can travel faster. Not matter, nor information, not even light, itself. But there is another thing believed to be tied to light speed: time itself. Think of it this way. If you traveled faster than light, you would get there. "Where?", You asked? Anywhere and everywhere before your reflection got there. But it goes beyond that. All that you are, the information that makes you, is not yet there. Yes, you would precede your arrival!

Think of it, like you would, the sound barrier on Earth. You hear a jet go by at supersonic speed. You look toward where you hear the sound, only to find nothing. Then, much farther ahead of its sound, you see the plane. That example is limited to sound. Just imagine now, as if it were traveling faster than light. It is obvious, that we could never see anything traveling faster than light, with the naked eye. But we do have cameras that are capable of capturing images of a photon of light. If you set up a camera, to capture a spaceship traveling at light speed, then, we could see it. You would, however, see the past. At the point you capture the image of the ship, the ship would be long gone. Logically, you would not see the ship fly by, only to see it later, where it once was. This, of course, would be true, if anything traveling at light speed behaved as in classical physics. Regardless, I think we are all on board, that time is also tied to light speed.

Now, that we have established that time is tied to light speed, we can proceed to show that space and time were not simultaneous. Space and time, to me, only became tied at the hip after the inflationary epoch. Prior to the emergence of light from that soup, in the beginning, time was eternal. Oh no. Please don't faint. This, too, will pass. Just keep telling yourself, these are the thoughts of a madman. You will get through this. Are you a bit more settled? OK, let's continue. The thought goes like this. In the inflationary epoch, space expands faster than light. If space is going faster than light, then, if we have an observer with a clock, within that expanding space, what will his clock do? Logically, you would think, that his clock should be running backwards. Well, logic has its limitations. There comes a point in time, or more accurately, in lack of time, that there is no time, even for human logic. Is it logical for you to extend your logic to a time, when there was no time? Can you be sure that your logic is logical, before logic began? Perhaps, I should have warned you to put the book down, a few sentences back. Perhaps, these last few sentences only make sense, if read at the time they were written. It is 4:30 in the morning. The world around me is in deep sleep. The only sounds are the occasional hum of my ac, the faint crowing of my roosters, and the tic tack of my keyboard. Confession: I am a half-speed, hunt and peck, typist. I never achieved using two fingers. I only use my index finger on my right hand and my pinky, or thumb, to hold the shift key. It's kind of funny. Most writers take a long time to develop an idea, and then, quickly type it out. For me, it takes longer to type out my idea, than it did to think it through. Let's get back to time. You see, we're talking about an observer in the beginning of the universe. His clock cannot turn backwards, because there was no time, prior to the beginning. We must conclude that his clock is standing still. It can't move forward, because he is going faster than light. Time simply cannot, and does not, wash over him.

Think for a moment, on the implications of this: 'time with no time' within a physical universe. You find yourself within the outer rim of the universe, looking out into nothingness. Turn around and look back to the future. Yes, back to the future. You are within a warp bubble, in the midst of creation itself. You were, no time ago, facing the nothingness beyond the boundaries of the universe. You were looking toward where spacetime and matter will reside, in the future. But, you turn 180 degrees, and you are looking at the future, flowing in the other direction, toward the center of the sphere, the physical universe. I gave you special imaginary glasses, because the place you are in, has no light. Why? Is it because light can't be emitted? No. Light cannot be seen, because you only see light, if you have time. There is no time, where you are, on the edge of the universe. Therefore, light does not travel. If there is no time, then, no information can be relayed to the physical world. I see that some of you have jumped up from your easy chair. "But wait a minute, Mister Farmer, we don't see light from this period, because there is no time. Our observer within this period has no time. That's why his clock is standing still. He is in eternity. That which has begun in eternity is never done. It simply can't end, because it does not fall under the passage of time." Eureka! You got it! If you did not get it, don't despair. You have time. Yes, the next chapter is Time.

CHAPTER 7

What Is Time?

TIME. WHAT IS it? We are always looking at our clocks, watches and phones, or asking what is the time? More important than 'what is the time?' seems to be 'what is time?' We are governed by time. More accurately, we are ruled by it. It is a ruthless taskmaster. It gives us no time to rest from its demands. It washes over us like a constant torrent. No matter how you respond to it, time keeps its unstoppable progress, until time is up for us. But time is undeterred. Even at our funerals, time still rules over our remains, and our loved ones. Your funeral and all it entails is ruled by time. Have you noticed how slow we travel in a funeral procession? It is man's feeble attempt to stymie time.

Time was something that was a total mystery to me, before understanding space as a self-replicating energy field. As a young boy, I saw it as a solid, written in stone. When I was in my teens, I thought it was flexible. Now, I see it as a result of replicating spacetime. As space goes, so does time. Let us explore time, all the while being mindful of not using too much of this precious gift.

Time - Presentism or Eternalism? I truly apologize for not having the time, to do time justice. We could devote the entire book to time, and we would still not do this topic justice. Presentism was first championed by Heraclitus. Eternalism was championed by Parmenides. I would suggest, that if you are not familiar with these terms that you look them up on the net. I will be giving you a basic understanding of these two opinions, on time. But these two will not be fully explained, and, they are, by no means, the only ideas for describing time. I will only cover these two, for two reasons. They are very ancient, and they are as opposed as can be imagined, when time is the subject. A summation of Heraclitus's (535-475 B.C.) Presentism: only the change or flow exists; or only the present is real, the past is just a memory, and the future does not yet exist. My summation of Parmenides (540-470bc) Eternalism: reality is an unchanging being. Past, present, and future are real. It is not that they were, are, or will be real, but that they are real.

The most important and relevant question is not whether or not Presentism or Eternalism are correct. The only thing that matters, in this book, is how replicating spacetime theory applies to any concept. I have thought long and hard about the application of these new concepts to the notion of time. The conclusion is as radical as the concept of replicating space, itself. Time is both eternal and fleeting. No, I'm not referring to the time before time, or the time when time stops at the end of the universe. I mean here, and now. The broad sense of time is not merely the tick-tock of a clock. We are talking about the time throughout the universe. Each observer within a particular frame of reference, has a different clock. This, by no means, can be used to say that there are many times within the universe. There are, definitely, many clock speeds, or spatial time zones. But, I believe that all of these time zones are within the same umbrella of universal time. Let's say that we could communicate in real time. If everyone took a selfie photo of themselves, at the same time, then those selfies would show that everyone existed at the same time. So, time exists as both variable, and fixed (stopped). It never fails that someone always objects when I deviate from current scientific dogma. Let me explain. We are fairly certain that, for the light which has traveled billions of years to reach us, time has not transpired. Yet, that same a 'time with no time', has been billions of years, for earth-bound observers. You see, if you accept relativity, then you already accept 'No Time', and Newtonian 'now time'. Time, without the effects of replicating space flow, and spatial pressure, reverts back to eternity. Before you get carried away, thinking that there is no time or reality, stop. Think through this experiment. I can easily prove to you the existence of reality and time. If you join me at my shop, I can make a believer out of you in 3 seconds, or less. We will put one of your fingers in the jaws of my mechanics' vice, verily holding it. When you say "go", I will start tightening the vise one turn each second. Before the third second, you will scream out "stop, I believe you".

How did time begin? You already know, from previous chapters, that I do not believe that time began at the beginning. If this is not confusing to you, you either don't understand time, or the statement. How can there be a place, or time, without time? How can a process progress without time? Well, in the case of the universe, it's really easy to explain. In the case of eternity, it's a bit harder. You see, as far as our physical world goes, it is well-accepted that, prior to the beginning, there was no time. How can there be a 'time with no time'. If we accept that time is nothing more than spacetime washing over you, then clearly, prior to the existence of spacetime, there was no time. But there is a legitimate question we must answer. At what point, in the beginning, did time emerge? Science says it was right at the beginning. So, did time really begin in the split-moment, in the beginning of the start of expansion? But wait a minute! Expansion could not begin without the energy from within that often-termed 'singularity' that contained all of the energy in the universe. So, what ruled before expansion? If expansion really started prior to time, then how could time continue, without there first being time.

We have come up with a 'chicken and egg' problem. Namely, which came first: the chicken or the egg? There seems to be only one way to solve the conundrum of space-without-time. Existence was real, prior to the advent of time. Whoa! Stop right there. Existence without time? That would mean that anything within that dimension, would have to be eternal. But then, there is no atrophy to maintain the Arrow of Time. Yes, to all. But this is not the time or space to unravel that conundrum. This is fully explored in Chapter 20. Now, how far did the universe progress without time, at least as we now know it? Obviously, we must accept that everything we see, when we look back in time through a telescope, is within time. But why? Well, what we see is light, and other information. Light and information travel within time. I can only conclude that time began at the split-second that time began. Was that helpful? I guess not. Let's be a bit more precise, then. Time began at the first sign of light, or any information. Now, that was definitive. As we all know, the first light and information we see is the CMB. This, then, marks the beginning of time (as opposed to the beginning of the universe).

The act of replication creates the Arrow Of Time. The Arrow Of Time is the origin of all movement, as space replicates, time expands to cover new space. You cannot back-flow past the outflow of time, from your time within time. So, why can't we reverse time? Because time does not flow unilaterally. The duality of spacetime means that time flows from every point in space, outwards, in every direction. If time emanated from one single location, I believe we could backtrack. But, if we try to backtrack, and time is truly emanating with space, then what? If time emanates from every point in space, it acts as a check valve. If you try to back-flow, you immediately arrive at No Time. Spatial time zones are determined by speed not locality. If replication stops, then movement stops, and everything becomes static. The universe would become a solid. Wherever there was matter in the form of gases or solids, it would become denser. So, if you had the power to stop time, you, yourself, would become trapped in a universe with no movement. Your diaphragm would not pull air, since air could not be moved. Your heart could not pump blood. You, along with everything else, would be static in a sea of frozen energy. Time is, therefore, the physical manifestation of energy in motion. Time is relative, because movement is relative. If everything moved at the same rate, everything would share the same time. Indeed, everything that moves at the same speed, is ruled by the same clock. This furnishes the illusion that time is a set entity for everything. It is our locality that gives us a shared experience of the passage of time.

Time begins, but what is time? Time is the energy of spacetime, traveling from you and through you. The fastest clock speed you would experience, would be if you were in deep space, outside of any gravity wells, and at a standstill. Under those conditions, the full flow of spacetime rushes from you, and through you. This flow, along with the spatial pressure it creates, would put you in the time zone of the fastest clock in the universe. Any acceleration of 'you with spacetime' or 'spacetime through you', changes your spatial time zone. Let's not forget that within a gravity well, you are also subjected to an acceleration. Acceleration diminishes flow in one direction and slows your clock. But why wouldn't it increase flow from the space through which you are accelerating? It is because you are not traveling through space, but rather, traveling with space. You started moving in one direction with spacetime, but the other side is still rushing through you, at the same rate. Remember you are your own reference point. When you are at a steady speed, space sees you as standing still.

Let's use Impersonating Thinking, IT (for short). Let's imagine we are a scene from your life, just a split-second image of the happiest moment in your life. Yes, the happiest, certainly not the saddest. Now, imagine 'you' as that moment, in picture form, traveling away from yourself, at light speed. Does that moment in time always travel away from 'you' at light speed? That is just not possible. From the time it leaves 'you' it starts traveling at faster than light speed. Why? Because, it is information in the form of light. It travels at light speed, with space. So, the speed at which it is moving away, is light speed, plus the expansion of space. This is true even if your image is traveling within the space of two gravitationally bound objects, such as galaxies. Remember, objects can be bound by gravity: spacetime cannot. Gravity wells affect spacetime flow, but only a black hole has the capacity to stop and hold your traveling image. Barring these extremes, the distance between 'you' and your picture, is the miles traveled by light, plus the miles increased between those two points, by the expanding space. This is a necessary part of a functional universe. Imagine, if light was to travel away from you at the speed-of-light or less, then, time would be static. We could see everything at the same time. Wow! We would see ourselves in the past, present and future. How confusing would that be?

The expansion of space brings with it, time. This makes each point in space its own reference point. If we were to stop expansion, time would stop. In a world without time, there would be no duality of space. Spacetime would be static. If anything ever happened, it would remain visible to everyone, everywhere, forever. The result of constant expansion is a separation of every point in space. As it stands now, a scene from your life travels out in all directions, never to be seen by you, again. Spacetime is, indeed, coming back to you in the same manner. Being that light is traveling away from you, and light does not reflect light, it is never seen by you, again. Does this expansion of all space create the mirage of multiple universes? Yes, the fact that each point in space is its own reference point, can lead us to this fallacy. Each point in space is its own reference point, because it is emitting spacetime. As spacetime replicates, it timestamps a unique reference point to each point in space. This constant movement of time produces the illusion that there can be multiple universes.

Many would tell you, that time is merely an arbitrary thing on which we base our experiences here on planet Earth. It is true that our unit of time is based on how our planet behaves, within this planetary system. But would you be free of time, if I placed you in deep space on a spaceship? No matter where you are, time is present. Or is it? Does light experience time? Is time present beyond the event horizon in a black hole? Is time eternal? Was there a time when there was no time? How much time did it take to make time? Is time real? Well, let's take them one at a time.

Does light experience time? As far as we can theorize, light does not experience time. I will give you an example that may be an eye opener for you. I once asked an individual from the power company this question. "Why are power poles always placed down the property line?" He answered, "So that we do not have to pay anyone for placing it on their property". Apparently, the center line between two properties is no man's land. Neither owner can claim that the pole is in their property because it is not. By straddling the property line, and being a service used by both owners, it pays no rent for using space. But wait a minute. It is partly in one's property. Yes, but there is a center line, and how can one say where the exact center of that line is? So the utility poles are truly in no man's land. I do not know if this is true, but it makes sense to me. I do know, that if they locate any infrastructure within someone's property, then they must pay for an easement. This is paid to the current owner and is recorded in the property deed. Well, light travels at the speed of light, but more importantly, at the speed of information and time, itself. Ask a light photon, from GZ-n11, which we see 13.4 billion years in the past, "How long have you been traveling?" The answer is "No time at all." Seems impossible, does it not? How can something which registers on our clock as 13.4 billion years old, have an age of zero years? The answer, no matter how unlikely, is that our photon from GZ-n11, has no time. It is in the boundary line of both directions of time.

Like the utility poles, light sits between property lines. This property line is the frontier between the duality of spacetime. No time runs over it, because it is running in one direction of spacetime, itself, on its property line. It is moving with spacetime, but being at the equilibrium point, it is not ruled by time. If spacetime creates gravity, then it must, by its very nature, create within itself a point of equalization. This point, within spacetime, is present at Planck length intervals or smaller. It sits within the center of the overlapping point of the duality of spacetime. The power pole analogy serves us well, in regard to time. Power poles, along the property line, are like things running at light speed in the universe. They pay nothing. The photon traveling at light speed has no time, the power pole on the property line pays nothing. We have covered travel at light speed. This analogy, however, can also be used to clarify sub-light travel. A pole on the property line can be compared to travel at light speed. A pole within private property lines can be compared to sub-light travel. When a pole is going to be moved within private property, an easement must be paid. Likewise, for any item traveling at sub-light speeds, if a change of spatial time-zone is required, then it must pay through exerted power.

Is time present, beyond the event horizon, within a black hole? We do not know, and possibly, we will never know. It doesn't mean that we can't imagine or theorize, from our vantage point of ignorance. Well, there is truly nothing new under the sun. When someone says that humanity is in ignorance, there will always be people who are offended. Incredibly, almost without exception, they tend to be the most ignorant among us. I stand behind my previous assertion, that humanity is standing in a vantage point characterized by ignorance. The more we learn, the more we see how ignorant we really are. For many years, I suffered from severe health issues which went undiagnosed. In one of my many visits to the hospital, in total frustration, I complained to the attending physician. "You call this modern medicine? One thousand years ago, it was called modern medicine. Five hundred years ago, it was also called modern medicine. Today as you stand here, you are practicing modern medicine. From my vantage point I see no difference. One thousand years ago, you bled your patient. Here today, you have bled me the same, and the only difference is, instead of a pan, you bled me into a vacutainer. The result is the same, no one knows what is wrong with me. No wonder you call your profession a practice, and you call your customer 'patient'. I don't have to tell you, soon after that, the good doctor and I parted company. I finally resolved most of my health issues on my own. The things that were out of range in my bloodwork, were that the good cholesterol was very low, and so was Vitamin D. I normalized my good cholesterol by consuming nuts and peanut butter. I also managed to bring up my Vitamin D with some premium vitamin supplements.

Back to time. We believe time is governed by light speed. No light travels out of the event horizon. It stands to reason that no light means no time. There is an obvious question that some of you are asking. "Does time run backwards in a black hole?" I do not accept that time can run backwards in a black hole. If it runs backwards, then it would do so until the time where there was no time. Is that not the exact situation in a place where there is No Time? So, if you attempt to run time backwards, since you have no time, you immediately arrive in No Time.

Is time eternal? I don't think that there is anyone who accepts that time is eternal. But then again, if some people honestly believe that the Earth is flat, then anything is possible. The vast majority would agree that time is temporal. If it had a beginning, it could have an end. We can conclude that although we can't fully comprehend the tyrant that is time, we accept its existence. We also accept that it had a beginning and possibly an end. Time could be forever, never stopping once it began. But just as our universe is believed to be temporal, so is time.

Here, I would like to tell you a story. Stories and illustrations are helpful to cement concepts into our minds. Years ago, I went fishing with one of my fishing buddies. We arrived at our favorite fishing spot, a reef with a lighthouse just off the coast of Key Largo, Florida. To our dismay, there was a sixty-five-foot party boat anchored right on top of our fishing hole. Being courteous, we found a place to anchor a couple of hundred feet from their position, so the current could not tangle our lines. We were going to concentrate on yellowtail fishing. A favorite way to fish for yellowtail is with a hand line, allowing the current to pay the line out of your hands. This method allows the chum and bait to flow down current to where the fish are. Back to the anchoring. I oversaw the anchor while my buddy handled the helm. We chose a prudent distance from the anchored party boat. I threw anchor, and as soon as the anchor caught, my buddy shut down the engines. With the anchor rope tied, I looked up to check our distance to the nearby boat. To my shock the boat was gone. I called out to my buddy, where is the boat? He looked up and was equally surprised. We scanned the area, and no boat. We scanned the horizon, no boat within our view. This was a clear South Florida day. We never heard their engines start. Mind you, these old boats are generally equipped with twin Detroit 671 diesels. These are good, durable engines, but quiet they are not. Even if we had not heard their engines, in the five minutes it took us to anchor, they could not have pulled anchor. Even if they had an onboard emergency, and cut the anchor rope, where were they? These boats are displacement, not planing hulls. They are very slow. We debated calling the Coast Guard but decided that we had no real information to give them. So we went about our business while we debated. What could explain what just happened? We finally agreed that, if it had been swallowed by the ocean, then we would hear about it in the next day's news. Then, we would call the Coast Guard, and tell them our story. We could supply them with the coordinates. We would tell them that the only explanation was that it had suddenly sunk....without as much as a scream from the dozens of people fishing on board. No boat was reported missing in that area the following day, or weeks.

To this day, I see this as a missing block of time. Similar things have happened in my life, but this is the only time when I was accompanied by another person. So, can we say that time can show anomalies? No. Even after this happened to me, I still think that there is a logical, real explanation for what we experienced. What that explanation is, I don't know. But I don't accept that time can locally, temporarily, change. Also, I do not accept that something, as large as that boat, can disappear without a trace. It's even more troubling that dozens of fishermen could go missing, and not be reported!

Was there a time, when there was no time? Absolutely, yes, and absolutely, no. How could this be possible? For the most part, we accept that time had a beginning. This guarantees that there was a time when, from our perspective, there was no time. Here is where we go into Lala land. We can agree that if time started, then there was a 'time with no time'. A 'time with no time'? Is that not eternity? If time now exists, and it was born out of eternity, does time not fit into eternity? If time is housed within eternity, and eternity, by definition, has always existed, then, so does time. This concept of time, within eternity, can, should, and will only be fully explored in Chapter 20.

How much time did it take to make time? Logically, you cannot use something as an ingredient to make something before the ingredient exists. So, the incomprehensible answer is that it took no time to make time. Time emerged out of eternity, manufactured out of a physical entity, namely energy. Yes, time is energy. Wait, why are you surprised? How many times must I prove that everything in the physical world is energy? Time is created by the spatial pressure created by the interaction of the fabric of space with itself. So, energy interacting with itself creates time. We can make this definitive statement: it took no time to make time. Since there is no time where time is made, then what began, is and will never stop.

Is time real? Not only is time real, but time is reality. Within a physical world, time is reality. If there is no time, then nothing happens. If nothing happens, then there is no movement of anything, including time. We will never see time. We will always see its effects. But make no mistake, it is as real as anything within the physical world. Being in the physical world, it is, itself, physical, and manufactured by energy. We could modify a well-known statement and say, I think within time, therefore I am. You guys are getting ahead of me. Someone is asking "Time makes reality, right? Aren't time and space made by the Fountains of God? It's their outward motion that makes our reality, right?" Yes, we are all in agreement, so far. More questions? "Then, if this process makes reality, at what point does reality emerge from what is essentially energy?" Well, I don't know how much further I can lead you guys. I'm afraid that the next book on this subject may not be written by me. If this concept of replicating spacetime is correct, then it stands to reason that the closer we get to the emergence of spacetime, the harder it is to distinguish reality from non-physicality. Does that make sense to you? Consider, for a moment, our experiences in the real world. You go to see an exhibition of the world's fastest car. It's sitting on the starting line. The light turns green, and it takes off. Just as the world's fastest car jumps off the starting line, a man on a moped speeds past. How can a moped outrun the world's fastest car? It's easy. It was speeding before the car even budged. At the time the moped passed the car on the starting line, it was already doing 40 mph, its top speed. The car, in turn, had just started, so for a moment, it was slower than the lowly moped. You can add many examples, like this one, to the list. We have tied ourselves into a pretzel. But don't despair, we will unravel this conundrum in the next paragraph.

Our experience in the real world shows us that things often begin gradually. We must, then, decide whether reality materializes spontaneously, or whether it follows the gradual path? Well, it looks like we have just stumbled on some cats. We can't tell if they are dead or alive, or both. If you don't get it, look up Schrodinger's cat. If you investigate the uncertainty principle, you will see that, in the world of the very small, reality gets a bit unreal. For instance, an answer gets very cloudy if you ask why atoms do not collapse onto themselves. The electrons revolve around the nucleus at a minute distance with enough force to maintain cohesion. Yet, with all this attractive force, they don't collapse into the nucleus. Here, I think, emerging spacetime equalizes with the nuclear force. How can I support that claim? Here is where size matters most. We are talking about the super small. Why would regenerating space act to stabilize the nuclear force? At this size, the electrons are not large enough to be subjected to the full duality of space. Almost gone is the dual flow of spacetime as it travels in the world of the big. At this distance, the effect felt is almost a constant outward push. This push is seen in the macro world to be weak. But, in this micro world, it is as powerful as its opponent. Regardless of what actually happens, the weird thing is that the electrons can't be pinpointed in both time and place. They are both everywhere and nowhere, at the same time.

Well, let's apply replicating space to this conundrum, to see if we can't simplify the problem. First, let's complicate it further, to shed some light. We are talking about an entity in the super small range. We are also talking about an orbit that, because of its speed and the small distance travelled, is close to the no-time mark to complete one revolution. Take orbit and revolution with a grain of salt. Both terms are more applicable to the macro world. At the distance and speeds that these entities operate, I don't think they truly orbit. To us, they appear and disappear. They move as a wave, or possibly as a vibration, as they seem to be everywhere at once. This is because we are close to the starting line of time and reality. We agree that spacetime/reality is magnitudes faster than the car we mentioned above. Not only is it faster, but it starts at full speed. As soon as it materializes, it's at its rated speed. We, in turn, are the guy on the moped. We are already in linear time, at our full speed. The only way we can see this little guy (the electron) is to stop him in his tracks. Speed is measured from two points, or two observers, if you will. The relative distance between the macro and micro world are immense. Compounding this are the size and time differences. Is this the answer to our dead cat and live cat problem? Perhaps, but I think the answer is even more basic. I think that we have advanced to a point where we are beginning to witness the beginning. Yes, here's a wild thought. If space is replicating, then the spacetime emanating from every point is brand new. Of course, it becomes entangled with the reality that has already existed. But, it emerges in a foggy state of uncertainty, because it is still not fully shaped into what it will be. So, what will it be? It will be what it needs to be, in order to conform to the reality, into which it is emerging. If not, reality in the physical world would give way to chaos.

Imagine a propeller. What happens when you move to its center? Closest to its center, movement stops: so does centrifugal force. As we get into the smallest of the small, time is no longer the same. The change is due to the way spacetime emerges. It does so from the center of every location. The closer you get to that center, the slower the time, or the closer you get to a 'time with no time'. Therefore, in the microscopic world, the Arrow of Time is not as obvious. In a way, it's not that there is no time in the micro world, it's that there is no space. If you have no space, you can't have time. Space and time are tied at the hip. The closer you get to the zero space, the closer you get to the zero time. Think of it this way. You are in a ship one mile long. You are traveling at 60 miles per hour. How long does it take you to clear a single mile-marker pole? It takes one minute because you are traveling a mile a minute. How about if the ship is 1/60 of a mile? One second. How about if we make the ship and the marker one atom long? No time, or close to it.

Time emerges with space, from every point in space. Your clock is governed by your frame of reference. Any acceleration of space through you, or you through space, will place you at a different spatial time zone. How far away is zero time, or a 'time with no time'? When you achieve light speed, there is no time. It depends on how far you have to travel to achieve light speed. This means that if you could, at the blink of an eye, achieve light speed, within one foot from your starting point, that is how far away resides zero time. This means that the Arrow Of Time is emerging from every point, everywhere. There is no past. It is just an image. What we call the present, is also a reflection of the past. The future is yet to be. If our reality is housed within eternity, then time is a manufactured event within eternity. You can look at reality as a wall. On this side of the wall, we see the Arrow Of Time. The arrow emerges from that wall which we perceive as the past. You are a child of your place of origin, for only as long as you share the speed, or spatial time zone. If, let's say, you blast-off in a fast spaceship, then you no longer belong to your place of origin. Not only are you no longer physically there, but you are no longer in that spatial time zone. As you speed away, your clock slows. You could say, you are traveling into the future of your place of origin. When you return, you might think you are coming back to your future. But it's the future of those you left behind. Your future is based on your own spatial time zone. The impossibility of reversing the Arrow Of Time is real to me. It happens because each point in space has time emerging from it.

So what causes aging, or its damage? Why would it be less in a fast spaceship, or in heavy gravity (when compared to standing still)? At a standstill, the full flow of spacetime is flowing from you and through you. As you accelerate through spacetime, or as spacetime accelerates through you, less spacetime emerges from you. The closer one gets to unilateral spacetime flow (the speed of light), the slower goes your clock. The slower your clock, the less spacetime flows out of you. The lower the energy flow, the less damage to your cells.

Think of it as if you are in a sandstorm. If you stand your ground, the sand will wear on your skin and clothing. If you could flow with the storm, then the closer you get to the speed at which it is flowing, the less damage you will sustain. You guys are impressive. But, someone is arguing, "Wait. You said spacetime is not unilateral. Yet, in the example you used, the wind carries the sand in only one direction!" Yes, the analogy is limited. I'm sorry. I can't tell you how it is, that omnidirectional space does not bombard you as you move through space. We will deal with that in Chapter 13, 'Travel and Spatial Time Zones'. I can tell you, it pivots on the fact that nothing travels through space: everything travels with space. Spacetime does not only degrade your skin and clothing. Since spacetime travels through you, it wears out (ages) all of you.

Picture someone at true rest. Remember that it may not be possible to be at rest in this universe. Orbits, rotation, and even the growth of space, add movement to everything. But, let's say you are in intergalactic space, and you find a way to come to a full stop. Now, you have the full pressure of space running out of you, and into you. This gives you the fastest clock, which means the fastest aging. This means that from the time we are born, we are being bombarded by time and we are dying. The reason why we actually die, is that the damage, caused by time, overtakes our ability to self-repair. You may think that you have always been the same, but you would be mistaken. The reason you believe you are immutable, is that you think with your brain. The brain cells (except for the hippocampus) are the only cells in your body that are never renewed. Your other cells are constantly wearing out and being replaced. The coding for that regeneration is in our DNA. The degradation of that information reduces our ability to renew. The evidence is easy to spot. As you get older, your body won't heal as fast. Your skin, which is constantly being replaced, gets thinner, and since it takes longer to regenerate, you look older. Stop reading right now, take a sip of your drink. Ponder on what you have just read.

I'm glad to see that some have taken my advice in the previous paragraph. You pondered on what you had just read. Some have found an answer, within the last paragraph, for one of cosmology's biggest mysteries (the timescale problem). Time, like beauty, is in the eyes of the beholder. Search the net for 'objects in the universe older than the universe itself'. Be selective: you will get about 40 million hits. There are, indeed, items in the universe which seem to be older than the universe itself. Allow me to present the mystery and its explanation. Science has found things that are older than the universe. To date, there is no explanation. By applying what you have learned, in the previous paragraph, the explanation is simplified. Everything within the universe ages, under the influence of its time zone. Let's say, you had a star that has spent time at a standstill. According to Replicating Space Theory, and to scientific observations, speed determines time-zone. If a star is at a standstill for a long time, it will age more than everything else that is in movement in the universe. So, the age of the universe is dictated by your frame of reference. How old would the universe be, to a person close to a black hole? That's right! Very young. How old does the universe seem, to a photon that traveled 13.4 billion years to reach us? If you could ask, it would tell you "The universe began just a split-second ago". Yet, to an Earth-bound observer, that light is 13.4 billion years old.

The flow of spacetime creates time zones. More accurately, spatial pressure directly governs the flow of spacetime. It is this static pressure that governs the frame of reference you experience. Those of you who have a well-developed mental sharpie, are racing ahead. "Eureka!" Some have screamed. "This is why speed, within spacetime, changes our frame of reference, giving us a slower clock. Of course, we have already learned that it matters not whether we speed through space or space speeds through us. As we speed up, we are relieving spatial pressure. Not being at rest prevents spacetime from creating, within us, an even greater spatial pressure. This also explains why the perception of time changes with the growth of space". Wow, how exciting! I'm no longer alone. You, too, are now basking in the full knowledge of Gods fountain.

The last paragraph has left us with a hard choice. Are we measuring the flow of time, or the flow of energy? Just like a scale actually weighs energy, a clock works by recording the rate of flow of spacetime. But we have already decided that spacetime flow is a flow of energy. It is easy to see how energy flowing through our cells would age us. But how can spacetime flow change clock-speed. Well, at the end of the day, all our time pieces are actually measuring the time needed to manipulate a set amount of energy. A clock can be pendulum-based, powered by gravity. We can use the same pendulum effect, in a rotating motion powered by a wound spring. The spring can be wound by your fingers, or by the movement of your hand. There are clocks that measure the time it takes to use up the current in an electronic circuit. A quartz time piece can measure the oscillations of a quartz crystal, as a current passes through it (32,768 times a second). The last time piece I will mention is the most accurate: an atomic clock. In atomic clocks, we use the oscillations of atoms. It is more accurate than quartz, because atoms are more stable. Atoms also oscillate at a higher frequency (9,192,631,770 times per second) giving us a lesser margin of error. All the clocks measure energy in the form of motion, quartz oscillations or atomic oscillations. Energy moves at the speed of the medium (spacetime). The speed of flow of the medium dictates time. All power is measured as work done in time. Anything that interferes with that process would change our clock.

Allow me to ask you a question. Your answer will determine how well you have understood replicating space. Will a self-winding wristwatch work in zero gravity aboard the space station? Wait. Stop. Don't read on until you have given me an answer. OK, are you ready to commit? What is your answer? That's interesting. Our readership is divided 50/50. The "Yes" group takes the prize. The self-winding watch works fine in outer space, outside of gravity. It does not depend on gravity, but on inertia. Of course, if you have understood inertia, you know it is everywhere. This is because inertia is supplied by spacetime. Science wrongly insists that inertia is a product of the mass of an object. For the "No" group, don't despair, you are in good company. Apparently, NASA was also concerned that the self-winding watch would not work in outer space. Perhaps, this is why the hand-wound Omega Speedster Professional "Moonwatch" was used by Apollo 11. To this day, this watch is still among the watches approved by NASA for space travel. By all accounts, this veteran time piece is the only watch that NASA certifies to be suitable for EVA extra vehicular activities (space walks).

What is time? Time is the movement of energy, created by replicating spacetime. This is why time is influenced by speed. The faster you go in any direction, the smaller the volume of replication from within you. The less those Fountains replicate and emanate (flow) from you, the less time flows through you. Any acceleration of 'you with spacetime' or 'spacetime through you', changes your spatial time zone. Time changes at different speeds because space replicates at different volumes. Whatever speed you achieve is associated with a replication frequency, which gives you your time zone. The evidence shows that spacetime is a replicating energy matrix in constant motion through replication. Its duality of travel gives space its peculiar ability to create a matrix conducive to all forms of travel. Its reproductive nature gives us a relative spacetime. The Arrow of Time only moves forward because once spacetime emerges, it displaces the current time into the past. If we could achieve light speed, the most we could ever do is to stop time in our frame of reference. Time cannot be altered because it is interconnected and relative and emerging simultaneously from every point in space. There are two common ways in which time zones are created. First, matter creates a low-pressure area causing space to increase replication, which increases flow and acceleration. The second way in which time zones are created is one in which entities create their own time zone as they flow with space at any given speed.

To conclude on time, in a timely manner: To me, time holds the theory of everything. Reality is governed by spacetime, just like the full speed of a moped is faster than the starting speed of the world's fastest car. Reality is governed by time. You cannot compare the very small with the very large, because it is a comparison of space and time. I remind you that matter is concentrated energy, or even more accurately, spacetime energy. Comparing the micro with the macro world would be like comparing the seed of a Redwood with a fully grown specimen. The theory of everything, therefore, is the theory of everything seen through the lens of spacetime. String theory, quantum mechanics, Newton's laws of gravitation, Einstein's relativity and general relativity, and if I may be so bold, Replicating Space Theory, are all stops along the line of reality. We don't need to make a new theory of everything. We need to develop these, to fill in the gaps between them.

CHAPTER 8

The Big Bang Echo CMB

T HE COSMIC MICROWAVE background radiation is said to be the echo of The Big Bang, the remnant of that long gone period where the dense soup gave way to a transparent universe. This light somehow permeates spacetime, and we easily detect it today. There is no person who has ever operated a TV or a radio, who can say they have not heard it. It is imbedded in the static you hear when you switch your TV or radio to a channel frequency that is not in use within range of you. Yes, part of the static you hear is the CMB. I just do not accept that any light information or time could be detectable prior to the universe becoming transparent Science believes that time, as we know it, starts with the beginning. I do not accept that theory. I'm convinced that time, in its current form, is beginning, yes in the present tense, at the moment space becomes transparent. I can just imagine that some of you who read my first book 'Let There Be Light', rolling up your eyes at this previous statement. In my first work, I had equated the CMB solely to replicating space. In other words, current space is doing the same thing it started doing in the beginning. Therefore, that is the CMB. Now, we must give you the full story. I believe that, hidden within the CMB, is indeed, the current local regeneration of spacetime, in real time. But the signal also includes the first light of the universe, the beginning of the beginning.

We are currently in a bind in the progression of this concept. Science, in my belief, is both right and wrong. Science states that the CMB is a signal of a bygone era, just an echo. This echo was supposedly emitted 380,000 years after the beginning. Here they are both right and wrong. What they hear today is most definitely from a bygone era. But it is definitely not an echo. It is the CMB emitted in the beginning, which is ongoing. What an interesting choice of word. Echo. Why would someone be compelled to use it to illustrate what the CMB really is? Well, let's muddle through this, because this word, alone, carries within it the unraveling of the current explanation of the CMB. An echo, as understood by the man on foot (an idiom from my old country, meaning common man), is the return, or bounce back, of something you emit, or already heard. Why use this word to make the CMB understandable? Quite simply, without this insertion, the common man would say that makes no sense.

If the event that caused this first light to be emitted was finite in time, then it would have travelled past us long ago, never to be detected again. Now you see why they throw in that useful, descriptive word 'echo'. How are we to believe that a signal composed of, basically, stretched light, can linger, in what science claims, is empty space. What did it permeate? If indeed an echo, what barrier did it strike to bounce back to us? If it is bouncing within the universe, which number bounce are we receiving now? Should the rendition of the latest bounce not show all of the distance it has traveled, cumulatively? Yes, cumulatively. Remember when you hear an echo, each bounce seems further. In the case of light, each bounce would be stretched further than the last. Lastly, if it is only an echo, how can it be so prominently picked up, by even the weakest receivers? Some of you are old enough to remember using the first remotes on TV sets. For you youngsters, the first remotes actually turned the tuner knob, mechanically, initially using a pneumatic squeeze bulb. Shortly thereafter, the tuner was rotated by an electric motor. These old sets lacked a volume-limiting circuit. If you tuned-in to a strong signal, the volume would increase to match signal strength. So, when you would come upon a channel with no station signal, a deafening static signal would be heard. Part of this signal is the CMB.

Well, take a sip of that favorite drink which I instructed you to put beside your easy chair, because, as the coffin says to the corpse, "get comfy, it's a long ride". Let's see how we unravel this carefully constructed web of light, radiation, echoes and other components which have been added to this conundrum. Are you ready? Let's go. The echo: is it possible? Absolutely not, in any way or fashion. The universe has doubled countless times. The doubling effect is very peculiar. When something doubles, there is more of it than there has ever been. The distance the CMB would have had to travel, in 13.8 billion years, would have stretched it into oblivion.

Why has no one stopped me? I would hope by now that someone has seen the elephant in the room, the one wearing a giraffe suit, dancing a waltz. It cannot be more obvious. Nothing can echo within the universe. Now you've got it. An echo is, by definition, something returning which you have already heard. Can an echo, which is information, make more than one trip? Information cannot travel faster than light, and neither can light outrun itself. No, don't confuse it with starlight traveling to us: that is a one-way trip. This CMB would have to be bouncing within the universe, since it was, according to science, emitted for a short time, eons ago. The light from, let's say, a galaxy started in its beginning and has been emitting ever since. That is why we can see light from galaxies that started long ago.

Allow me to illustrate. Let's imagine a dark night, a flashlight, and two friends, walking down a straight dark road. The slower guys says, "You go on ahead, and I will shine the light once, to let you know I'm OK". The faster guy, being faster in speed and mind, says "No, you keep shining the light. That is the only way I can see the light, continually. If you shine it once for a short period, I must be looking for it, in order to see it, and even then, it gives me only one report". "Yes", says his slower friend, "I know that". That's why I will give you this mirror. I have another. We'll keep them aimed at each other, and the light will keep bouncing between the mirrors, and you will know what's up with me". Well, although creative, that won't work either. You see, light can't stay focused, as it travels with space, because space is not only expanding forward, but also sideways. So, the light will scatter, and get weaker, in each subsequent bounce. The same would happen with light emitted in the beginning of the universe, even, if it had a place to bounce from. But after all is said and done, it cannot echo, because it only had time to travel to us, once.

Let's explore the possibility of a bounce, or echo, further. As a New Yorker would say, "Fuhgeddaboudit". The very nature of expanding space would negate any possibility of a structure, or reflective area, from which light could bounce back. There is, however, a more clear and present danger to this 'echo' nonsense. According to science, the light was emitted long ago, for a relatively short time. If there was such an echo, it would not permeate the universe, but would travel as a pulse. Mind you, a severely stretched pulse, but a pulse, none the less. Well, the patience of the learned ones is wearing thin. Frankly, they are getting tired of being told why it can't happen, all the while knowing it is indeed happening. The question they have been asking is, "If all the possibilities you mentioned are not viable, then explain why we read the CMB in our instruments."

Here's the nitty gritty of the story. This light would, indeed, be a pulse if it had been emitted for a short time at the beginning. But, as you already read in Chapter 5, 'Creation of Matter, is it Ongoing?' the beginning has not ended. The beginning did occupy the center of the universe, in the beginning. It now occupies the rim of the universe. Why is the beginning ongoing? It's simple. The beginning is expanding at greater-than-light speed. Greater-than-light speed outpaces light, but more interestingly, it outpaces time. The beginning has not and will not ever stop. Unlike all other beginnings, this one will always keep on keeping on. It is as new and fresh today as it was 13.8 billion years ago. You could say that it should actually be getting younger. But, since it is responsible for starting time, itself, it can't stop, nor get any younger than zero years of age. You could say that it has no time to stop making time. Its only choice is to sit between eternity and the physical world, doing what it began doing, a job that has no end. It reminds me of my business years. I would show up for work, even when I was very sick, to open the shop. It never failed that someone would ask "Why did you come in to work, in your condition?" I would always tell them that I tried calling in sick, but no one answered the phone. A similar thing happens with the beginning, when it tries to stop, it has no time to do it in. If you could reason with it, and you asked, "Aren't you tired of doing the same thing?", the beginning would sound like a skipping needle on a broken record. It would say "just started, just started, just started... ". To you youngsters, ask Grampa what I mean.

There is a final key factor in the story of this CMB. I cannot disclose the last piece of this, the oldest cosmic puzzle, because it is intertwined with the concepts of Chapter 14. To give you the full story of this CMB mystery, I would have to disclose most of the contents of Chapter 14.

CHAPTER 9

Relativity Made Easy

RELATIVITY IS A term familiar to everyone who has a basic level of knowledge of the universe. A portion of people probably think that humanity has always known that we live in a relativistic universe. However, relativity has been known since 1905. In 1905, Albert Einstein published his theory of relativity. This theory would quickly dethrone the ruling understanding of time and space which had been set forth by Isaac Newton in 1687. So, what is the difference? A Newtonian universe is one where time and gravity are the same everywhere. Meaning, no matter the frame of reference of an observer, time is a constant. This would also mean that gravity is felt at every point in space simultaneously. Curious to me, is that both of these men were so brilliant, that even when they were wrong, they were right. How can somebody be wrong and right at the same time, you might ask? Let me explain. Newton's laws of gravitation are still used in calculations involving distances within our solar system. Even if they were based upon the wrong premise, they are accurate on that scale. In my opinion, Einstein's use of warped space to explain gravity, is inadequate. Einstein's vision of warped space was a static picture, which explained space in Newtonian terms, rather than through relativity. I believe that mass creates a flow differential in spacetime, resulting in gravity. The curious thing is that if you produce an illustration of curved space, and put it in motion, as relativity demands, then you will observe space flowing into matter. The fact that Einstein and Newton were right, even when they were wrong, proves, like nothing else could, their tremendous intellect.

So what is relativity? And, more importantly, what causes relativity? Relativity is the absence of absolutes, as we deal with space, time, light, and gravity. In other words, what an observer sees and experiences, is dependent on his frame of reference. For instance, the Sun's light takes eight minutes to reach us, on Earth. Gravity, having the same speed, reaches us at the same time as light. Clock speeds are influenced by speed. If you dig deeper into the Sun's light it gets more bewildering. The light we see from our Sun is actually at least 150 thousand years old before it reaches us. It starts within the Sun's center and travels outward. If I'm right, and matter is made of compressed energy (the most basic of which is spacetime energy), then this means that the radius of the Sun is equivalent to 880 quadrillion miles of space, derived by the product of the 150,000 years (and eight minutes) x (times) the distance that light travels in a year. Double that to include the entire diameter of the Sun. I'm sure you realize that this means matter creates a time dilation, because it 'is' compressed space. I can think of no better supporting evidence for replicating space. What else could drive these light photons from the center of a star, to emerge and then grace us with their light and warmth? Only replicating space could be responsible. Clearly, light travels with space, outward from its source, deep within the stars.

Replicating space also demystifies relativity. If space replicates, then it is not Newtonian. It is relative. The relative effect of spacetime is best seen in the 'twin paradox'. Make a quick search on the net, to become familiar with this thought experiment. I've read many articles on relativity. Every article discusses the function of relativity. The effect seen in the 'twin paradox thought experiment' was a mystery to me until I discovered RST. You could say that relativity is the law of how space functions. I, however, do not understand laws which have no explanation, as to why it is so. If something is observed to happen, then there is a cause. No cause, no effect. If you think you have found an effect without a cause, then you're mistaken. The Arrow Of Time demands that the cause precede the effect. If you claim that some effect precedes its cause, then you are ignorant of the mechanism that gives you such an illusion.

Up until the writing of my first book, I was dumbfounded by relativity. How can a clock, irrespective of whether it's a mechanical or digital electronic device, be influenced by the speed at which it is traveling? And even more confusing is, why would a gravity well cause the same effect as speed? The universe came alive to me when I realized that nothing moves through space. Everything moves with space. This revealed to me, that every point in space is its own reference point. If you fully understand this, then you realize that when you are accelerating, you are moving away from yourself. Space only sees you under acceleration. In contrast, at a constant speed, within light speed, you are as if standing still, yet flowing with space at that speed or spatial time zone. What does this have to do with relativity, you may ask. This is relativity. The movement of space from you, and through you, creates relativity. Think of spacetime as a river. You are flowing in this river. If you are anchored in the river, and the river's current is flowing at 10 mph, then ten mph of water is rushing beneath you. If you are flowing with it, at the speed of the current, then no water rushes past you. But, if you are moving with the current at only 5 mph, then there is still 5 mph of water rushing past you. Now, let's take it to space. Spacetime flows at light speed from every point in every direction. This means that if you are flowing with space at its full speed in any direction, then no time flows over you. Given that every point in space is replicating, direction of travel matters not. If spacetime was static, then we would have a Newtonian universe at the macro level. You will learn, in later chapters that at the micro level, size and speed create a situation where relative time gives way to Newtonian static time. I have called this state a 'time with no time'.

I have been asked by many readers of my first book to explain travel as it relates to replicating spacetime. Let me try to simplify this concept. Space is replicating, not from the center where it began, but from every point. If space was expanding solely from where it began, then space would be unidirectional. Unidirectional space is not conducive to a functioning universe. At least, not one that could support life. Life could not survive in unidirectional space. Formation of planets, orbits, buoyancy, and gravity would be impossible. Imagine you were on a planet which suddenly materialized in such a universe. You would be pushed off into outer space. Every bit of matter within such a universe would travel outward, from the center where it began expanding. Not having any opposition to its outward flow, it would increase in speed. Everything would dissipate into the nothingness outside of that universe. In contrast, all indications in the way this, our universe functions, provides evidence that space replicates from every point. This sustains a universe that expands omni-directionally, from every point within it.

Let's say, for the purpose of this illustration, that you are facing north. In front of you, spacetime is rushing north from your position. In back of you spacetime is running southward. To your right, it's running eastward, and to your left it's running into the west. Now, I stand in front of you facing south. In front of me, space is running southward from my back northward, and so on. This demonstrates several things: the duality of space, the omnidirectional nature of the flow of spacetime, and lastly, that every point in space is its own reference point. This ability of space, to replicate from every point, allows us to see from every point, as if it was the center of the universe. Do a search of the observable universe, and you will see that it's always a sphere. Our telescopes see an equal distance in every direction. This spacetime, traveling in all directions from every point, creates a spatial pressure. It gives every item in the universe the ability to stay still, or to stay in motion, at whichever speed it has achieved. Propulsion is not caused by any law of equal and opposite reaction. Propulsion is, indeed, pushing on something. It is pushing on replicating space. This acceleration gives you a push, like gravity. Everything in the universe is a push. Nothing is a pull. This, to my surprise, was easily understood by the readers of my first book. You cannot pull anything. You must reach behind everything, and then push it toward you. Why is it impossible to pull anything? Because it isn't there yet. You must reach to where it is and push it toward you.

I could not, for the life of me, understand why speed would give you a slower clock, no matter the direction of travel. I always thought that if I sped away from a starting point, that my clock would slow. Turning around and heading back to my starting point should speed up the clock. This, I reasoned, would synchronize the clocks upon arriving back at the starting point. Factor in, that every point is its own reference point, as a result of replicating space, and it now makes sense. There is no link between two moving objects. Each object is its own reference. Regardless of direction, if traveling in a straight line, you are flowing with space, at whatever speed you have achieved. When traveling at a set speed, you are in a spatial time zone. Every point in space is identical. It is an energy fabric. This fabric is growing, not merely stretching. This growth creates a flow. The differences in this flow create gravity. This flow, rushing over matter that is traveling at less-than-light speed, determines your spatial time zone. Everything traveling at the same speed, shares the same clock, regardless of direction. Everything traveling at differing speeds, have differing clocks. Replication gives us omnidirectional flow of spacetime. Spatial pressure, created by this omnidirectional flow, gives spacetime the ability to exhibit variations in flow volumes. Differences in flow volumes create every push felt in the universe, including gravity. There is another product of spatial pressure that is less obvious. Time is also a product of spatial pressure. The irrefutable proof is that a difference in the flow of spacetime results in a time dilation. The closer you are to any massive object in the universe, the more time slows for you. Of course, only in relation to another location experiencing less flow of spacetime. Being your own reference point, you see no difference from within your frame of reference.

We think of gravity as a unique force. Actually, once you have understood replicating spacetime, it is but one of many names describing the same thing. Among these names are gravity, centrifugal force, inertia, kinetic energy, momentum, and angular momentum. All these forces are a result of the relativity of spacetime. There is no force in any entity within the universe. All these forces, as we've observed and labeled them, are the result of relativity pushing on them. Energy is not conserved within the mass of any object. Energy is always within spacetime. Let me give you an example that may bring this thought home. Make believe that you are an asteroid. You are barreling toward Earth at 20,000 mph. As you approach Earth you start picking up speed. Nowadays, science says it's because you are increasingly affected by Earth's gravitational field. The statement is right. But what is gravity? No, it is not an attraction. It is space accelerating into a low spatial pressure area caused by Earth's mass. How does low spatial pressure in space look, in the realm of time? It is a time dilation. You see, the asteroid cannot increase its mass. Neither can it increase its energy. What is happening is that the asteroid is being pushed by accelerating spacetime. In a manner of speaking, spacetime is the one who is conserving energy. In order to have the same energy move within the same time, the flow of spacetime, itself, must increase, proportionally. The asteroid, being within the same medium, is subjected to the same increase in the flow of spacetime. In other words, now more spacetime energy is flowing past the asteroid. The result is that the asteroid picks up speed. Upon the impact on the surface of the planet, the asteroid has zero kinetic energy within its mass. It is spacetime giving the energy to the asteroid, because it suddenly accelerated to a stop.

I can hear the objections raised by some of you. "If that were true, then, all objects would have the same impact speed, regardless of mass!" Actually, they do. Regardless of mass, they all accelerate at the same rate. On a planet, without an atmosphere, a feather and a cannon ball fall at the same rate. This, alone, puts to rest the current picture of the object possessing kinetic energy. The energy always resides in spacetime. At the moment of impact, both a feather and a cannonball do have the same speed. They fall at the same rate, because flow increases closer to the planet. The speed of gravity does not change, but the flow does. The closer you get to a planet, the more spacetime flows into its surface. If it were true that the energy resides in an object's mass, then it would dictate the rate of fall. The difference in mass, however, does make a difference. Spacetime gives each object the force that its sudden acceleration to a stop, demands. This, of course, is directly related to its mass. This paragraph is more at home, earlier, in Chapter 2, The Key or Rosetta Stone. But it is here, because, if you understand relativity, then you understand gravity, and vice versa.

I know there are many of you who are still stranded. You just can't free yourselves from years of conditioning. You just can't accept that an object's mass has no energy. The funny thing is that the irrefutable proof is within your mind. Let me ask you a question. How much do you weigh? Please don't tell me. Just bring the dreaded number up in your mind. Now, why do you weigh that much? Is it for your love of chocolate? How about donuts? Perhaps the love of rice and beans? Is it because of your mass? What determines weight? Is it your mass or is it the mass of the planet on which you stand? Wow! We're not fat. It's the Earth that's fat.

The Earth's heavy weight causes the time dilation which causes spacetime to accelerate through us. That's right. Your mass is meaningless in deep space, is it not? I can only put you on a scale if you are under an acceleration of spacetime. Who has not felt weightlessness, when traveling in an airplane? If you hit turbulence and the aircraft suddenly drops, do you not feel weightlessness? When, in a car going over a raised railroad track, or a dip in the road, do you not get the same feeling? You see, within your experience is evidence that your mass has no intrinsic weight of its own. If you skydive from an airplane with your bathroom scale, can you weigh yourself as you free fall to Earth? The only weight you would detect is the air resistance of the scale being pushed by your body. Your scale can only weigh you, when it is resting on terra firma. If you are on a ship in deep space, at rest or at a constant speed, do you weigh anything? This one is actually a trick question. In this case, you actually do have a weight. But it is too small a weight for your bathroom scale to measure. Yet, all matter creates a time dilation. This time dilation creates an inward acceleration of spacetime. Any acceleration creates a gravity response. So yes, you weigh something against the ship. It's just very little, because you and the ship are very tiny. Replicating space gives us a plausible explanation for that pesky equivalency principle. A bowling ball and a feather fall at the same rate, if there is no atmosphere to cause resistance. The reason is that energy does not reside in matter. It is the sole property of spacetime.

One last thought: Is there any atomic energy within your mass? I believe, even here, the power rests in spacetime. You see, the power which matter releases, when it loses atomic cohesion, is also not its own. Upon losing cohesion, a release of energy is caused by spacetime. If you lose atomic cohesion, spacetime propels all your energy outward. The same energy used to bring your atoms together and form a solid, has now been released. Yes, you understood that right. Spacetime is always trying to explode you, and all the other matter in the universe. The fact is that, because you are made of compressed energy, your atoms are held together by the nuclear force. But clearly, if the inward force was not kept at bay with an opposing outward force, then things would collapse upon themselves, at the atomic level. I hope you have all understood the concepts in this chapter. If not, at least you can walk away saying, "I'm not fat, the Earth is the fat one."

CHAPTER 10

Dark Matter, Dark Energy

T HERE ARE COUNTLESS hours being spent by our top minds on the hunt for this mystical duo. We see their effects on normal matter. We can calculate their relation to normal matter. We can adjust our telescopes to extrapolate what percent of an image is composed of these troublemakers. So far, for all our efforts, we see the effects, but the two movers and shakers remain anonymous. Far be it from me to challenge so much brain capacity, and instrumentation. I whole heartily agree that the data is correct. I believe they have documented, accurately, the shenanigans of this mysterious caped dynamic duo. I suspect some of you know what is coming. It's "but", and a big "but" at that. But although the effects are real, the wrong players are being blamed. First, neither of them exist, at least not as described. Second, they have been in existence longer than the universe, itself. The biggest "but" of all, is that these mysteries are not only responsible for the expansion of the universe, but also for keeping it together. For the unlearned reader, please relax. We all tend to tense up when topics, beyond what we know, are brought up. Especially if we think that others are masters of the topic. Well, relax. There are no masters of this topic. We do have brilliant minds who could give us extensive lectures on the observations. But none can tell you the 'who, what, where, why, and how' of dark matter and dark energy. There isn't even a clue about what these dark operatives are made of. No one knows when they sprang into existence. We haven't a clue which mechanism they use to interact with normal matter. How something dark can come from a visible universe is dumfounding. Picture a wild-eyed odd-haired scientist, screaming and pulling out his hair. This is an accurate picture of what these two troublemakers, Dark Matter and Dark Energy are driving our scientists toward. Well, in my humble opinion, the cavalry has arrived.

Early on, I realized that replicating space had the capacity to explain many things. Foremost, it was a thing unseen. If you want to hide something successfully, hide it in plain sight. Years ago, I went fishing with a salty old character. We got to the boat ramp, started to undo the straps, and just then I saw that we had a problem. He forgot to take down his toolbox from his truck. I discretely asked if I should put it in the truck cabin and cover it up with stuff. To my surprise, he said to pay no attention to it. Leave it in plain sight. Well, this is a very large city, and this is one of its busiest boat ramps. I told myself his tools are toast. To my surprise, the tools were safe and sound, when we got back from a half-day fishing trip. I told him I had been sure he was going to lose his tools. He told me he has done this for years. He hides them in plain sight. His theory is that the more you hide something, and secure it with boxes and locks, the more people think it is worth. Once it comes to their attention, someone will try to get to it. The dark stuff dilemma is caused by a player that is hidden in plain sight.

Just how does replicating spacetime create the effects we attribute to dark matter and dark energy? First: how does it drive the universe apart? That is simplicity, itself. We already have many analogies to explain it. As spacetime replicates, it gets bigger, so all of its contents are driven further apart. Of course, the contents that are gravitationally bound, do not go with the flow. One analogy would be 'galaxies painted on an expanding balloon'. Another, a loaf of raisin bread, as it grows. Why, then, does it not drive the components of individual galaxies apart? Because, this is a crafty player, indeed. Its outward force is outstripped by its inward force. When matter is present, it creates a time dilation. If you change time, and keep space undisturbed, then spacetime creates a gravity response. The previous sentence sounds simple enough, but it is not to be underestimated. I need you to understand the relation between time and space. Whatever you do to one, affects the other. When matter creates a time dilation, there can be no other response than an increase in flow. In other words, spacetime must accelerate to maintain the relationship between its two components. This inward flow of spacetime energy keeps cohesion. It also has the side-effect of showing up as an increase of energy in, and around, the galaxies. Of course, any increase of energy will give you the appearance of more matter of the unseen, so-called dark variety. When in doubt, select the simpler, more elegant choice to explain the universe. Why use two unseen forces, when one will suffice?

"All well and dandy", someone has said. "I see how replicating space can account for the effects seen in and around galaxies. But how can a force pushing outward, throughout the whole of space, also hold the universe together?" I'm so glad you guys are here to make these topics flow. The answer is also in the flow. Go with the flow, young man, go with the flow. As you learned in Chapter 5, Matter Creation, is it Ongoing? regenerating space is self-limiting. Its outward speed is limited by its growth. Once the universe reached what can best be described as critical mass, it began controlling its outward speed, all done through the rate of flow of spacetime. I hope these concepts are studied by greater minds than mine, one day. One tantalizing outcome might be that we may deduce the total size of the universe, by its spatial pressure. Here I would like to give you a titbit, as to how big the universe must be. We know that as space gets older, it expands. So I believe we can use age differences between galaxies to extrapolate the total size of the universe. The Milky Way is 13.2 billion years old, compared to the furthest galaxy we have seen to date, GN-z11 at 13.4 billion years. How large must the universe be if a 200 million year age difference gives us such a separation? Perhaps I'm being overly optimistic. This reminds me of an old preacher's illustration. A large colony of ants was being decimated by an elephant who would routinely come by and trample their mound. The ants called a meeting. It was decided they would climb on a tree, wait for the elephant, jump on him, and kill him. The plan went well until the elephant began to shake all the ants off of him. As one ant was falling, she looked up and saw another ant holding on for dear life, on the beast's neck. The falling ant screamed "Strangle him, choke him to death!" Eugenio Castaneda. By comparison, finding the size of the universe would make an ant strangling an elephant with its bare hands, child's play.

The key to tying dark matter and dark energy to replicating space, is in identifying replicating space. And, I think I have an idea how we can do just that. We may never be able to see a single particle, or packet of energy, that makes up the fabric of spacetime. But I think that we have already observed the fabric itself. It is what science calls quantum fluctuations in a vacuum. Since the beginning of this journey, I have known that spacetime is an energy fabric that is ever-present. It was no surprise to me to learn that 'they' have detected energy emerging from nothing in a vacuum. This is the exact observation I would expect to see, if I had the tools to test for replicating space. It's funny to me to hear people say that a vacuum is a place with nothing in it. A place with nothing in it does exist, but not within the universe. The nothingness outside of created physical space is a true place with nothing in it. It is so absolutely empty that it does not exist. Nothing visible, or having volume, or location, or anything else that can be described, is empty. I challenge you to describe the nothingness outside of the universe. If you think that the universe is infinite, then try to describe the nothing that preceded it. The only way to describe what does not exist, is to give it existence, so that you can reveal it. As soon as you reveal it, you have failed because its nonexistence gave way to existence.

Back to the task at hand. How can we prove replicating space is real. These so-called quantum fluctuations in a vacuum are a manifestation of replicating space. How can we prove this? It is elementary. If I'm right, there will be a measurable difference between these fluctuations in different gravity wells. Matter creates time dilations. Time dilation creates gravity by increasing spacetime flow rate. We know that galaxies have greater levels of dark energy and dark matter than empty space. This, again, is consistent with replicating spacetime. I propose a test of the power output of quantum fluctuations within different gravity wells. The results would reveal replicating space. By the way, remember, all forces caused by acceleration are the same as gravity. A test can be carried out using a NASA G simulator. I have heard great men of science say that these quantum fluctuations gave us the universe from nothing. That would be the ultimate free lunch! I wonder if the folly of this statement ever occurred to these brilliant men. They equate space under a vacuum with the nothingness before the beginning. It is not that these fluctuations caused the universe, initially. These fluctuations are only possible within a physical creation. Why would I believe that? Energy is the basic unit in everything physical. Energy, or any of its creations, can only exist within created space. Curiously enough, energy must create space before it has a place in which to materialize. The quantum fluctuations we see today are actually creating space from within created space. They are creating, or to be more accurate, growing the universe right before our eyes.

Silvio Gonzalez

At the end of Chapter 1, we asked where is all the missing energy. This is known in science as the vacuum catastrophe. I will not try to fully explain what this term means, to the satisfaction of the learned ones. I believe it would be silly for a farmer to try to tell scientists what it is that they mean by this term. But please allow me to explain it to the man on foot. There is a great discrepancy between what is calculated to be the content of energy in space, versus what our experiments show. Quantum field theory is said to be one of the most reliable theories, outside of its prediction of the energy found in space. Just how much of a discrepancy is there, you may ask? Well, according to our best estimates, there should be enough energy in one cup of space vacuum to boil all of the oceans on Earth. For those of you who have ever tried to boil a large pot of water, enough said. We are talking about an insane amount of energy. This farmer is here to tell you that I find that calculation right in line with what I expected. Not only is the calculation right, but I think we already have the tools with which to confirm those calculations. I would give my left hand for the capacity to express things in mathematical terms. Try as I may, I can't master advanced math. Let me give you math geniuses a tip on where to focus your attention. Take a good look at a black hole. Calculate the amount of energy right at the event horizon. I believe that you will find that the energy manifested by a black hole is proof that quantum field theory is correct. The reason why science cannot see this potential energy within space is that they still think space is empty.

Science has accepted quantum fluctuations in a vacuum. This does not do space justice. Space is composed of the first and only essential field. It is an energy grid composed of nothing but energy in its most pure elementary and irreducible manifestation. It is the elementary field that serves as the venue for all other fields. All other fields, and by logical consequence, everything else in the universe, are composed of this energy. It has the ability to reproduce at whatever volume is needed to fill any low pressure in space. I know

142

some of you will be tempted to say that the energy manifested in and around a black hole is the result of warped space. I personally find the notion of warped space nonsensical. This idea that four dimensional spacetime can warp and cause an effect that manifests itself as a two-dimensional occurrence, is just plain wrong. In the case of a black hole, how can a push be exerted past the event horizon? Clearly, spacetime cannot warp, as depicted by all the examples given to show gravity. A warped fabric is two dimensional and can only show the manifestation of gravity. It cannot be used to say that it is gravity. It is merely what gravity does, when you stretch a two-dimensional fabric horizontally, and add a heavy mass on it, like a bowling ball. The most incredible thing is that warped space could only work in a Newtonian world. Warped space is stationary. Replicating space flow is Einsteinian.

I think quantum field theory is exactly right. Space does contain a huge amount of potential energy. Let me present a simple illustration to show you how this is possible. Let's say you tap into the output of Grand Coulee, the largest electric power plant in North America. The first thing you do is install some work lights. These lights draw a mere 10,000 watts of power. You take a reading, and you conclude "Wow!" such a big power station and it only puts out a mere 10,000 watts of power? No, I assure you the capacity of the Grand Coulee is 6,809 megawatts. So, why is it not manifested under a load? Because, it will only have an output to match the load it is put under. Science has measured the basic load of our local spacetime fabric, but they only measured the load to keep the lights on. If they had measured the load on spacetime, right at the event horizon of a black hole, then they would see just what space energy output capacity really is. I expect the energy output results of space, tested near a black hole, to equal those predicted by quantum field theory. Let me give you just one more bit of evidence, for why I think quantum field theory is correct. Most people have no idea how deep the deepest part of the ocean is. Well, the deepest part of the world's oceans is in the

Pacific Ocean in the Marianas Trench. The deepest part found in this trench is 37,070 feet. How is this relevant? More people know the height of the highest point on Earth, than those who know the depth of the deepest part of the ocean. But with a bit of common sense, you could assume that the highest point above sea level would be mirrored by the lowest place below sea level. Mount Everest is 29,031 feet above sea level. Here is where this comparison ties into the vacuum catastrophe. What is the densest matter known to man? I think, hands down, neutronium is the densest matter known to man. How much energy is in a cup of neutronium? I think it is logical to assume that a cup of neutronium and a cup of fully energized space vacuum are close in energy content. If I had to choose, I would say that neutronium takes it by a nose.

Let's have a little fun. Quantum field theory says there should be enough energy in one cup of space to boil all of the world's oceans. Remember, in Chapter 2 we said that neutronium weighs 5 trillion metric tons per teaspoon? Well, there are 48 teaspoons in a cup 5x48=240. This means that there are 240 trillion metric tons per cup of neutronium. Converting metric tons to U.S. tons, we take 240 x 1.102 = 264.48 trillion US tons. You may remember that a two-hundred-pound man has as much energy as a hydrogen bomb. A group of 10 two-hundred-pound men weigh one US ton. We multiply our 264.48 trillion tons by 10. This will give us the total amount of men. That would be a whopping 2,644,800,000,000,000, that is over 2.6 quadrillion men. Each man has the energy of a hydrogen bomb. The approximate amount of Hiroshima bombs needed to boil the ocean is 170 trillion. Given that an average hydrogen bomb is 1000 times more powerful, it would only take 170 billion hydrogen bombs to boil all the world's oceans. A cup of neutronium has 15 thousand times the energy required to boil the oceans. Now, I know the more astute of you think that I have made a mistake: "The neutronium was made under the pressure of a neutron star. So, we cannot use its weight as a measure." I beg to differ. Remember, I do not believe that the energy of gravity resides in any object. The energy that crushes a neutron star is not its mass. Rather, it is the energy of spacetime, flowing unilaterally inward toward the star. I grant you that the mass, being propelled ever faster by the inflow of replicating space, will supply the hammer blow. Replicating space supplies the energy to crush every proton and electron, thus creating a neutron, which turns the core of the star into neutronium. I remind you that matter tells time how to dilate; dilated time tells spacetime how to flow; and flow governs how matter moves.

I debated with myself as to whether I should include the following two paragraphs in this book. One reason against it, is that it takes a very large book to do justice to the topic I'm going to mention. The only link in this book to this idea is that the universe could be a free lunch. I'm but a lowly farmer, but that is exactly what qualifies me to tell you, that there are no free lunches. Believe you me, each morsel you put in your mouth has caused you, or someone else, to work for it. But perhaps more importantly, we farmers had to wrestle that morsel of food from a relentless adversary. Who is this adversary, you ask? It is cruel Mother Nature. I laugh when I hear people talking about Mother Nature, as if she is a benevolent mother. As farmers, we struggle tooth and nail to scratch, from its grasp, enough to feed an ever growing world population. Most people, today, have no idea the precarious position humanity is in. Let me give you the world stats, found in different sites on the net. World food reserves: 74 days. Lowest reserves in 40 years. In five of the past ten years, humanity has eaten more than we farmers produced. America became a net food importer many years ago. To make matters worse, most of our agricultural might is in soybean and corn, and it's not easy to live on those. America's fall from food self-sufficiency is not well known. This is hard to decipher, but it can be found in a few articles, or gleaned from stats, on the internet. This comes as a surprise to most Americans. It shook me to the core when I read it, over a decade ago.

This, and the preceding paragraph was written 4/26/2020. The world is in the midst of an unprecedented historic worldwide shutdown. The reason? A coronavirus pandemic. The stats above are pre-shutdown. The situation is so fluid and complicated, that I dare say no one has a clue of current reserves. Farmers, all over the world, are losing their crops. Most restaurants are closed to prevent the virus spread. Millions of pounds of potatoes are rotting since restaurants are not selling French fries, or baked potatoes. For the same reason, millions of gallons of milk have been lost. Tons upon tons of fruits and vegetables.… My own farm lost the first crop of the year. It usually gets sent to New York, to be used mainly by restaurants. In my case, I made no adjustment, because that crop came from decades old trees, so there is, I hope, next year. For dairy, and most farmers, they immediately adjust to the new demand. "Why", you ask? We farmers work on incredibly small profit margins. One or two failed crops, and most farmers are done. So fields must be left unplanted, milk cows must be culled and so on. If we compare the world to flight, we are an airplane, not a helicopter. We cannot hover. We either fly or nosedive, crash, and burn. Humanity's biggest enemy is, by far, famine. Here is a list of some of the peoples and civilizations destroyed by famine: The Akkadian Empire; the Mayans; the Vikings; the third millennium BC Cambodian Khmer civilization, and again their late 20th century Khmer Rouge regime, under Pol Pot; the Anasazi, or the Pueblo people of North America; the Indus Valley Civilization; and the Sumerians. There are many more that could be added to this list. It is safe to say that the majority of empires and civilizations are in this list. Famine has directly or indirectly been the driving factor in most human upheavals. The bottom line is that the world is suffering from collective insanity. We have backed away from a charging lion (covid19) into the jaws of a T-REX, namely famine. By shutting the world down, millions of humans are already condemned to death.

Now, back to our concepts. I can't complete the subject of quantum fluctuations, without pointing out a few oddities. These will expose one of man's greatest weaknesses. Man is ignorant of that which man ignores. If man knew what he ignored, he would no longer be ignorant. Why do we test for quantum fluctuations in a vacuum? Are they not present in the Earth's atmosphere? Are they not present within matter? I have no doubt that they are present everywhere. Why, then, do you always see quantum fluctuations associated with a vacuum? We must test for quantum fluctuations in a vacuum, because we need to remove the interference. "What do you mean, Mr. Farmer?" Put simply, particles and matter, itself, are made out of this same stuff. Energy/quantum fluctuations. Why are you surprised? How many times must I tell you, that energy is all there is, in the universe. Spacetime, matter, and energy are all one thing: energy. Let's explore the folly of the current thinking, that there is nothing inside of a vacuum. First, what is a vacuum? A vacuum is defined as space devoid of matter. Does it exist in the universe? Of course not. There are particles, seen and unseen, in the deepest, darkest parts of intergalactic space. How about a man-made vacuum? Is that not a true vacuum? No, not at all. First, which material can you name, that is not porous? The only materials we have, to construct a vacuum vessel, are made of matter that the universe has made. All matter is 99 percent empty, so the vacuum vessels are porous. That's strike 1. Our pumps and plumbing are made of the same materials. Strike 2. The neutrino is a particle known to pass through matter. Strike 3. There is no true vacuum within created space.

From now on, when you hear mention of a true, full, or complete vacuum, you can chuckle a bit. Beyond this mystical vacuum, there is an even bigger problem with our current thinking about quantum fluctuations. Not only can we not find, nor create a true vacuum, but if we could remove, and block all matter from re-entering the vessel, we would still have space. Space is spacetime. It is the construct, the medium, the plexus, the matrix. It is energy. If you could remove everything else, the energy of space would remain. Out of this existing energy fabric, comes more of it, through duplication, procreation, or regeneration.

I know some of you have gotten a glimpse of another elephant in the room. There is another reason why a true vacuum could never exist. Actually, within any vacuum chamber, there must be spatial pressure. It's quite simple when you factor in spacetime. Even if you do not yet believe that spacetime replicates, you must believe that it stretches. If spacetime is stretching, then a finite vacuum chamber is constantly housing more space than it did, milliseconds ago. The chamber, itself, maintains its size. But the space within it is growing. The question that comes to mind is, why does the growth in space not increase pressure? It does. So why don't we see it? Because the vessel is porous. The atoms making up the vacuum chamber may have enough cohesion to keep its form, but it is still porous. There is no matter that can stop spacetime. You guys are great. Someone just screamed "Eureka! There can be no true vacuum within the universe. A true vacuum can only be a place that has nothing in it. Within all created space there is a spatial pressure created by replicating space. This pressure creates reality." Give that man his doctorate. He has fully understood replicating spacetime.

There is one more thought on which I would like to elaborate. Can there be too much energy in the universe? Why would science be so concerned about the energy and matter content of the universe? They must be very concerned. Under their accepted model, all of the content of the universe existed from day one. Their model demands an exact content, to keep cohesion. They have not fully embraced relativity. They work into their equations, the total combined gravitational effect of the universe, as a whole. Do a net search. Does everything in the universe exert a gravitational pull on everything else? The answer is a resounding yes, according to science. Let's take this argument apart. Science is dead wrong. The force of gravity has been proven to travel at the speed of light. How can anyone claim that matter can exert gravity on other matter beyond the information horizon? Ever-present gravity is not relativistic. It is Newtonian. Furthermore, they choose to ignore the law of gravitation. When distance doubles between two bodies, the gravitational force is diminished by a factor of 4. There is no doubt that the universe is much bigger than what we see. Simply, the news of the existence of things very far away has not reached us yet. Remember, light and gravity travel at the same speed. Mr. Scientist, how can I feel the gravity of something whose light has not reached me, if gravity travels at light speed? If this belief in "gravity at all distances" was correct, then all black holes would swallow their host galaxies. The answer, once again, is given to us by replicating spacetime. The reason why gravity dissipates so quickly, is that, as soon as spacetime emerges out of matter, its flow starts to equalize with its surroundings, to normalize. At a finite distance, spacetime flow normalizes and no more gravity is felt. There is no pull from everything to everything. That belief is a remnant from the 1700's. Yes, just after the Dark Ages.

There is one final problem to solve, with this concept. If all spacetime is indeed replicating, then there is way too much energy. Under the current, accepted scientific concept of the universe, which began with all its energy, we are coming up short. With my concept, it would logically seem that we have too much energy. How can we have self-replicating energy, while still keeping energy balanced within the universe? Spacetime is capable of increasing energy output, in the face of matter. Matter creates a time dilation. This means that, in and around a galaxy, there is an increase of flow of spacetime. There is very little matter in the universe. This means that the propensity of the universe to create an increase in the flow of spacetime, which causes gravity, is small. In the rest of the universe, in the absence of matter, spatial pressure keeps the flow of spacetime constant. In conclusion, I believe that dark matter and dark energy are both one thing: regenerating space.

CHAPTER 11

Big Freeze, Big Crunch or Big Rip?

L ET'S START BY getting familiar with the three most common beliefs of how the universe could end. They are the Big Freeze, the Big Crunch, and the Big Rip. Why do I call these three ideas beliefs? I would say that anything, no matter how logical or easy to understand, that has never happened, can only be a belief. The universe has, to the best of our knowledge, never ended. We have not seen it end, nor is there any real scientific proof that can sustain such a notion. We do, however, have irrefutable proof that it started. What proof you ask? Just look around you. I think no one can deny we exist. Why, I wonder, do we think the universe will end? It is simple. A physical finite being cannot fathom the eternal. Then, there is the evidence of death and finality, all around us. Even those things which we hold as pillars of regularity and continuity, are here one day and gone the next. Let's just get into one such thing. Our Sun, how much more trustworthy and regular can you get? Never have I gotten up in the morning and learned that the Sun called in sick. Every morning, my roosters crow, and the Sun rises. So, is this bulwark of trustworthiness eternal? By no means. According to NASA, this ball of fire in the sky is using up its fuel at a rate of 600 million tons of hydrogen per second. Wait - don't panic! It still has about 20 solar years left. Oh, that still did not calm you. Slow down, each solar year is about 230 million years. No need to cash in your 30-year CD's just yet. The Sun should be with us another 5 billion years or so.

Back to defining the Big Freeze; the Big Crunch; and the Big Rip. The Big Freeze is a theoretical end to our universe that would see, in laymen's terms, an equalization of energy throughout the universe. At that point, no further energy in motion produces no further movement, nor heat of any kind. Everything freezes and comes to a screeching halt. The Big Crunch is similar, in that the universe runs out of energy to expand, and then, gravity collapses the universe into itself. Just think of stretching a large rubber band until you can't pull any more. When you have lost all strength, the band brings your arms back to where you started. The Big Rip also has to do with a lack of energy. But this time, matter within the universe has dispersed to such a distance, that gravity can no longer keep its expansion in check. The universe then speeds up, and flies apart at the seams.

The Big Freeze. Let me see if I can bring this concept to life, in your mind. Many years ago, when I was in an automotive repair class, the teacher asked the class how brakes worked. Most of us said "by friction between the drum and brake shoes". Some said, "by stopping the rotation of the tires, like on a sudden stop". None of us really understood the science. Our teacher explained that the brakes turned the car's energy of motion into heat energy. I was one of the most vocal opponents. That's when the teacher went in for the kill, and he exclaimed "OK, if I'm wrong then explain brake fade!" Brake fade is the point where the brake components are so hot, that no further heat can be generated, nor transferred, and you have no further braking action. This is why we have those runaway truck ramps in the downhill direction on mountain roads. It is a last resort for a truck that has overheated its brakes. At that point, the driver has no choice but to take this off-ramp where a road of sand slopes back upward, stopping the truck quickly in a pit of sand.

It is a fact of life that if there is no difference, there is no movement. No movement, no time, no growth, no decay, and no life. Here in the theoretical death of our universe, is hidden in plain view, the greatest evidence for regenerating space. For the benefit of the thinkers among us, let the rest of us take a break, and sip our coffee or tea. Let's give them a minute…. OK time is up. I know some of you got it. Where is this irrefutable proof, in light of the Big Freeze? Spacetime must be regenerating in all of the universe, in light of the theory of the Big Freeze. Here goes. In order for the universe to function, there must be movement of energy, not just in one region, but in all of created space. There can be a difference in the magnitude of the movement of energy, but there must be movement. OK, with that as a foundation, let's build on it. Let's take a make-believe trip to deep intergalactic space. We find ourselves in an area of darkness, at a temperature just above absolute zero, with no gravity. What keeps this region of space from falling into the Big Freeze? If space is merely stretching, then the temperature must drop. Temperature is energy. You cannot allocate a set amount of energy into a larger amount of space, without the temperature dropping. Replicating space brings with it a set temperature. This added energy prevents even the deepest parts of space from falling into a Big Freeze.

Here's the only thing I've seen, where the more you share, the more there is to go around. If it were not so tragic, then it would be hilarious. As you know, I lost my old country (Cuba) to communism. Even as a child, I noticed something peculiar. If we shared our food with others, we would run out more quickly. But we could share our hunger with more and more people, and there was always more hunger the more we shared it. Why? Because food is finite. We only had so much of it. But hunger was generated by each new arrival. The answer then, is that each regenerating spec of spacetime brings with it a set temperature. The capacity to regenerate keeps spacetime in motion. This means that space may not have begun hot. Space could have begun at the same temperature as today's average. We do see evidence of heat, but this heat was not created by The Big Bang, but by The Spatial Hammer (covered in Chapter IV). This heat is not key to the uniform temperature we see throughout space. This heat energy is key in the process of creating matter. The uniformity we see in temperature, throughout space, is solely dependent upon replicating spacetime. This addresses why space maintains a temperature, and why we have not succumbed to the Big Freeze.

I do not accept that a set temperature can be kept through space and time, without the benefit of replication. That is Newtonian. Not to mention the problem of locality (flatness problem). How can space maintain the same temperature without the ability to communicate and adjust? Spacetime is relative, not Newtonian. Space can only maintain a set temperature, if it is replicating, growing everywhere in every place, at all times. This growth would give us an unexpected consequence. If I have understood Replicating Space Theory at all, space is not only holding its temperature. Are you ready? Space must be getting hotter! Why? It's obvious. If energy content is increasing, then space must increase its temperature. We must remember to include stellar heat, collisions, friction and all other processes that create heat. And here, I would like to propose that, rather than a Big Freeze, the universe would end in a "Big Burn".

The Big Crunch is the theoretical end of the universe, where the universe stops expanding, and starts contracting. Like everything pertaining to the universe, it is very complicated. But we do not need to get into the specifics, or the math. Most of us, including myself, would not benefit from such details. The very learned and gifted would understand it all, but for the most part, they already know these details. Suffice to say, that the universe ends up in a complete collapse. The final outcome would, I think, result in an unimaginably massive black hole.

Monumental men make monumental mistakes because they work on monumental endeavors. I will lay before you evidence that most of the luminaries in cosmology have stumbled over the same obstacle. Stumble may not be the right word. They are not aware that they have stumbled. Here is the hidden obstacle that these great men have crashed into, without them even knowing they have done so. The universe can never collapse on itself because gravity acts on heavenly bodies, not on spacetime itself. The evidence is this. No one has ever suggested that spatial expansion is not happening within areas encompassed by gravitationally bound bodies. This means that even if the impossible were to happen, only matter would collapse onto itself. Even if gravity could act on everything that is present in the universe, which is nonsensical, matter could never return to the beginning to create The Big Crunch. What these luminaries have missed is this, let's say that ever-reaching gravity was possible. Let's imagine that gravity eventually stops everything and starts bringing it back to one central point. And how would a central point be chosen? There is no one point with overwhelming gravity. Let's say such a central point existed. How fast would the furthest bodies from that central point have to travel to outstrip the outward expansion of the universe? Bingo, they would have to break the light speed barrier. Everything in space is traveling away from everything unless they are gravitationally bound. But bodies also have movement independent of spatial expansion. We can then conclude that bodies are not stuck to space in a rigid form, like a sticker stuck to a sheet of paper. Space and matter are two individual entities that can and do travel independently of one another. The concept of The Big Crunch has given rise to the speculation that our present universe is merely a result of a previous Big Crunch. Can you imagine the cataclysmic explosion that would result from all of the matter in the universe crashing together at multiple times the speed of light? I remind you that no scientist believes the universe began with an explosion. If matter and spacetime were to collapse inwardly, that would violate the law of entropy. The only possibility remaining, is that time would have to run backwards. Time running backwards or breaking the law of entropy would mean that the universe is no longer bound by the laws of physics.

Here is yet another enigma that RST has caused me to investigate. After writing the paragraph above, the following question materialized in my mind. Mind you, this is something I have never heard anyone address, in a lecture, paper or book. Is the space that is encompassed between gravitationally bound items, such as a galaxy, under negative, positive, or static expansion? This, of course, is never addressed because, under warped space, the question cannot even be considered. Those who hold the nonsensical idea that warped space is the cause of gravity, see no linkage between gravity and expansion. In comparison, RST demands that spacetime be different between gravitationally bound bodies as compared to intergalactic space. The following questions are not only valid, but necessary. Is space collapsing into galaxies? Is the space within galaxies expanding? Could gravitationally bound space be static? Well, get ready. The answer is totally unexpected. The correct answer to the three preceding questions is yes. I can only imagine the distress this causes some of you. Each case seems to be mutually exclusive. How can they all be true? At the center of a galaxy, spacetime is collapsing into itself. Did you already forget that there is a black hole at the center of our galaxy? That is all that is needed to create an area of space where more spacetime is flowing inwardly than outwardly. But this zone does not end at the event horizon. The zone into which space is collapsing extends all the way out and beyond the furthest gravitationally bound body. The reason why the black hole does not swallow everything in a galaxy, is that orbits create equilibrium for the bodies that inhabit all galaxies. The positive growth is seen within gravity wells where spacetime accelerates replication to equalize the spacetime vacuum created by matter. All of the bodies within the galaxy create (and absorb) these collateral currents. Even though there is a tremendous amount of space replication within a galaxy, there is no positive net gain of expansion. The reason is simply because it is a unilateral increase of flow which is absorbed by the bodies that create it in the first place. At a distance beyond that last gravitationally bound body, there will be a static point. This is the point where space is at an equilibrium, not flowing in or out. Beyond that point the duality of space reasserts itself. This marks the beginning of regular expanding spacetime. In conclusion, I believe that the space within galaxies sees no net expansion. The interactions of gravity wells create an island within the flowing ocean of energy that is the universe. Spacetime gradually changes replication rates at the outer border of the galaxy. This acts as an expanding joint to secure a non-growing island to the ever-growing sea of energy that is spacetime. While basking in the light of Replicating Space Theory, I heard one of you cry out, "There can be no net gain of expansion within a galaxy because if there was, it would tear the galaxy apart". Wow! You really get it. Yes, indeed, it is the growth of space through replication that causes expansion. Wherever there is expansion, there is movement. Gravitationally bound galaxies are in that state because their combined gravity has cancelled expansion. Yes, gravity is a net unilateral flow of spacetime. We cannot separate gravity from spacetime flow because just as space is tied to time, gravity is tied to flow.

The Big Rip is the opposite of the Big Crunch. In the case of the Big Rip, the universe would literally fly apart at the seams. All matter would fly apart at the atomic level and dissipate into the emptiness of the nothingness. I would imagine that being so stretched; it would cease to exist. Reality itself would not be possible. Everything including spacetime would dissipate. This fallacy can only be contemplated, if you believe that spacetime is stretching, which dictates that you believe gravity is Newtonian. Speculative calculations peg gravity as having the ability to surpass the light-speed information barrier. You must believe that every item in the universe asserts a gravitational effect on every other item. This, regardless of distance. Supposedly, it is this ever-present gravitational effect that holds the universe together. It counteracts the effects of expansion. This, of course, is complete nonsense. Gravity is known, by science, to travel at the speed of light. It is relative, like everything else in the universe. Even if gravity was ever reaching, which is nonsensical, how could it attract something that it can't sense? For all practical purposes, one end of the universe is completely independent of the other. The only reason the universe looks the same is that it all emerged in the same way. Not only in the same way, but from the same thing: energy. Could a Ford Model T be built today, identical to one produced in 1920? Yes, it can, if it was built with the original materials and tooling used in 1920.

There is a misconception within the belief that the universe could end in the Big Rip. If we are to believe that space is empty, then the growth of an empty medium should not rip gravitationally bound galaxies or groups of galaxies apart. If the misconception that space is empty is true, then the only thing that would happen is that all of those galaxies which are not gravitationally bound to us in the universe, would disappear from our sight. None of the galaxies within our local group would move away from us. How interesting it is that scientists have perceived the expansion pressure created by the movement of space. They are correct about the expansion of space being capable of ending in the Big Rip. Replicating space theory proposes that as spacetime accelerates through matter, a gravity response is created. In the proposed runaway expansion of the Big Rip, the outward flow of space creating the outward gravity would overwhelm the inward gravity being caused by the mass of the galaxy. The galaxies would eventually fly apart. But that would not be the end of it. The continued acceleration would also overwhelm the cohesion of matter, down to the atomic level. There is no way that this is possible, if space is empty. On the other hand, if replicating space theory is a reality, then they might be right. A runaway expansion would end the world in the Big Rip.

These three concepts are governed by one ingredient: energy. In case you didn't know, it is the only physical ingredient which makes up the universe. We live in a triune, or best yet, a triplex universe. Matter, energy and spacetime. These are three distinct things, but they are all composed of the same thing: energy. In the case of the Big Freeze, it is believed that the universe has a set amount of energy from the start. This energy is manifest throughout the universe, in many ways, but always moving toward atrophy. In the case of the Big Crunch, we start again with a set amount of energy. This energy is the cause of the expansion of the universe. When that energy is used up, gravity wins over expansion, and a rapid collapse begins. In the Big Rip, the expansion takes the universe to a point where gravity can no longer maintain its cohesion. The universe just flies apart and dissipates.

Of course, these three models are purely imaginary. We have no evidence that it has happened, or that it has started happening. Nonetheless, we have the capacity to imagine what could be. So, it is a valid point to discuss. The current consensus is that the universe is a closed system. They believe that the energy within such a system cannot increase or decrease. If that was true, then all of these scenarios are equally possible. But while I do believe that the energy balance can give us a universe of the type we enjoy today, I see no possibility that an ever-expanding universe could be sustained from science's fixed-energy universe. We can conclude that energy is the key to all of the physical processes in the universe. Then let's go head long into energy, to see if we can believe in the Big Freeze, the Big Crunch, or the Big Rip.

It is easy to see why energy would be the key to solving the question of the end of the universe. After all, if the universe was made out of something else, other than energy, then, that 'something else' would be the key. It is unfathomable, that all of the energy in the universe was once packed into an area the size of an electron. Here, I would like to remind the reader that everything within created space is composed of nothing but energy. Energy in various forms and concentrations. Did you know that it is believed that a person with a weight of 200 pounds contains more energy than a hydrogen bomb? Now, expand your mind carefully, to put that in perspective. Let's just deal with the observable universe. I don't think mankind will ever have a clue as to what is beyond that which we can observe. In the observable universe, it is guesstimated that there are between 200 billion and 2 trillion galaxies. I'm a conservative man, so let's use half of the low side of the guesstimate. 100 billion galaxies with an average 100 billion stars in each. That gives us 10 sextillions stars, or 1 followed by 22 zeros.

Let's talk about stars. You need to know that the Sun, our own star, is not the big kid on the block, or even in the universe. Yet, it still comes in at a 'guess' weight of over 4 nonillion pounds, that is, a 4 followed by 30 zeros. This means that our Sun weighs 22 octillion (22+27 zeros) times the weight of a 200-pound man. Now, imagine the weight of all the stars and planets, and comets and asteroids. If the mass of one person contains more energy than a hydrogen bomb, then how much energy is contained in the mass of all of the matter in the universe? Now the picture is somewhat more complete. There is an elephant in the room. How can any person believe that all that energy was contained in a point approximately the size of an electron?

We did not name all of the matter in the universe. There is one more item I would like to name. Let's not forget what are, possibly, the most massive things in the universe: black holes. An example would be the black hole at the center of our galaxy Sagittarius A. It is estimated to contain 2.6 million times the mass of our Sun. It is speculated that most of the galaxies have, at least, one in their center. OK, this is a good time to take a sip of your drink and allow your brain to cool for a few seconds. If you are not flabbergasted yet, you will be, with our next statement. All told, visible matter is only 4 percent of the mass and energy in the universe. So, all of the visible matter in stars, black holes, planets, comets, asteroids, dust, and all of the rest that is visible, amounts to 4 percent. Now add the 96 percent of the unseen. Keep in mind that you, alone, have more energy than a hydrogen bomb. Just how can any sane person believe that all of the energy in the universe, could be contained in a speck the size of an electron?

Most sane people would say that there is no need to beat this dead horse any further. But there is a white elephant in the room. This pachyderm is very stealthy, and only the astute among you have perceived its presence. There is a whole category of energy that I have left out of the equation. This illusive item is information. We will deal with information in Chapter 17. But we must include information here since it is energy. If we are to believe that our world is predictable, then all information was present in the beginning. So, information is power after all. Not only is it power, but being energy, it can be neither created nor destroyed. This would mean that the information of your body existed in that initial singularity. Now, I think your mind has met its match. Imagine everything which has materialized in the universe, throughout its existence. We can all agree that there have been a massive number of objects in the universe through its history. Now, how massive is the information cache that describes each of those items, down to their most minute detail? This vast cache of information would, in my opinion, be more energy than the total energy in visible matter. To those among you who do not believe that information is energy, please keep an open mind. You will need it, when you get to Chapter 17.

It is easy to see how science would theorize that The Big Freeze, The Big Crunch or The Big Rip would be the end of the universe. It is logical that a universe with a constant energy content would succumb to one of these three endings, or perhaps one totally unexpected. But replicating space theory has the capacity to maintain the universe in its current state, and throughout its development, forever. The constant addition of energy keeps the temperature from plummeting throughout the entire universe. A constant and stable temperature prevents the universe from falling victim to The Big Freeze. The expansion caused by the growth of space keeps a constant spatial pressure, keeping The Big Rip at bay. Likewise, the constant outward expansion provided by spatial growth prevents The Big Crunch. Therefore, you can relax. The universe is here to stay. Its beginning should puzzle and mystify even the greatest and most learned of minds. But the concept of its continued existence is as plain to see and accept as Creation, itself.

CHAPTER 12

Inertia and Momentum

INERTIA. FIRST OF all, forget the 'item at rest' statement. It's doubtful that an item at rest could even exist in the universe. We, ourselves, are rotating with the Earth, orbiting around the Sun. The Sun orbits within the Milky Way, and our galaxy rotates around the local galaxy group. Even if something could be found at rest, it resides within expanding space, so it's at rest in relation to what? Here is something that emerges as obvious, as soon as you accept replicating space. Everything in the universe is its own reference point. As odd as it sounds, when you accelerate, you are actually moving away from yourself. Space does not see movement. Space sees only acceleration. When you are not accelerating, as far as space is concerned, you are standing still. How can this be possible? Stated most simply, spacetime is emanating from everywhere in every direction. Any movement is actually flowing with space. Nothing moves through space, everything moves with space. This is why speed of travel changes clock speed, regardless of the direction of travel. No matter where you are headed, spacetime is also headed in that direction. The faster you go, the less spacetime washes over you, and the slower your clock goes, in relation to someone who is traveling slower than you.

If you were traveling in a very fast spaceship, your clock would slow, in comparison to Earth's clock, whether you were traveling toward the Earth, or away from it. Let's throw a twist to the old 'Twin Thought Experiment'. Let's put both identical twins in separate spaceships. Let's send them in opposite directions at the same high rate of speed. Do they age differently? How about, if they turn around and head toward each other? Is there any age difference when they pass each other? Now, staying on course, headed away from each other, have their respective clocks changed? As long as each ship maintains the same speed, their heading is irrelevant. This omnidirectional effect in space, confirms that spacetime travels in all directions, from all directions. We also see that everything in the universe is its own reference point.

Probably, the hardest thing to imagine, from all I have written, is that everything in the universe is its own reference point. Spacetime replicates from every point. Hence, we are all ground zero, along with everything else in the universe. This explains why we can travel in one direction, without being stopped by oncoming spacetime. Think of it this way, as you travel at whatever speed you are going, you are standing still. Why, because all of space is traveling with you in that direction. So, at what speed is spacetime traveling, in all directions? At light speed. Anything traveling within light speed, is traveling or flowing with space. Spacetime is actually emanating from you. In a way, you are moving as a wave of energy through a sea of energy. Acceleration is the only thing that is seen by spacetime. Acceleration includes speeding up, slowing down, and turning. Rotation is also an acceleration, since you create an axis, toward which you are accelerating, but never reach. If rotating around a planet, or any other body, you can achieve a stable orbit. At the right speed and distance, you can orbit without using any more power. This is why we see people in the space station floating. I guarantee you; they are still within Earth's gravity. Their rotational speed, however, equals that push of gravity. Their acceleration toward Earth creates an artificial, outward gravity. At the right speed, the outward rotational push is equal to the inward gravitational push.

How about in space? Is it possible to achieve a stable orbit around an imaginary axis? That is not possible. Without a planet to create a gravitational push, it is a one-sided acceleration. The faster you accelerate toward your axis, the greater the flow of spacetime emanating from that axis, flowing past you. This is also gravity. But it is a unilateral push from the axis. Of course, this means that centrifugal force is gravity. It is what we now call 'artificial gravity'. Just as gravity diminishes very quickly as you move away from a planet, so does centrifugal gravity. The tighter the circle, the closer to the source of gravity. The less pronounced the circle, the straighter the path and the less gravity response. "But wait just a minute", said the reader in the nice plush, blue recliner. "The spaceship circling an imaginary axis is traveling at a constant speed. Why, then, is there a gravity response from space. They should be flowing with space". Now, allow me to explain. The circling craft is not at a steady rate of speed. It is traveling to the center. But not merely traveling, it is under a constant acceleration inward. Imagine, in your mind's eye, a ball in deep space. Now, imagine that out of this ball, there are rays of energy flowing in every direction. Now picture your spaceship circling that ball and breaking through these rays of energy. Can't you see how you encounter each ray with the tip of your ship? Do you not see, as you keep circling, that you gain ground on that ray? By the time the ray clears the back of the craft, you have diminished the altitude compared to the axis. Now, put it all in motion. Do you see, now, that you are accelerating toward the axis? Traveling in a circle, you accelerate inward while always maintaining the same distance.

Think of it this way, you are surfing in the outflow of spacetime that is emanating from your axis of rotation.

I know some of you just saw that white elephant in the room, again. You know, the one in a zebra suit dancing to the Tango. If centrifugal force is not a pseudo-force, then where does that leave centripetal force? As it stands now, science says that centrifugal force is a pseudo-force, and that the only true force is the centripetal force. I tell you they are both real. The centrifugal force is the outward acceleration of space as you accelerate toward the axis. In an orbit around a planet, the inward gravity push would be the centripetal force. But what about circling in deep space? What is the centripetal force? Do you see it a little clearer now? In a circling spaceship, in space, you have to use thrust to counter centrifugal force. It is beyond me how any person with a normal IQ can say that one is real while the other is a pseudo-force. They say that when centripetal force disappears, so does centrifugal force. That is nonsense. These two forces both disappear in the absence of the other. Let's go back to our spaceship circling in outer space. What happens if I shut down the engines? That's right, both centripetal and centrifugal force immediately disappear. How about if we could shut down the flow of space from the axis? That's right! The centrifugal force would disappear. The ship would take a straight path corresponding to the angle of thrust. No further centrifugal force means no further centripetal force.

Let's talk about a ball and string. If you spin a ball around your head, you will feel the string pulling directly outward from the axis. That would be the centrifugal force, the so-called pseudo-force. The pull of the string on the ball would be the centripetal force. When you let go of the string, the centrifugal force mysteriously disappears. The ball stays on a straight path, rather than going directly outward in the direction of the pull. The new path is a straight line, tangent to the axis. Why? Because the ball is no longer forced to fall toward the axis. Its path goes straight out from where it was released. That steady, straight path no longer has a gravity push from the center axis. How about if we rotate the ball in space. What would happen if we could turn off centrifugal force? The ball would stay in a circle. If the axis is moved, then what? I think that the ball would reach the end of the string, and bounce instead of circling. The bounce would depend on how close to the circle the axis point was shifted. The number of bounces would depend on the elasticity of the string. That is what I think. What are your thoughts? I hope to meet you one day and get an answer. The bottom line is that centrifugal and centripetal forces are both wings of the same bird. In the case of an orbit around a planet, they are both caused by an acceleration. They are both real, since they are both a gravity response to an acceleration.

I can't hope to convince you of the concept of replicating space, if you do not understand mass. Ask anyone what is mass? The most common answer is that mass is the quantity of matter in an object. But ask what matter is? Very few would say that matter is energy. Ask someone what they are weighing when they put something on a scale? They will most likely answer that they are weighing the amount of matter in it. As hard as it may be to understand, what we actually weigh on a scale is energy. Everything in the universe is energy. Understanding this will allow you to understand why a moving object shows more mass, than one at rest. Example: two identical steel balls, each exactly the same except for their temperature. Which will have more energy? The hotter or the colder one? It's easy, right? The hotter one. Now, the hard question. Which one weighs more? Science will tell us the hotter one weighs more. The bigger question is, why? Do we really believe that there is more matter in the hotter ball? I don't know about you, but I do not, and I do. I like cake. Here I can have cake and eat it too. I know that no more atoms have materialized in the hotter ball. This means there is no extra matter. Both balls are still identical. Or are they? For the life of me, I could not wrap my head around how metals expand as they get hotter. Now, it makes total sense.

At the atomic level everything is moving, orbiting, dancing, or vibrating. Take your pick. The consensus seems to be vibrating. Although, from our linear time, it seems to be an act of magic. At these levels, things seem to occupy different places at the same time, as if they were a wave. It also seems that things pop in and out of existence. It's like a game of peekaboo. I have heard it said that babies understand quantum mechanics better than adults. To an adult, covering your face and revealing it is not funny. We know your face does not disappear, just because it can't be seen. But to a baby, it seems that your face pops in and out of reality. This, of course, is hilarious to them. To us adults, the micro world is a peekaboo world. Things seem to occupy different places at the same time. They also seem to appear and disappear, just as in the children's peekaboo game. How is this related to materials expanding, and mass seeming to increase with increased energy? If things at that level jiggle more, then they occupy more space. If each component occupies more space, then the item must expand. The expansion must happen so that each component can keep the same proportional distance. The item has expanded along with an increase in atomic agitation. This will mimic the volume of a larger item. Although the mass did not increase, even by one extra atom, the result is more weight. Now we have clarity. An increase in volume of the same matter creates expansion. The pseudo increases in mass increases resistance to the acceleration of gravity. Now, energy, or mass increased by movement, makes sense. There is one more nugget I can take away from this. I'm an amateur blacksmith. I had not understood, until today, why metal becomes so pliable when heated. As metal is heated, it expands. When it expands, each nuclear component gets further away. The attractive force drops. This, then, must be why it is so easy to bend and shape hot metals.

There seems to be just one loose end in this line of thinking. Why do gases react opposite to matter, in regard to weight? For instance, if the principle was true for gases, then hot air would fall, and cold air would rise. We all know that in order to light a fire, we need to put the fire under the wood. Who has not seen a hot air balloon rise into the air? How about the flames of a fire, rising into the air? If a volume of air is heated, it contains more energy than before. Energy adds weight. So why does hot air rise instead of sinking? It's a matter of density and buoyancy. When you heat air, you do so within a medium. The medium is, of course, more air. The air does, indeed, expand like a piece of metal. But rather than becoming heavier than the medium, it becomes lighter. In the case of metal, it is a solid. Solids are denser than gases. The density of solids gives them the ability to expand, without developing holes, if you will, between their atomic parts.

In a solid, the heat-agitated parts vibrate more, but they still remain dense enough to impede the free flow of spacetime. This is not the case in gases. They are already spread thin, so any more distance between their atomic parts allows spacetime to flow more freely. This lack of resistance to the flow of spacetime reduces the weight of the gas. Let's imagine two sails on a boat. Let's make one sail out of wire mesh and the other out of a rubber mat. Both sails are elastic. If we stretch the wire mesh sail, it will catch less air. In turn, if we stretch the sail made of rubber, it will catch more air. The same thing happens with air. The hotter air gets, the bigger the gap grows between its atomic parts and consequently, the less resistance it offers to gravity. Hotter air does, however, displace the cooler air. The cooler air, being heavier, pushes the hot air up. Remember, it's all a push, never a pull.

There are two examples that come to mind, which are as counter intuitive as hot air. Years ago, when I started my adventures in boating and fishing, I learned something very odd. One day, I was out fishing in a twin-engine boat. One of the engines quit, and I had to limp to shore on one engine. I put the stalled engine in neutral and started motoring with my good engine. I noticed that there was a lot of drag and pull from the side of the stalled engine. But why, if the prop was freewheeling? Well, I engaged the prop on the stalled engine, and to my surprise the drag diminished greatly. Very puzzling, what was happening here? Well, it turns out that if a prop on a stalled engine is allowed to freewheel, then it will start turning and become a virtual disc. If you keep it from turning, you are only dragging the separate blades through the water. The second example is even more puzzling. A fellow farmer called me one day. He needed help. He had installed a brand new 5 HP electric irrigation pump. When he tested the pump it overloaded the circuit and tripped the circuit breaker. He had made no changes to the system; the pump was an exact replacement. The problem turned out to be a very strange occurrence. He had not yet connected the outlet of the pump to his sprinkler system. Without any backpressure, the pump was free to pump too large an amount of water. This increase in volume required more power to pump, than would a smaller volume at a higher pressure. It would seem that the greater the restriction and pressure, the greater the power requirement. But, it's the other way around. In a centrifugal pump, the less back pressure, the more water gets pumped. The increased volume causes an increased load.

Just when you thought you had that figured out, here is a monkey wrench in the works. Does buoyancy only work with gasses and liquids? No, the same forces are at work in solids. If we could heat only a portion of a metal ball, namely its center, what would happen? If that heated portion had the ability to move within the ball, would it fall, or would it rise? This is a question for a metallurgist. I personally think it will not rise or fall. It will stay in the same place. I think the increase in volume will weigh exactly what it displaces. How about a metal ball in motion, in space? Which exhibits more mass on impact? A cold or a hot ball? The hot one of course. The energy resides in spacetime. The sudden stop is an acceleration. The hotter ball will offer greater resistance to the acceleration of spacetime through it.

One last beating for this dead horse. Not all energy is heat energy. Let's talk about one more form of energy. If we have a piece of machinery in operation, does it weigh more than when it is stopped? It will weigh more. The reason being that movement in the macro world also increases the contact that the existing mass makes with the acceleration, causing gravity. In conclusion, no amount of energy truly increases mass in an object. There is, however, a measurable increase in what I would call temporary, or pseudo, mass. After all, what is mass, if not energy?

Energy falls broadly under two general headings. First, kinetic energy: these forms of energy include all energy in moving objects. The second heading is potential energy. This is energy that is stored. There are many different types of energy that can be listed under these two headings. Energy cannot be created, nor destroyed. Instead, it changes forms. I must remind you there is nothing but energy in this physical world. All that is physical is energy. Not only is matter energy, but so are the rest of the contents of our universe.

There is no kinetic (accumulated) energy in anybody in the universe. The power is in replicating space. Let's say you are traveling very fast, in space. Your ship hits an asteroid. Is it the kinetic energy that delivers the energy upon impact? No, it is the sudden acceleration. All changes in speeds are accelerations that create a gravity response. You are traveling in a spatial time zone equivalent to so many miles in so many hours. By changing your speed, space delivers to your mass roughly the same amount of energy that it took to get you to the speed you were traveling. Why does science believe that matter is the bearer of kinetic energy? The answer is very simple. We blame what we see. If what we see is corroborated by what we experience, then that seals the deal for sure. We see matter. We do not see spacetime energy. Does this change any of the tried-and-true formulas and observations of inertia? Not at all. Inertia is real. We just attribute the energy to the wrong player.

There is a very puzzling statement out there, related to mass. Mass increases with speed. This misunderstanding comes from the error of assigning the energy of an item to itself, rather than to space. If you read deeper, you will find that no one really believes that mass changes. Then, what are they talking about? Let's say you weigh 300 pounds. You are a football player. Is it possible that a 100-pound skinny guy could take you down? The logical answer is, of course not. OK, let's experiment. You stand there, and we will put the skinny guy in front of you. The skinny guy will push you to move you out of his way. Who will move? Even though the skinny guy is doing the pushing, you will stay put. He will move. Why? It's simple. It takes three times the energy to move you, as it does him. Now, you stand still, and he comes running at you very fast. Upon impact, will he move you, or you him? He moves you. This is proof that mass increases with speed, right? Wrong, this is the Achilles heel of energy, being attributed to an item, instead of to spacetime. Nowhere does this great blunder become more apparent, than it does as we approach light speed. As matter approaches light speed, it disproportionately increases its mass. We believe the energy needed to propel it to light speed would equal all of the energy in the universe. I do believe this is theoretically correct. But I believe it is catastrophically misstated. Why, then, can a 100-pound man bring down a 300-pound man, when the 100 pounder is charging at a fast speed? Factor in replicating spacetime. As the skinny man picks up speed, he achieves an ever-slower clock in relation to the 300-pounder standing still. Upon making contact his energy is delivered at a set time. When you factor in time, you realize what happens. The one-hundred-pound guy delivers 100 pounds at speed to the 300-pound guy at rest. When the two guys collide, their clocks synchronize. So, the skinny guy delivers 100 pounds for a longer time compared to the 300 pound guy who was standing still. Both are under an acceleration. However, it takes less energy to accelerate the stationary 300-pound guy, than it did to accelerate the 100 pound guy, who was going very fast.

"What are you talking about?" someone just complained. Yes, both are accelerating. The 300 pounder is standing still and starts moving on impact. That is easy to understand. The 100-pound guy, however, is already moving and slows upon impact. Why is he also accelerating? Please factor in replicating space. The medium is moving. With a medium moving in all directions, all changes of speed or direction become an acceleration. I plead with you to unlearn your bias in this matter. You are your own reference point. Any change in your speed in any direction is an acceleration from your current speed. Any acceleration within a moving medium will bring with it a gravity response. Yes, I have named the push we feel as we accelerate 'gravity'. Why, because it is that 'thing' of which we were first, and most, aware. Who did not fall countless times as a toddler? Yes, harder to admit as a grownup. Gravity dominates us almost as ruthlessly as time. Interestingly, they are cause and effect. Gravity is caused by a time dilation caused by matter.

I love the unexplained. Nothing has helped me more, in my journey, to prove replicating space than the unexplained. There is a great mystery in cosmology and physics, as it relates to the galaxies. You may look this up on the net. Do a search on any search engine; "What keeps galaxies from flying apart?" Science does not know why this is so. This problem has given birth to much speculation. One such wild idea is that a halo of black matter around the galaxy keeps it together. They have also theorized that if Dark Matter is responsible, there must be another force. Are you ready? "WINPS" "weakly interacting massive particles". These hilariously named particles supposedly respond to gravity, and another, as yet unknown, force. The force, similar to the weak nuclear force, would possibly create, among other things, radioactive decay. Do you still think this old farmer has a vivid imagination? I can't hold a candle to these learned ones. Let's think this through. A halo of matter is adding gravity, through its mass, to hold the galaxy together. But wait a minute. Is a halo not on the outside? If you add a halo of mass, will it not pull the galaxy apart? Is Dark Matter producing antigravity? If Dark Matter is producing antigravity, then what keeps the halo from dispersing throughout the surrounding intergalactic space? Enough said. It should be abundantly clear that I do not believe Dark Matter exists. There is still, however, a real problem. Without invoking some, as yet unknown force, our own galaxy should fly apart at the seams. Considering the distances and speeds at which the outer edge of our galaxy spins, it should not exist. So what holds it together? Here is where you go to your hat rack, and get your best thinking cap. I believe that it is because inertia is delivered by spacetime and is not inherently within an object. In other words, in the outer rim, centrifugal force diminishes, and gravity is exerted inward by the acceleration of the stars' outward motion. Whoa! That did not go so well. The learned ones had a fit. The regular folks are lost. OK, let's recap inertia and centrifugal force, to see if we can't get everybody on board.

Centrifugal force, according to Replicating Space Theory, is a real force. It is a gravity response created by an acceleration of a rotating object, as it falls toward the axis. In the case of our galaxy, the outer rim is one million light years away from the center. If it were true that inertia and momentum reside with the object, then the galaxy should fly apart. The reality, however, is that, at that distance, there is very little centrifugal force, or more accurately, negative gravity, exerted on the outer rim. Replicating space is exerting an outward gravity push through rotation. Yes, centrifugal force is a real force. It is the flow, or acceleration, of spacetime from the center of rotation. But at such a great distance, the push is very weak. Even a weak push, should fling the galaxy apart. It seems logical that the outward force should be more than the gravity exerted by the combined mass of the galaxy. Here, however, a very odd thing happens. The inrushing spacetime creates an inward push of gravity. As the galaxy spins, the spiral arms accelerate outward from the center. This outward acceleration creates an inward gravity push. Let me explain this further. Remember, all items in space, unless accelerating, are at a standstill, as far as space is concerned. Picture the galaxy stationary in space. Now, put it into a spin, as it normally is. Do you see how the spiral arms continually seem to accelerate outward? Since all of spacetime travels in a straight line, the stars in these arms are actually accelerating outwardly. The spiral arms are gravitationally bound all the way back to the galaxy's center. However, their arc makes them accelerate outwardly, as they rotate. Can you see, it acts not as individual stars, but as a gravitationally bound strand? Both forces balance out and keep the galaxy together. Yes, I know there is a loose end. What, then, is that halo which science has identified as Dark Matter? This halo is the mass of the spacetime in motion, rushing into the galaxy. It extends from well beyond the outer rim, to the center of our galaxy. Of course, we can only detect its mass outside of the galaxy. The inrushing spacetime, within the galaxy, is masked by the mass of the galaxy itself. If a learned one with access to space-born telescope data reads this, I suggest the following experiment. Look for galaxies which are colliding. These collisions happen at great speeds. I believe the halo of the inrushing spacetime would be seen emerging out of the galaxy's mass. Yes, I think that for a short time, inrushing spacetime will be observed, separate from its attracting mass. This will give you a clear picture of the flow of spacetime, not of dark matter.

Momentum, or mass in motion, has also lost its meaning to me. Here is what I believe. All observations and formulas are correct, but the assigned root cause of the observed effect is incorrect. Yes, it is true that mass in motion exhibits energy in proportion to speed and direction. But I believe that which causes these effects is the medium. Space is not empty. Space, or more accurately spacetime, is a replicating energy field. This field permeates, like a fabric, every nook and cranny of the physical universe. All of the characteristics of the universe are caused by this constantly growing energy fabric. Indeed, reality itself is made by the replication of spacetime. The universe is unimaginably large. Yet, all of the universe must be governed by the same spacetime continuum. If the universe is not under the same reality, it is no longer one universe. I believe reality is supported within an observer's observable universe, through relativity. The regions from which information cannot be gathered, cannot maintain reality through relativity. Relativity, therefore, maintains reality within the informational range. With this short- and long-range system, reality's cohesion is maintained. For those of you who feel lost, about reality and entanglement, don't despair. These concepts will be made clear in the next chapter.

CHAPTER 13

Travel and Spatial Time Zones

T RAVEL. WHAT AN enjoyable experience. I know that all of us have had trips we would rather forget. It could be, because we were traveling to the funeral of a loved one, or a trip that just turned bad. But traveling, for the most part, is a great adventure. We can leave our everyday surroundings, and experience new things. Most of us, however, have never given a second thought to what makes travel possible. Travel is only made possible by the duality of spacetime and replicating space. We do not travel through space; we travel with space. One of the hardest things for me to understand was how objects travel in space. Objects can travel at speeds approaching the speed of light, and it's as if they were standing still, facing no resistance. This is because space travels in every direction at light speed (actually a bit faster). Since space is emanating through replication from every point, the duality of spacetime creates equilibrium at any speed, up to close-to-the-speed-of-light. This equilibrium allows everything to travel unilaterally, unopposed, at any speed, in any direction. Yet, the acceleration of an object, or the acceleration of space through an object, creates a gravity response. You have removed yourself from equilibrium and are encountering spacetime energy when you increase your speed in any direction. We can travel only because space is going where we are going. It's going to and fro, from everywhere to everywhere. It starts wherever you are, in every location, and travels out in every direction. No matter what course you take, spacetime is going there. Here I must remind you, that it always travels in straight lines. This travel, in straight lines and at a constant rate of speed, is pivotal in giving you a gravity response, upon any acceleration. A decrease in speed is treated the same as an increase. But so is a change of direction. Replicating space is responsible not only for time, but also for space.

Just as a fabric has intersecting points where strands intersect with one another, the fabric of space is composed of energy strands, arranged in a three-dimensional pattern (plus the one dimension of time). The Fountains of God emanate from where the strands intersect. Spacetime emanates from every point in space and flows in every direction. If the fabric of space was not replicating, then travel would be very difficult, if at all possible. A stationary fabric would mean you would be going through space, like you go through the atmosphere when you travel on Earth. This would, at the very least, give you the gravity response that you feel, when under a sudden acceleration.

Perhaps you are still having a mental block on this concept of the duality of replicating space, and how this facilitates travel. Allow me to explain it further. I have told you many times that in space you are your own reference point. This occurs because your speed determines your clock speed. At whatever speed you travel, the speed of light is constant. Not because it remains constant, but because speed changes your clock. We could say that as you speed up, light speed changes in regard to you. But since your clock also changes proportionally to your speed, light speed remains constant for you. Remember, speed has two components: distance and time. Let's say you are traveling at 100 miles per hour. That means in one hour's time, you travel 100 miles of distance. By traveling a longer distance, or by traveling a longer time you would not change your speed. To change your speed, you need to travel a greater or lesser distance within the same amount of time. In space, neither distance nor time is set in stone. If you travel faster your clock slows, if you slow down, your clock gets faster. From within your frame of reference, you cannot tell anything has changed. At any speed below light speed, the speed of light remains constant for you. Space, therefore, emanates from and through you at a set rate, as long as you remain at a constant speed. Light traveling with space will always seem to travel at the same rate as seen from your reference point. This change of clock speed upon any acceleration places you at equilibrium at any speed you have achieved. You will remain at equilibrium, flowing with space as long as you do not accelerate.

As a mechanic, growing up in the muscle car era, I became aware of the effects of atmospheric drag early on. The fastest I ever took a car was 110 mph. Even at this moderate speed, the wind resistance is fierce. I was in a stock Buick Skylark with a 350 cid engine and a two-speed Power Glide transmission. As you get into those higher speeds, you become aware that your enemy is friction. The friction between your car and the air. This is why you hear of very fast cars having insanely powerful engines.

We can imagine what would happen if spacetime was not replicating in every direction at light speed. On Earth, you would battle atmospheric and space pressures. The more incredible thing is that our atmosphere would not react to rotation. So, as the Earth rotates, the air on Earth's surface would try to remain motionless. At the equator, it would give us a wind speed close to 1000 mph. With replicating space, the atmosphere responds to friction, and it spins with us. In space, there is no atmosphere, but there would be space pressure. The results would be like what happens on Earth, now. Let go of the accelerator on your car, and air friction immediately slows you down. If spacetime did not replicate, then nothing man-made would have ever left our planet.

The only reason that we can send a rocket out of our planet's gravity is replicating spacetime. We send our rockets eastward, with the direction of Earth's rotation. Interestingly, not against, but with. Why? Because the surfing effect of spacetime is maximized with rotation. As a result of spacetime replicating and traveling in straight lines, like an energy fabric, spacetime swirls into Earth. Since the Earth rotates, it makes spacetime swirl. This swirl mimics a ramp that we use to increase the lift of our spaceship. It is not unlike an airplane, on take-off, powering directly into the wind. At the end of the day, all we do is surf on the outrushing spacetime. When we reach escape velocity, we are free of Earth's gravity. At escape velocity, the increased outrushing spacetime, created by rotational travel, is equal to the inrushing spacetime. This rotational travel is actually an acceleration toward Earth. The faster we orbit around the planet, the faster we fall toward the planet. We are weightless at the point where the speed of the fall toward the planet equals the gravity created by the inrushing spacetime. Weightlessness is not the result of the centrifugal force caused by the mass of our ship. It is the falling toward Earth that gives us an acceleration which equals that of gravity. Gravity, of course, is caused by the uneven flow of spacetime. This flow is greater toward Earth. This flow is caused by the time dilation created by matter.

Thankfully, travel is easy and possible. Travel on Earth is easy to understand. We start learning from the time we take our first steps. We learn about gravity, balance and travel, all at once. Little by little, we master walking, running, bicycling and driving. For some of us, fast travel becomes an obsession. The human psyche is fascinating to observe. On a memorable sailing trip through the Caribbean, we visited Bimini in the Bahamas. One of my children made an observation, "Dad, these people are obsessed with speed!" He pointed to a man getting into a golf cart. "Look closely", he said. My son was right. No sooner had he sat down on the golf cart, than away he went, full throttle. The speed with which he pressed the accelerator was so, that a loud clank was heard as the pedal hit the metal. Looking at him you got the feeling that he was still trying to push that accelerator, further. Then my son said, "Let's watch the boats". We turned to the marina where we had our boat moored, and sure enough, here came a local to his boat. No sooner had he released the ropes, than full throttle he went, causing all kinds of havoc with the boats moored there in the marina. If you have never been to Bimini, it's a speck of land, amid a beautiful turquoise sea. We concluded that the size of the surroundings caused a desire in the populace to increase speed. Although it seemed counterintuitive, this increase in speed somehow made things look bigger to them.

I would like to delve into space travel. Local Earthly travel is our daily experience, and we don't have very many questions about it. In space travel, I would like to first mention that propulsion has nothing to do with action and reaction. In space travel, you are, indeed, pushing on something, with that something being spacetime. This concept was covered almost ad nauseam in my first book "Let There Be Light". If you don't believe the concept, or don't understand it, read it in the other book. For the most part, almost everyone that read the other book understood. Not that everyone accepted it, but they did understand the concept. In a nutshell, as you create an acceleration with the rocket exhaust, you are pushing back against spacetime, flowing in your direction. The acceleration gives you a gravity response. Yes, the same thing pushing you toward Earth, is pushing your rocket forward, namely gravity. The flow of spacetime accelerating into the Earth is pushing your rocket toward Earth. The acceleration of gases being expelled by your rocket gives you a gravity response, pushing your rocket. This is why a constant flow from a rocket in space gives you an ever-increasing speed. Please try really hard to keep an open mind. We have all been programmed to believe that for every action there is an equal but opposite reaction. I don't want you to ignore that. Think of it this way. I am merely telling you why it is so. You are accelerating exhaust gasses backward, so you are getting pushed forward. Did you understand the statement? When you sit on the launch pad, the rocket exhaust accelerates back into spacetime. Any acceleration gives you a gravity response. Since the exhaust never has to return to you (because it is a gas), the push is continuous. Obviously, you cannot propel yourself by the sudden movement of anything attached to yourself. Even in zero gravity, accelerating your arms, for example, would not propel you. You can accelerate them in one direction but stopping them is also an acceleration. So, if the accelerated item is physically attached to you, nothing is achieved. Agree or disagree, but just accept it, so that we can continue our excursion into space travel.

I can sense that I have lost some readers. More importantly, many of those who remain are reaching a mindset of disbelief. How can a mere farmer express himself so assuredly against the genius of Newton and Einstein? Well, it's time to give you some irrefutable evidence. Early on, when I had understood replicating space, I came up with a troubling thought. If this energy is so ever-present and abundant, there must be a way to harness it. This would give us mastery over the universe. We could, basically, have all the free energy we wanted. We could do so from anywhere in the universe. It would give man the ability to rid himself of all pollution coming from our current energy sources. It would also give us unlimited lift and propulsion for all of our space travel. I was going to begin experimenting on a device to do just that: to harness replicating spacetime energy. Well, thankfully I found that I did not need to spend a lot of money and years of my life. The device already existed. But, interestingly enough, its inventor and a host of college professors had no idea why it worked.

The device I intended to build would consist of two gyroscopes, opposed to one another on a rotating carriage. I would like you to put the book down for a moment. I have a treat for you. Do a search for "Sandy Kidd anti-gravity machine" Did you see how this machine cancels gravity? Do you realize, even that prototype installed on a spaceship, would give a craft unlimited speed? Mind you, this device does not interact with air, fluid or any solid. More importantly, it does not depend on action and reaction. This device harnesses the power of spacetime, as it replicates, in every point throughout the universe. The inventor, Sandy Kidd, had been inspired to build the device, after he had seen a presentation on the ability of gyros to seemingly defy gravity. The invention process proceeded like most inventions, through trial and error. It is no wonder that its inventor, nor any of the scientist that have seen it, can understand why it works. But to this farmer, and to those of you who are a 'quick study', it harnesses a force we know to be replicating spacetime.

There is a second type of reactionless drive device that is equally as exciting as Mr. Kid's device. It is called the EmDrive. As I understand it, the device is nothing, but a metal funnel closed on both sides. Within this funnel, they manage to bounce radiation. The test results have been all over the spectrum. The problem with testing this device is that the power output is minute. The total output is equivalent to about the weight of a Zunzuncito (A bird you will learn about in chapter 15) or about the weight of a penny. I do not understand how they can keep radiation bouncing within this device. I do conclude that if, indeed, the radiation bounces at least a few times, and if it can be created with a small energy expenditure, then this drive is viable. Not for liftoff, but for planetary and near-interstellar travel. It will be a sub-light drive. It also has the handicap of only being able to accelerate to the halfway point of long voyages. The second half of the trip must be used to slow the ship, so that it can stop at its destination. This drive definitely violates the action and reaction law. This is a closed reactionless drive. It works by utilizing the power imparted on the particle by replicating space. The particles that make contact with the sides of the funnel cancel out. But they will travel back until they hit the small side of the cone. There, they will hit with less force after having had contact with the sides. Then they are redirected forward. When striking the front, larger side of the cone, having had less interactions with the walls, they impart a net push by their momentum. This momentum is the push given by replicating spacetime. There is one very large handicap. It is the same shortcoming as the solar sail. It must be huge, because the power harnessed from each particle is minute. This drive does not violate the law of conservation of energy. The fact is, that it harnesses a source of regenerating energy that has been always with us. Amazingly, until the writing of my two books, no other human being knew of its existence. Welcome to the knowledge of Replicating Space.

Let me give you an overview of the implications of space travel and why it is so. There are many terms that will be used, but their meaning has changed. For instance: thrust. The rocket engine does not propel the craft with thrust, or action and reaction. It is a gravity response from space that propels the craft. You are pushing, or accelerating, exhaust gases into the spacetime that is rushing your way. You are pushing on something, indeed. Any acceleration creates a gravity response. This is because acceleration is changing the relationship between time and space. Remember, everything is a push. There are no pulls in the universe. So, the exhaust gases are pushing on spacetime, and spacetime pushes back, as a gravity response. I remind you that all forces in the universe are gravity responses from spacetime. This explains why, when the speed of the exhaust is reached, the craft continues accelerating. If it was merely 'action and reaction', then further acceleration would cease at the point in time when both speeds equal one another. Furthermore, 'action and reaction' cannot explain why mass increases as an object approaches light speed.

Let's make believe we came up with a method to make rocket fuel, on the fly. With unlimited fuel, we could have unlimited acceleration. Normally, a rocket-powered craft is limited by fuel. The more fuel you add, the more fuel is needed to propel the extra fuel weight. So, there comes a time when it is impossible to gain further advantage by adding more fuel. But this is imaginary. We are not limited by facts. So, we get into our spacecraft, with unlimited fuel, with no weight per pound of fuel. We fire up the engines, and we race into intergalactic space. With unlimited, no-weight fuel, we have no speed limitations. Or do we? As we approach light speed, we pick up extra drag, or push, from the front. Wait. How does this fit into 'action and reaction'? It does not. But it is explained easily by Replicating Space Theory. As you pick up speed through space, you are merely traveling with space. This will continue until you get close to light speed. At this point, you will truly start traveling through spacetime. Spacetime, heading into you, will make contact and push on your ship. This resistance will quickly rise as your speed rises. You are losing the effects of traveling, or flowing, with space, and encountering the forces of unilateral spacetime headed your way. Why do we see this happen prior to light speed? There is an overlap of spacetime travel on both sides of light speed. This is what actually locates light at this particular speed. This overlapping creates an equilibrium between the two opposing forces of spacetime flow. This is why light resides here. It's like a stable orbit around a planet.

I sense some frustration among you. Some of you don't accept that light can react to an equilibrium point. You don't believe that light has mass. Well, you already know that light has mass. What is light? I hope all of you believe that light is energy. Did you forget $E = mc^2$? Energy is mass and mass is energy. If Einstein does not convince you, I'd like to ask if you know how a solar sail works. What does it harness? Yes, indeed, it harnesses the energy from light photons, as they are reflected by the sails surface. Interestingly, it is theorized that solar sails could propel a craft to within 90% of light speed. Why not light speed? Because only light is light enough to be nestled between the overlapping fronts of spacetime. Fascinating. I wonder if the word "light" was also adapted to mean "little weight", because we assumed light was close to being weightless. You really need to accept this fact. "Everything in the universe is energy". If it exists physically, then it has mass, because it is made of energy.

Before we leave this thought zone, we should demystify 'overlapping spacetime'. It is easy to assume that everyone understands what you, yourself, have understood, and hold as an irrefutable fact. To me, space and time are as clearly understood as 2+2=4. Let's see how we can all share in this clarity. The Fountain of God emanates spacetime from every point in space. Clearly, this means that spacetime is clashing with itself. The constant travel, in all directions, demands this clash. Spacetime does not travel unilaterally. Spacetime is omnidirectional. At every point that spacetime clashes with itself, there must be overlap. We are dealing with the lightest of all energy. This overlap in the clash zone creates, at its center, equilibrium. There is zero force, zero space, and zero time, within this center. "Wait a minute, Mister Farmer. Why, then, does light get propelled by this overlap, while the other contents of the universe stand unaffected"? Light is small enough to fit between the two fronts of overlapping space. Can you fit an elephant in a thimble? Of course not. But I'm sure you would agree that we can easily fit a flea in a thimble. Only those things small enough to fit within the boundary of spacetime can travel at light speed. I remind you, they see no time, because for all practical purposes, they take no space. If you are size challenged (use little to no space) you also use little to no time to exist. Light is not unique in this list, the tiny neutrino is also included. I'm sure there are many other particles that travel at light speed, which are still undiscovered. "How far away is this equilibrium boundary from everything in the universe"? You did not ask the proper question. The question is "how fast away is this place?" It is at light speed from itself. If you insist, I will tell you how far this overlapping boundary is from itself. This boundary is at Planck length distance from itself. As soon as you achieve light speed, you are there, because 'there' is everywhere.

I just saw a great many bulbs light up above the heads of our group of learned readers. "Wait just a minute. Planck length is the distance that light travels in one unit of Planck time". Yes so what? "Don't you see what this means"? No, I'm sorry. I'm only a farmer. Do tell us. "This means that light is free to travel back and forth, within this boundary, possibly creating the appearance of a wave. The wave will collapse upon contacting anything in linear time. Since this boundary has no time, it can give someone, observing from linear time, the illusion that this photon can show effect before cause. This perceived reversal of the Arrow Of Time is not valid. It is similar to the apparent breaking of light speed as galaxies recede from us. This perception of time reversal is caused when an observer, who is governed by linear time, views a 'time with no time'. Everything traveling at light speed is trapped within the boundary of spacetime, in a place with no time, flowing with spacetime. It will remain in this place until it is forced into linear time, by contacting anything in linear time". Well, I guess I will have to take your word for it. That is a bit more complicated than planting corn.

Travel at everyday Earthly speeds is easy. But space travel is a whole new animal. Even before we went into space, we knew that outside of Earth's atmosphere, human life stops abruptly. In order to survive, we must create an artificial atmosphere. We must supply the gases, pressures, and temperatures to sustain life. We must also shield ourselves from harmful solar particles and radiation which would end human life very quickly. Only after all of these requirements are met, can we dare be in space. Recently, NASA has learned of new dangers in space. We have known that we lose bone density and muscle mass in space. The new studies have also shown that we develop blood clots and suffer fluid imbalances, the most worrisome in the brain cavity. The things we currently know are probably the tip of the iceberg. Let's detach from these issues and let the great people at NASA deal with them. You and I are not hampered by any human limitation. Our imagination has neither budgetary nor human frailty limits. Are you ready to explore the universe? OK, then let's go.

Let's imagine our ideal spacecraft. Here, you will be surprised and shocked. After factoring in replicating space, I concluded that the ideal spacecraft mimics a galaxy. It is round but not spherical. It would be a saucer. Full disclosure: as you will learn in Chapter 20, I do not believe extraterrestrial UFOs exist. I actually thought about other shapes, but the saucer shape won. The runner up was square. But square is ideal for a personnel transport or a garbage scow, but not for a ship of exploration. Among other things, a saucer-shaped ship can be rotated, if needed, at high speeds without uneven structural loads. In building this ship, we were limited only by our imagination. After all, it is an imaginary ship. First, let us explore the propulsion system. There is only one choice for interstellar or intergalactic travel. Spacetime propulsion. Man will only shed his travel limitations when he learns how to control gravity effects, by utilizing replicating space. This craft would have an outer skin, with the ability to control the effects of spacetime. Imagine this flying saucer at a standstill, hovering 100 feet above your head. How does it hover? It reduces the flow of spacetime from above, to match the spacetime rushing up from Earth. It is neutralizing gravity. In the horizontal plane, it is under an equal flow, so it stays still.

The isolated cabin is no longer under any effect of gravity. By allowing a disproportionate flow of spacetime within the cabin, we can maintain a steady gravity, oriented toward the bottom of the craft. The orientation of the craft within our atmosphere would not matter to the occupants. They would always be stuck to the floor, no matter where the floor would be. The only reason why we would keep the craft oriented top to bottom, is to see the Earthlings upright. Propulsion is achieved by allowing more flow to contact the ship from a given side. We can achieve, in this craft, light speed, in no time at all. But wait. What would we use for inertial dampeners? In a sudden acceleration, we could be smeared onto the walls of the ship. No problem. Inertia does not reside with the object. Inertia is the effect of an acceleration. Did you already forget the previous chapter? Since our cabin is under full spacetime flow control, we feel no effects of any acceleration. The common areas are governed by Earth's clock and Earth-like gravity. The crew quarters are under the control of each crew member. They can vary gravity as they prefer. Care has to be taken to equalize the spacetime flow, before opening and closing compartments. If a compartment is opened without equalization, a gravity response could kill crew members, due to differences in spacetime flow, which would show up as accelerations. Likewise, the entire ship has to be equalized when the ship has landed on a different planet, since it is normally set up with Earth's gravity in mind. In my first book, I christened my ship SG1. We will christen this one SG2. Are you ready to take her out for a spin? Take the wheel.

Let's take SG2 for a quick spin around the block and visit the Moon. We start ascending directly to the Moon. Gone is the need to use orbiting and centrifugal force, to help us defeat gravity. We can now travel in direct lines. The only thing to do is factor in relativity. Of course, relativity would be important on long range trips, but not on a skip to the Moon. On long range trips, we need to travel to where the target will be, not toward where it is. To travel to the Moon, if we punch it, we can be there in 1.3 seconds. Gone is the gradual acceleration and deceleration. It would take longer for the captain to give the order than it would to get to the Moon. In a day's work, we can visit all the planets in our solar system. The ship handles like a dream. Are you ready to go interstellar? OK, let's go!

We have decided to go to our nearest star. Proxima Centauri lies 4.2 light years away. But wait! That is a 4.2-year trip at light speed. Not to worry, let's engage our interstellar/intergalactic drive. This drive exploits the overlap in the frontier between light speed barriers. Light sits nestled between the duality of spacetime. But spacetime flow overlaps the speed of light in both directions. This is why light is in this location. This is where its mass experiences gravity equilibrium. There we go again. Someone just said that light has no mass. If it exists in the physical universe, then it has mass. Have you already forgotten what you read, just a handful of paragraphs back? I will assume you have understood. Once we break through the light speed barrier, we can utilize spacetime to accelerate through to the next light speed, and so on. We can, therefore, achieve any desired warp speed. This brings us face to face with the following. Light speed is not exactly zero time. It is only zero time for those within that time zone. All else stays within its sub-light time zone. In order to get to Proxima Centauri in one Earth day, we would have to travel at 1532 times the speed of light.

Someone has asked three important questions. "Firstly, why didn't we figure in our calculations the extra space that grows between these two points? Secondly, why if we are traveling at light speed (with no time), must we go beyond light speed in order to decrease our time of travel? Thirdly: What would be the pressure exerted on a ship, whose outer skin is creating a place with No Time, within the macro world?" Firstly, these two points (Earth and Proxima Centauri) do not recede from each other, because they are gravitationally bound. Spacetime is, indeed, replicating within these two points. Being gravitationally bound, the growth of space cannot push them apart. The new spacetime washes over these two bodies. Undoubtedly, this is a factor influencing their time zones. Secondly, we need to increase speed, because, if you remember, we have set our cabin to Earth's time zone. This means that for both the Earth and the cabin, the trip to Proxima Centauri takes 4.2 years, at light speed. This, since they share the same frame of reference. Think of it in this way. Both Earth and the ship's cabin are under the influence of linear time. You could argue that the cabin of the ship is its own self-contained universe. This may be true, but both are within a universe of replicating spacetime. In both cases, their reality emerges from a 'time with no time'. Both Earth and the ship's cabin, being under the same speed and acceleration, share the same time zone and frame of reference. Even though these two places are unique standalone universes, for all practical purposes their clocks are the same. Thirdly, at light speed, the pressure on the outer skin of the ship is manageable. This craft has an outer skin with the ability to control the effects of spacetime. The artificial spacetime, created within the ship, also aids by supplying an outward force to counter the inward force.

Once we approach light speed, we are faced with a set of problems which are very troubling. What happens to time? As we go faster, does our clock aboard SG2 slow down, in relation to that of the people we left on Earth? In the relics of the past, it was so, but this is SG2. We have full control of gravity and speed within the cabin. By simulating Earth's gravity, and its speed through space, we match their clock perfectly. Did it click yet? The clock of any observer is determined by their speed. Speed determines spatial time zone, or clock speed. As you will learn in the second half of this chapter, speed determines clock, and acceleration determines gravity. But gravity is actually spacetime flow accelerating through you. This is the same as if you were accelerating in spacetime. The implications of these spacetime controls, in the ship, are varied. Outside the skin of the ship, there is linear time. The skin itself is in No Time. The inside of the cabin is on Earth time. Wait, I just heard someone scream "that means we are traveling through space and time". Yes, we are essentially in a time or warp bubble. We can control movement by our interaction with spacetime. We control the contact of the flow of spacetime with the ship's outer hull. This determines direction and speed. Yet, by controlling how much spacetime flows through us, inside the ship, we control time.

"Eureka!" Someone said. It's a space and time machine. Yes, and no. Not so fast, Greenhorn. We can, indeed, slow time to match any time in the universe. But we cannot reverse the Arrow Of Time. I believe you can go into the future of your past, but you can never go into the past of your past. I was tempted to write the past of your present, but everything we experience through our senses is the past. Where you are in spacetime is associated with a place and a time. If you traveled fast enough, you could slow your clock in relation to your starting point. But you could never reverse the clock of your starting point. If we land on a planet and go outside of our bubble, then we will be in a time controlled by nature. Not only are we very far in distance, but also very far in time. We can board our spaceship, and head back to Earth, under Earth's clock. We could even simulate a slower clock, to shave off some time. But I don't see how we could arrive on Earth before we left. The logic is this. Matter cannot break the light barrier. The bombardment of spacetime flow would reduce you to your basic ingredient, energy, if not through the physical contact, then through the paradox of occupying a time when your information does not yet exist. In other words, the news of your existence has not yet arrived. While you are traveling in SG2, your interaction with spacetime is controlled. We simulate Earth's gravity well and its speed. By controlling gravity and speed, you control the forward speed of time. However, while within the warp bubble, you and your information arrive intact, and emerge out of the bubble. Of course, you would have had to emerge upon landing on a planet whose speed is within light speed.

If one achieves light speed, one stops time at the moment one achieves light speed. At that point, all of the visible objects are perceived by you as if stopped in time. If you could choose to emerge by, let's say, a planet on the other side of the universe, you would experience no time between your entry into light speed and your exit near the chosen planet. But for someone in linear time, he could find you anywhere along your route, in all of the possible places you could be, at any moment within his time. That is right. He is governed by the passage of time. You are not. This means, that in relation to him, you are everywhere along your possible route, at the same time. So, wherever he looks for you, he will find you, according to the law of probability (Born's Law). I know, you don't have to tell me that sounds ridiculous. How can something be everywhere and nowhere, at the same time? Your answer is within your question. Something cannot be everywhere and nowhere at the same time. But I assure you, anything traveling at light speed is everywhere and nowhere 'with no time'. Not being governed by time, someone traveling at light speed is, indeed, everywhere and nowhere, in relation to someone governed by linear time.

Let's imagine you are twelve billion light years away from Earth, in a spaceship capable of light speed. You decided to make a trip to Earth at light speed. As soon as you achieved light speed, you could have emerged anywhere in the universe, while perceiving no time lapse from your frame of reference. But let's say that between your point of departure and Earth, there was a planet with an advanced alien race. They turned on a device that collapsed your warp bubble, and your ship dropped out of warp near their planet. How long did the trip seem to take? No time. How much time did it seem, to the aliens to take? To them, you and the light originating at your time and place of departure, arrived together. Let's say that your ship's engineer was able to nullify the speed trap, and you escaped within 5 minutes after dropping out of warp. How long would the trip seem to have taken? It took just the 5-minute layover, at the speed-trap planet. How long would it have taken from the point of view of the Earth? You would arrive 5 minutes after the light that left with you from the original departure point. As you were traveling from the other side of the universe, you traveled through the images that Earth has reflected over time. Your final destination will not be where you saw the planet, just previous to your departure. The object is no longer where its light had indicated it was. You would, in essence, be traveling to that planet's actual position, since you are traveling at light speed, rather than the position you observed from your original departure point. Wow! Both Newton and Einstein were right. There is a Newtonian time, for everything traveling at light speed, and a relativistic time, for everything traveling at sub-light speeds.

Nobody has realized that we did not cover a key issue in the previous paragraph. What is the perception of each observer? In this case, we have the two observers, with different frames of reference. The Earth-bound observer is governed by linear time, while the spaceship-bound observer is governed by Newtonian time. We did theorize that for the frame of reference aboard the ship, no time will elapse while at light speed. But, if he can see the Earth, what time would he perceive Earth is experiencing? At light speed, he sees no time. He will see Earth standing still in time, while he is traveling at light speed. At the moment he drops out of warp, near Earth, he will emerge into Earth's linear time. Seems counterintuitive, but I assure you, it is perfectly rational. You cannot expect Earth to conform to the spaceship's time. The spaceship, at light speed, has no time. You cannot give what you don't have. On the other hand, Earth is in linear time. Everything within Earth's spatial time is in the same time zone. Logically, the ship is the one assuming Earth's frame of reference.

One of our learned readers is very insistent upon adding something to our discussion. "There is a more powerful reason for why the ship, traveling at light speed, must conform to Earth's frame of reference, and not the other way around. Of the two, Earth is the one with the greater entropy. If the Earth was to be pulled into the ship's frame of reference, then that would violate the second law of thermodynamics (the law of entropy)". Thank you, I see it now. If it was the other way around, then we would be reversing the Arrow Of Time. What could be further from entropy, than a 'time with no time'? This Newtonian time is literally the antithesis of the law of entropy. We have left the best for last. The Earth is not the one traveling to the ship. The ship is traveling to the Earth. Since it is the ship that matches Earth's speed, it must be that the ship conforms to Earth's time. After all, speed determines spatial time zone. When two objects under different speeds share the same locality, whichever of the two that accelerates to match the other's speed, assumes the other's spatial time zone. How about from the point of view of Earth's inhabitants? Well, they don't see the ship, until they see the ship. Did you understand the statement? The ship is traveling at light speed. This means that they are, for all practical purposes, a beam of light. Can you see light before light arrives at your location, where it's stopped by your eyes or telescope? Of course not. Then, how can you think you would see any light reflected from a craft traveling at light speed? If it was approaching Earth below light speed, then its reflection would arrive before the ship. But at light speed, the ship and the reflection arrive at the same time. Upon dropping to sub-light speed near Earth, the ship is visible because it is in linear time, within a frame of reference shared by Earth and the spacecraft.

By now, all of you should understand time as easily as you understand the pronunciation of your name. Of course, by this, I mean time, as understood through Replicating Space Theory. I'm puzzled why none of you are excited with how the two previous paragraphs prove RST. Can anyone tell me how Replicating Space theory is proven in the previous paragraph? Well, I must say, some of you are very close. Let's put forth the evidence. Back on the spaceship, as you achieve light speed, all objects are seen in real time, Newtonian time or a 'time with no time'. You pick which description of time you like best. Why do you see all objects in the universe in real time? Because light traveling to you at light speed takes no time, from your frame of reference (at light speed), to get to you from anywhere in the universe. Just like it takes you no time to travel anywhere in the universe at light speed, all emitted and reflected light gets to you in no time. If you do travel to the edge of the universe, it takes no time, from your frame of reference. While you stay at light speed, time doesn't pass

194

for you. Once you emerge into sub-light speed, you emerge into linear time at the time and place at which you emerge.

I hope you understood "you emerge". That's right. You emerge with spacetime, as it replicates out of a place with no time. This is proof of RST. This also proves that the most we could do is to stop time, but we can't reverse it. Because time emerges with space, from every point in space, this creates relativity. The light emitted, from any object in space, travels from it at light speed, plus the speed added by the growth of space. Time, therefore, has an irreversible arrow, The Arrow Of Time. Its perceived progression forward is influenced by the emergence of spacetime flow, but the most we can do is to stop time. It cannot be reversed. If this is all true, and I believe it is, then space does not stretch. It must replicate. Stretching space would allow us to reverse The Arrow Of Time. If space stretched, then it would also stretch time. This stretched time would allow us to reverse course, and reverse The Arrow Of Time, similar to what the Doppler Effect does to sound. With replicating space, time does not stretch, but rather, space and time (spacetime) grows from every point in space. This gives us no time at light speed. At light speed, you are traveling within the border of spacetime, at its exact speed. It also explains why, no matter your heading, your clock slows as you accelerate.

No chapter on 'travel' can avoid dealing with time. I see no way to explore 'travel' while leaving time out of the discussion. After all, time and space are tied at the hip. They make up spacetime. Even when we discuss travel in a 'time with no time', time is in it, even if absent. Of course, everyone should realize that time travel cannot be ignored. We travel through space, (actually with space) but we do so in time. It is, then, no wonder that I still sense a bit of confusion. If SG2 can control the flow of spacetime in its cabin, and if it can travel at any speed, then why can't it travel backward in time? Furthermore, why does the math in relativity seem to allow time travel into the past? Years ago, when my younger son was in high school, he came home one day with a very funny story. In math class, a boy had stood up and asked the teacher what was the use of algebra? My son could not stop laughing. No, not about the question, but because the boy was wearing a tee-shirt that read "Never underestimate the power of stupid people in large numbers". As funny as this student's mindset was, I think the other extreme is just as funny. The mathematicians among us tend to think that math is always right. That is an equally funny statement. The figures can be right, while what they show is wrong. If a man weighing 300 pounds goes on a diet, losing 1 pound a day, what will he weigh 50 days later? It's easy, 250 pounds. How about in 150 days? That's right, he will weigh 150 pounds. Here is where math fails. What will he weigh in 150 years? He will weigh about 15 percent of what he weighed when he died. That would be the weight of his bones. One thing is certain. Bones would be all that is left. If the diet did not kill him, old age did. Math can give you an answer that is not possible in a physical world.

Let me give you an example from my own experience. A few times in my life, I have had a negative bank account statement. I guarantee you; I had no negative dollars in my account. Why am I so sure? Simple. There are no negative dollars. That just does not exist. But the math says it does. Yes, but it is a tally to keep track of what I owe, not what I have. Time is more elusive than money. Time requires no effort to use it up. It flows, whether you are running a marathon or taking a nap. Time is made by the emergence of spacetime, and its subsequent travel. If you travel at the speed of light, the best you can do is to stop time, to the extent that stopping time is possible. But you can never reverse time, because once it emerges, it cannot reverse. Reversing The Arrow of Time would be traveling into the Fountain Of God quanta particle. That is not physically possible. This was proven each time an atom bomb, or a hydrogen bomb was exploded. Man does not split the atom. Emerging spacetime splits the atom. Any time you try to ram matter into the epicenter of emerging spacetime, the matter is shredded back into its basic component:

energy. That energy is then expanded at tremendous speed, as it tries to reach light speed, being propelled by spacetime.

Einstein taught us that matter is energy. This was truly revolutionary. But I think that Replicating Spacetime Theory leads us to a thought that is much more mind-blowing. When matter is turned back into energy, it reverts back to its original indivisible form. The explosion, caused by the sudden release of energy, in any of its manifestations, is the result of a growth of spacetime. Matter, then, is concentrated spacetime energy. If matter is dismantled, it expands to become spacetime energy. Matter is energy, and energy, in its most basic irreducible form, is spacetime. One last thought. This means that the push, felt after an explosion, is not solely the movement of atmospheric gases. We are feeling a gravity response, as spacetime abnormally accelerates through us. This sheds light on what creates waves in spacetime. Waves are caused by explosions, and collisions in space. These waves are caused by matter reverting back to spacetime. WOW!

You are associated with the time of your origin. The time in which you originate, will continue to move forward, no matter what you are doing. Here, you need to be reminded that you are your own reference point. This means that under an acceleration, your point of origin is the place you just left. Why is this important? We must remember this fact, so we can understand that as you accelerate with spacetime, your time zone is ever changing.

One last thought. I need to clarify that a 'time with no time' exists only at exactly light speed. Zero time exists at a multiple of the speed of light. When you have broken the light speed barrier once, it does not matter how many additional multiples of the speed of light you attain. For all practical purposes, there exists only one light speed barrier. A 'time with no time' exists only at exact multiples of the speed of light. When you speed past one of the multiples of the speed of light, you are again subjected to linear time. Speed of light plus any extra speed would subject you to the fastest clock in the universe.

Additional speed would slow your clock. The closer you get to the next higher multiple of the speed of light, the slower would be your clock. So, the closer to the lesser multiple, the faster the clock. The closer to the next higher multiple, the slower your clock.

The alternative to this concept would be to accept that, as we break the light speed barrier, we would experience a break in the space time continuum. This would force us to concede that there are multiple universes. This, of course, is something I do not accept, as even remotely possible. If we could time travel, we would need to use a measure of travel that would integrate both distance and time. Being unable to travel through time would require a different way of measuring speed. Our non-time speedometer would display a warp number, plus a fraction of the warp speed we are currently traveling. This gauge of additional speed past the exact multiple, is best, because only the fraction of light speed past the multiple, affects our experience of the relationship between time and space.

Is time travel possible? I believe traveling back in time is impossible, from within this physical world. If time travel were possible, how could you go back to the past of the future? Yes, imagine time the way I have taught you to think of the duality of spacetime. In the duality of spacetime, there are three locations: the center one, and the two opposites from that center. Time has past, present, and future. If you are in the present, and you go back into the past, you have just killed your future. You have stopped your existence from moving forward in time. How could your future continue, when you are no longer a participant in it? Now, imagine you went back to the past. If you changed something, then you are killing the future of your past. There's a wild thought. If you went back into the past, your future becomes your past, because it has already happened. This means that any changes you make in the past, do not change your future. They only change your past. Even though you may think you are changing your future, if you have already experienced it, then it can only be considered your past. Perhaps, by going back in time, you would make a new timeline. But at what point does that timeline skew? If your answer is that your timeline becomes skewed at the moment that you went back in time, then what would be the outcome upon making a change in the past? As soon as you made a change in the past, you have changed the future. But, if your answer is that your timeline became skewed immediately upon going into the past, then you have dissolved what has already happened. In the true sense of the word, you cannot change the future, since the future has not yet happened.

We are physical creatures living in linear time. If you traveled back in time today, then you stopped your future as soon as you went backwards into your past. If you could change your particular future, then you would be changing only the past. Only the past is certain. You can forecast what may happen tomorrow, but the only certainty is what has already happened. Why would you think the past is solid enough to relive, but you believe the future is fragile enough, that it would vanish by changing the past. In order to go back into the past, or forward into the future, time must exist as a block. Past, present, and future must be real and already consummated. But the concept that you could change it, negates its existence as a pre-existent, monolithic entity. I must conclude that time emerges with space. It does so from every place in the universe. You could say that there might be a Newtonian time, except that it would have to be relativistic. In other words, time is the same in the entire universe. All of reality emerges out of 'now' time, a 'time with no time'. Once it manifests, it becomes that which it needs to be, in order to match its surroundings. In other words, it emerges out of all possibilities into reality, that is, out of eternity into linear time. This negates the possibility of traveling back into the past. It would be like trying to put Humpty Dumpty back together again. Once the egg is broken, it is no longer an egg, but it is a broken egg. Once the present is used, it becomes the past. If you attempt to travel back to it, you are stopped by the present emerging out of Gods Fountain. The past, then, is the result of the consumed 'present'. Once the present is used up, it is no longer available to be remolded. There is no way to flow through the emergence of the present to gain access to, and relive, the past. If you have really and truly and completely understood the last two paragraphs, I'm surprised. This is because I wrote them, and I don't fully comprehend them. If you know me, or meet me one day, would you be so kind as to explain them to me?

There are aspects of time and information that are very intriguing. Is there a record of all the information throughout time? I think, as we speak, that most, if not all, that has happened in the universe is recorded within energy. At first glance, this idea may sound like science fiction. But here I would like to ask you a question. Let's say that we could send back in time a DVD containing a famous movie (each of you choose which one). Let's send it to Einstein in 1910. Could he play the movie? Remember this is one of the smartest men who have ever lived. Of course, he could not play the movie. He had no DVD player, nor TV, in 1910. As a matter of fact, it would take a long time for mankind to discover what the disk is made from. Our first plastic Bakelite had just been invented three years earlier. My point is this: I think everything that happens is recorded as it happens, within the energy of the universe. We currently have no player to read that kind of information. We might advance to a point where we can witness the past. This, because I think the past is not lost, it is recorded in the universe. But just like a movie in a DVD, we could never interact nor change any part of it.

I can't ignore the complaints any further. There are a few readers of the opinion that time travel is part of relativity. They are putting forth the Twin Paradox, as evidence. Let me point out your error. I do believe that the twin who stays on Earth would age faster than his twin who travels at great speeds. So, you could say that the twin who returns, comes back to the future. But what no one mentions, is that the twin on Earth sees the past in his brother's face. One has aged, the other has not. You may think this means that one twin is in the past, while one is in the future. This, however, is wrong. When the younger traveling twin looks at his brother, he is seeing his brother's time, not his. The same with the elder. At the moment that the one brother changed his speed, they were no longer in the same spatial time zone. This means that neither brother time traveled. Both decoupled from each other's spatial time zone. This misconception comes from thinking that Earth-time is the valid time. But time, like beauty, is in the eyes of the beholder. Remember, both twins had 60 seconds to a minute and 60 minutes to an hour. They definitely did not share the same clock speed. But as far as time duration, nothing changed from each brother's frame of reference. Here's how I would define time travel. Time travel is the ability to move from the present, to the past or the future, without the traveler experiencing any time. If you are not specific, then we are all time travelers. No one stays stationary. We all move forward in time, every second. Furthermore, depending upon your distance from Earth's surface, your time clock changes. This effect is caused by the acceleration of spacetime flowing into Earth. Yes, it is minor, but there is a definite difference. So, the homeless, street-level dweller ages more slowly than the rich man in the skyscraper's penthouse.

Within the last paragraph, there is irrefutable evidence for Replicating Space Theory. I'm surprised that none of you have alerted us to it. Time travel is always associated with fast travel. In all of the movies, they associate traveling back in time with somehow exceeding light speed. In the movies where space travel is not part of the movie, light is used to signify travel through time. Not once, however, is returning to the future coherently explained. As a matter of fact, in some cases, they use the same process, when they backtrack their steps. But we are certain that the direction of travel does not matter. Any time you speed up, your clock slows in relation to your place of origin. If we were to follow the Sci-Fi method, and travel really fast, we would simply go further into the future, in relation to our target place. If we retraced our steps, we would compound our mistake.

How, then, can we travel into the past? According to everything we know, it requires slower than stop-speed. That is not possible. Space is emanating from every point in space. With space, of course, comes time. They are inseparable. Regardless of the direction toward which you speed, the result is the same. Your clock will slow, in relation to your point of origin. Everything we experience, and all we know about time supports Replicating Space Theory.

There is one more thing that has become clear to me, as far as time travel. True time travel demands replication of the traveler. If you do not replicate the traveler, then how can the traveler witness himself living in the past, or more troublesome, in the future? Without replicating the traveler, he could not witness himself in the future. He stopped his future as soon as he left his present. But if, as a clone, he witnesses his future, then he is only witnessing the future of his donor. Replicating the traveler has some real issues. What would you do when you came back to the present? How would you reintegrate the clone with the donor? If you do not, then you are no longer looking at your future, your past, or your present. If you tell me, one stops existing, then you must choose which one. If you tell me, it's the one who time traveled, then everything he learned is gone with him. If you say it's the one who did not travel, then the traveler is ignorant of what happened while he was traveling. As a clone, you could only look at your donor's time. Apply this to the Twin Brother Thought experiment. In this scenario, they are very similar, being that they are twins. But as I stated previously in this chapter, when they look at each other, they look at each other's time, rather than their own. At the moment that one of the twins sped up in relation to his brother, they no longer shared the same spatial time. The fact that one person cannot travel at different speeds, while alive, means that we are stuck in our own time.

As we go through the process of editing this book, my editor and friend, Jeffrey Sterling, has asked repeatedly, "Just how do you come up with these concepts?" Well, Jeff, I sense that others want to know, also. I will answer all of you now. Let's take the last paragraph. I, like most people, was none the wiser when Sci-Fi movies used speed to travel into the past. Not being trained in any of the sciences, I simply did not see any problem with it. Again, I saw no problem when they backtracked their steps, to return to the future. Everything changed, when I accepted that The Fountain Of God was replicating space from every point in space. If this is happening, then any direction toward which you speed, slows your clock, in relation to your point of origin. This occurrence is caused by several reasons. You are flowing with space, so less time washes over you. You are also relieving spatial pressure. You may remember spatial pressure is instrumental in creating time itself. By further refining our thought, we realize that as you accelerate, your point of origin is the point you previously occupied. This point of origin is always moving forward with The Arrow Of Time. The final distilled answer, then, is the following. Everything you read in this book, and the previous work, is a result of applying Replicating Space Theory to the unknown, as well as the known.

What would happen if we could develop a spaceship like SG2, capable of faster than light travel? As you traveled away from Earth, the faster you went, the slower went your clock, in comparison to Earth's clock. So, what would you see, when you looked back to Earth? If traveling below light speed, you would see Earth's past getting older. No surprise there. All we ever see is the past, no matter what you look at.

How about if you are traveling faster than light speed? If you were traveling faster than light speed, looking back to Earth, theoretically, you would not see Earth. Even if close to Earth, it could not be seen. That, or anything else, for that matter. No light could overtake you. No light would be gathered by your ship's rear-looking telescope. How is that possible? It's simple. Remember, nothing travels through space. Everything travels with space. Since you are outrunning spacetime, nothing can be seen overtaking you from behind. So, as you travel away from Earth at greater than light speed, how can you observe it? Get ready, this will surprise you. I believe it's possible that your telescope would need to be set up, facing forward in the direction of travel. Wait, just a minute. How can you see Earth, looking away from it? Did you forget that replicating space replicates from every point in space? So, your observation platform is governed by the duality of spacetime. When you are limited to sub-light speed, you can look toward the Earth to see its reflected light. But, when traveling above light speed, you are outrunning spacetime and light. Yes, indeed, you would be chasing down the light reflected in Earth's past. Upon overtaking that light, it would strike the collector and reveal the Earth. Here, we have a few issues. How much faster than light speed will you need to travel? If you're not fast enough, you will not gather enough photons to get good resolution. If traveling too fast, it could have the effect of Earth appearing too bright, with no contrast. Like a camera shutter left open for too long, it all becomes an over-exposed blur. There is still another major issue. Will you get any discernible features, viewing, basically, the wrong side of the photons? I can imagine it would appear like a movie seen from the back of a transparent screen.

If you traveled far enough, at greater than light speed, could you see further into Earth's past than when you left? Yes, I think that is possible. Would it be that you have traveled into the past? No, it would just be a reflection of a past event. That was not so hard. Now, you had better take a good sip of that cold drink, to cool down your brain. The next illustration is a real problem child. What would we observe, if we turned around, and headed back toward Earth? Below light speed, we would see Earth through our forward telescope. The picture, although of the past, would be that of the progression of time moving forward. Maintaining your course, what would happen if you traveled faster than light speed? In the old country, we had a saying to signify something becoming hard to nearly impossible. "Here is where the sow twists her tail". Without giving it any thought, the answer is that you would start seeing Earth's past, and it would be getting younger. But when you think it through, your brain locks up. Here is an easier way to think about it. Time is determined by the outward flow of spacetime, in every direction, at light speed. If you sped toward Earth, at faster than light speed, you would reverse the reflected images from Earth. The picture you would see, at the end of an hour, would appear in less than an hour's time, because you are headed toward Earth, faster than its light is headed away from Earth, toward you.

Stop screaming! You are going to hurt your vocal cords. I heard your question. "Why, if we are reversing the time of the image we observe, are we not reversing time itself?" It's because the best we can do is to stop time. We cannot reverse it. There comes a time, within our race back to Earth, where we no longer have any time left to reverse, and that means you have arrived on Earth. No longer is the reflection of Earth being emitted, in relation to your frame of reference, because time stops at light speed. When you were at light speed, traveling toward Earth, you worked yourself backwards over that static reflection of Earth. At what speed did Earth-time stand still for you? At light speed. At what speed did you start rolling back the reflected time of Earth's history? At greater than light speed. At what point in time did you arrive back at Earth? At the same point in time that you achieved light speed. From your vantage point, Earth-time stood still. Please understand it is not that Earth's reflection stood still, as it traveled through space. What I mean is that from your frame of reference, Earth no longer sent out a reflection. This is because, from your frame of reference, time was standing still. This means that wherever you headed in the universe, you would have arrived at the same time at which you achieved light speed.

Let's try to make this time and reflection business easier to understand. Light travels at light speed. At any given time, away from Earth, a particular picture of Earth's past is seen in a particular location. So, for this example, time has stopped in the universe.

Now, get into your ship, and proceed toward Earth. Events appear to be moving backwards, not forwards, right? Well, a stationary snapshot of the universe, is what happens at light speed. Time stops. Things that move at light speed still move, but their movement is no longer governed by time. When traveling at light speed, from any location, we see Earth at a standstill. Here comes the logical follow up question. At what speed does that happen? My belief is that it happens at light speed. Light speed, after all, is the speed of the medium. Light does not travel through space. Light travels with space. One last thing: from the point of reference of someone on Earth, how long did it take you to reach Earth? Even though you were headed toward Earth, at light speed, in a no-time zone, Earth's time never stood still for the Earthlings. From the perspective of an Earth dweller, it took the same amount of time as did the light traveling from those stars present at your departure point. At the speed of light, the universe is a snapshot of itself.

If we had a way to see through time, what would we see when we viewed Earth, while traveling toward it at light speed? If your view was not interrupted by the reflections which have already been emitted, you would see Earth in now time (a 'time with no time'). That's right. From your vantage point, everything in the universe has stood still. I can guess that telescopes would be sort of useless in a 'time with no time'. They would either see nothing at all, or all of the reflections throughout time, from each item viewed. One thing is certain. As you travel at light speed, you would be traveling to your destination, experiencing no linear time. Consequently, you should see all of the universe in now time, or in other words, Newtonian time. Remember, this applies only to you. All other spatial time zones, moving at sub-light speeds, would see time passing at their particular rate. How is it that you would arrive at your destination at the same moment that you achieved light speed? Easy! You are traveling at light speed toward your destination, but light is also traveling at light speed toward you. If, at light speed, it has taken you no time to reach your destination, likewise, it takes light from your destination, the same no-time to reach you. I really hope you are still with me. If you think that's easy, I suggest you go back and read it, again. If, on the second reading, you still find it easy to understand, you have really impressed me. But wait, we have more.

Take another sip out of that cool drink. Are you ready? Let's forge ahead. Now, we are going to have the two points moving in relation to each other. So far, we have assumed that the Earth was stationary. For those who read my first book, you may remember that Earth is anything but stationary. Earth spins on its axis with a speed, at the equator, of about 1,000 miles per hour. It rotates around the Sun at 67,000 miles per hour. The entire solar system rotates around the center of our galaxy at 514,495 mph. Let me take you one more step, and we will stop there. Our galaxy is part of a local group. This entire group of galaxies is moving at about 1,000,000 mph toward the constellation Hydra. To me, this means that nothing is at rest. It also cements the idea that every separate body in the universe is its own reference point. Now, some of you have stumbled upon a curious thought. We're traveling at those tremendous speeds, yet we believe that our time is the right time. The big question is: what time are we in, if we are traveling at these speeds? I'll leave you to ponder that.

Let's talk about traveling at speeds relative to another body. We are fairly certain that nothing in the macro realm can travel faster than the speed of light. But that statement references two objects in the same spatial time. Two separate bodies can be traveling away from each other, at greater than light speed. We have seen galaxies doing just that. It would be like two cars running away from each other. Their total speed would be the sum of each car's speed. But galaxies can move away from each other, at speeds greater than the sum of their individual velocities. The biggest reason is the expansion of the universe, or more accurately, the growth of space between them.

I know there are still a good number of you who can't comprehend how one's frame of reference can have no time, while time is passing for someone with a different frame of reference. Let's see if we can make this concept simpler to understand. Let's say, you are 10 billion light years from Earth. You are in a ship traveling at light speed. How long would it take that ship to travel to Earth? You must specify from whose perspective. From the perspective of the observer in the ship, it takes no time. From the perspective of the observer on Earth, it will take 10 billion years, plus the time to travel that space which grew between the two points, over those 10 billion years. Let's slow down, so no one is left behind. Let's agree that there is a now-time across the entire universe. In other words, right now, you are reading this book. But, on the other side of the universe, something is happening at the same time. We can then agree that there is a now-time, or a Newtonian time, in the universe. Obviously, we cannot see it in real time. However, we will see it, eventually. For instance, we are only now seeing what happened at the edge of the universe, 13.8 billion years ago. And a point at that distance is only now receiving the reflection of Earth's past, 13.8 billion years ago (if Earth had existed back then). I think we can all agree, though, that if two points exist simultaneously within the universe, then they are under now-time, even if one could not be seen from the other's location. So, we see 'now time', but with a delay caused by relativity.

What makes time? You have already read in the previous chapters that time is created by the emergence of spacetime, from every point in space, emanating from God's Fountain. It is not hard to understand, that when you are traveling within the boundary of the medium, from which time is emerging, that time does not wash over you. If you travel to Earth, at light speed, then you travel in no time, because time is not washing over you. A person on Earth, though, is in a different time zone. By the time you arrive, he perceives your trip as taking billions of years. What explains this? Within your frame of reference, time stopped when you achieved light speed. Then you traveled through space and time (spacetime) until you reached Earth. You may not have been aware that time was moving forward in the universe, but that is just your perception from your frame of reference. The conclusion is that in a spaceship, at light speed, you cannot perceive time, because you are not traveling through space. You are traveling with space and time. Yes indeed, you are traveling in spacetime, at the speed of the medium.

We should further explain this new concept: spatial time zone. These time zones are not determined by locality, but by speed. A spatial time zone is a given speed that locks time and space to a particular relationship. All speeds are their own time zones. Under any constant speed, spacetime sees you as standing still, flowing out at whatever speed you have achieved. Once you have achieved a particular speed, you are identified with a particular spatial time zone. The time zone is equivalent to 'distance divided by time = speed'. On each side of you now, reside slower or faster speed zones. Accelerating or decelerating has the same effect. Accelerating in any direction will remove you from free-flowing spacetime to an acceleration. The result will be a gravity response. Objects traveling at the same speed are in the same spatial time zone. Objects traveling at different speeds will have a different clock speed in relation to each other. Objects at light speed will see no time from within their frame of reference. Where does velocity fit into the picture of travel in space? Velocity and vectors are irrelevant in space. Velocity is speed and direction. There is no direction in space. Why no direction? Because, if you are traveling toward any direction marked by a heavenly body, that body is no longer there. Even the patch of space it was in, is no longer there. On the surface of a planet, direction is meaningful, because it is a constant. Speed in any direction gives you your spatial time zone, and acceleration is the means to change your time zone.

Let's see what happens between two bodies hurtling through space, at speeds both within and exceeding light speed. First, replicating space gives us a spatial time zone, at a given speed. Barring the effects of a gravity well, all bodies traveling at the same speeds share the same clock. Direction of travel is not a factor, since space replicates from every point outward at light speed. Some of you may have realized that in one of the previous paragraphs, something did not make sense. I told you that our craft, SG2, moving at greater than light speed, would lose its view of a body behind it. But I also told you that we would not lose sight of bodies moving away from us, at greater than light speed, due to expansion. These statements contradict each other, yet they are both true. In order for us to lose sight of an item, either we or the item must go faster than light speed. But why, you may ask? If the combined speeds are greater than light speed, is it not the same? Here's the difference. Things traveling at or beyond light speed, can neither emit nor reflect light. At and beyond light speed, nothing is visible. Even if something passes by only ten feet away, you will never see it. There are several reasons. The human eye's refresh rate is 26 frames per second. This means that, in the time it takes for your eyes to snap a picture, an object traveling at greater than light speed, would be out of your field of view. My point is, that if an object travels at greater than light speed, then it can never be seen.

As long as nothing in the universe exceeds light speed, we will never lose sight of anything we currently see, because it is traveling in a replicating medium that will eventually wash over us. Think of it as two items with a rubber band between them. As they pull further apart, the rubber band stretches, but they are still connected. They will remain connected, until the rubber band fails. I can imagine that there could come a time when light would be stretched to the point of not being detectable. It is also true that you cannot see something which is not old enough for its light to have reached you. But as long as enough light is emitted, you will always see that which you now see. The only exception is if something forms in between you and said item. Then your view will be blocked, if not lensed. Science maintains that after the universe reaches 19 billion years old, we will start losing sight of the rest of the universe. This would be right, if light traveled through space. I think most of you have already accepted that light travels with space. There is nothing that travels through space. The only way to travel through space is to overtake space. This, of course, means traveling faster than light.

Don't get too hung-up on light speed. Light does not travel. It has no speed of its own. Light flows with spacetime. Its speed is the speed of the equilibrium point of both fronts of spacetime. The fact that spacetime replicates from every point in space in straight lines, means that it must clash with itself. At the point it clashes, it does not stop, but overlaps equally in both directions. This overlap creates a center point devoid of gravity or time. This is the home of light.

Let's explore how light travels, a bit more. If light was to travel 'through' space, then what would propel it? If you say it needs nothing to push it, once it is moving, then what set it in motion? If something sets it in motion, then it is defeating the tremendous gravity of a star. Only one thing makes sense to me. Light starts moving from a central location in the star, moving outward with the outflow of spacetime, as it zigzags its way through the star. Light, therefore, is traveling not through space, but with space. So how are we to explain what happens when it encounters an obstruction, let's say a mirror? It's simple. Its forward travel is impeded. It has no alternative but to bounce back, reversing its direction. Of course, it becomes a mirror image. What exactly causes the mirror effect? The duality of time, of course. The image is now traveling in the opposite direction. Why does it bounce? Because, as it is brought to a stop and not absorbed, spacetime, coming from the other direction, propels it. OK, so why do different surfaces reflect a different percentage of light? Here, color has a lot to do with the result. If a material is painted with bright colors, it will reflect more light. The darker the color, the less light is reflected. There is, however, nothing so dark that it does not reflect light. Or is there? Here is an exception to the rule: A black hole. To begin with, the reason it is called black is because it neither reflects nor emits light. On surfaces where light is not reflected, it is turned back to energy, in the form of heat. After all, it was heat energy which produced light to begin with. Remember, there is nothing but energy within the universe.

There seems to be some dissent amongst my readership. It's been building. The concern? How does SG2 avoid collisions? At the speeds this craft travels, it's an atom smasher. As it travels in a straight line, through an evenly distributed universe, collision is inevitable. Yes, I should have known better than to try to put one over such an astute bunch. But I remind you how this ship was conceived. It is not a product of the famed Lockheed Martin's Skunk Works but was conceived in the workshop of imagination. The Skunk Works brought us the U-2, SR-71 Blackbird, F-117 Nighthawk, F-22 Raptor and the F-35, among others. But, as fabulous as they are, none of them hold a candle to SG2. Our ship is equipped with a quantum multicore computer. Its computational capacity is much more than the combination of all its predecessors. It has tremendous storage capacity, storing mankind's accumulated knowledge. It is self-aware AI, accessing that knowledge, to make decisions. Every day that it is in service, it compiles more data than mankind's entire knowledge base. On its first day, it solved every mathematical problem which men have failed to solve. This computer, named Alpha, for being the first of its kind, navigates the ship. All of the universe's data, gathered by man, is at her beck and call. The sub-system that is tasked with controlling spacetime, calculates gravity effects of bodies in our path. Course corrections are made at Planck length intervals. No course correction is needed for bodies with less mass than our ship. Anything smaller is manipulated to end up at a safe distance from our travel route. This creates a corridor for our return trip. When needed, we replenish energy stores. Smaller bodies are allowed to impact our advancing spacetime wake. We harness the energy released, as they are threaded into spacetime. I know what you are thinking. I WANT ONE OF THOSE SHIPS!

Now that you have read both chapters 12 and 13, I think you are ready to see how Replicating Space Theory brings the concepts together. Let's create a scenario which will demonstrate how Replicating Space Theory explains inertia, momentum, travel, and time zones. I think the best way we can cover these concepts is to employ the launch of a conventional liquid propellant rocket. For the sake of this illustration, the rocket will be carrying a deep space probe. We begin this illustration with the rocket sitting on the pad at Cape Canaveral, ready to start the countdown. 10, 9, 8, 7, 6, 5, 4, 3, 2, 1. The rockets ignite, and we have lift off! The current scientific explanation, for why we have lift off, is that for every action, there is an equal and opposite reaction. The action is the exhaust of the rocket being propelled out of the rocket nozzle. The reaction is the thrust created, lifting the rocket skyward. So long as the pounds of thrust exceed the weight of our vehicle, our rocket will climb. How does Replicating Space Theory explain the lift off? If the accelerated exhaust is greater than the accelerated inflow of spacetime coming from above, then we have lift off.

Our vehicle has climbed and has reached stable orbit. NASA's science says that a stable orbit is reached when the pull of Earth's gravity equals the object's momentum. How does Replicating Space Theory, (RST) explain a stable orbit? As a craft circles Earth, it is falling toward Earth. This means that it is accelerating its fall toward Earth. When the combined flows of the inrushing spacetime (coming from outer space) and the outrushing spacetime (coming from within Earth) are brought into equilibrium by the falling effect of the craft, we get a stable orbit. Remember, momentum is not a quality of the object. Rather, it is imparted onto a moving object, by the flow of spacetime. How does our vehicle break orbit? We fire the rocket engine and increase the speed. When the vehicle's speed reaches a point where it is falling faster than the inrushing spacetime flow, it starts to surf on the outrushing spacetime flow. The vehicle will travel into space, leaving orbit in a straight-line tangent to its curve of rotation. Why does it stay in motion? Is it because, as science says, that an item in motion stays in motion until something acts upon it? Not according to RST (Replicating Space Theory). Our probe stays in motion because it has reached a specific spatial time zone. This time zone is identified by a specific speed. So many miles traveled in so many hours…. It has nothing to do with inertia and momentum, as defined today's science. There is no power stored in any object. All natural forces in motion emanate from the moving medium that is spacetime. Why do we need to exert more power in order to change the speed or direction of our probe? Is it caused by inertia? No, not at all. The cause is replicating space.

Here I must remind you that, as far as spacetime is concerned, any item moving at a steady speed is at a standstill. It is only acceleration that is relevant to spacetime. Here is where the rubber meets the road. Why? Because, at a steady speed, you are your own reference point. Spacetime is emanating from you at a steady speed in all directions. How can you envision this? It's easy. Any light that you reflect is traveling at light speed, is it not? Well, light, according to RST, travels with space at spacetime speed (plus spatial expansion). When our probe fires its thrusters, it accelerates in one direction. The probe moves away from itself. This acceleration away from itself creates a gravity response that must be overcome by thrust. The gravity response is caused by an unbalanced spacetime flow. The flow is a response to a time dilation. Yes, you read it right. I'm positive that upon acceleration, the accelerated item is experiencing a time dilation. Why is it so hard to understand? Matter creates a difference between inflow and outflow of spacetime. A difference between inflow and outflow of spacetime creates a time dilation. Why wouldn't a forced flow in moving objects cause a dilation, resulting in gravity? Doesn't the accelerating object change its clock speed? Well, what is a time dilation, if not a change in clock speed?

This unbalance causes a gravity push from the direction of travel. But why doesn't the increase in flow in the other direction pull on you, equalizing the push from the direction of travel? Have you forgotten that there are no pulls in the universe? Only pushes exist. One must reach to where the item is, in order to push it toward you. To pull an item, you must pull it from where it does not yet reside.

Under an acceleration, you are no longer within the boundary of the duality of spacetime. This takes you out of phase with spacetime. You are changing your speed, which changes your clock. Remember that the speed of travel changes clock speed. It should be clear that if you are changing clock speed, then you are witnessing a time dilation happening right in front of your eyes. At a constant speed, you are stationary in space in a constant time zone. All flow of spacetime through you and from you is equal. This is why no gravity effects are felt when traveling at a constant speed. It is very different on Earth because you battle atmospheric gases, and you are traveling atop a stationary medium. But in space (where our probe is) you are in a vacuum, traveling within a flowing medium. Once the probe's thrusters are shut down, the probe is once again flowing with spacetime within its new spatial time zone. The probe's clock speed has now changed to match that of all other objects traveling at the same speed within the universe.

For those of you who have understood this chapter, I will explain travel in the light of RST. As you travel in any direction, space is also traveling there. You are not traveling through space, but rather you are flowing with space. Nothing travels through space: everything travels with space. The faster you go in any direction, the smaller is the volume of replication from within you. The less those Fountains replicate and emanate (flow) from you, the less time flows through you. Any acceleration of 'you with spacetime' or 'spacetime through you', changes your spatial time zone. The reason why time changes at different speeds is that space replicates at different volumes. Whatever speed you achieve is associated with a replication frequency, which gives you your time zone. Stated more plainly, the faster your speed, the less spacetime can replicate from within you. The faster you move, the less time you spend atop a particular locality. Since spacetime is relative, you are only under the influence of the time that is replicating through you in a particular locality. The only way travel would not change clock speed is if time were Newtonian. Nowhere is this seen more clearly than in a gravity well. Within a gravity well, your clock is determined by your distance to the surface of the body causing the gravity. Even at free fall, your clock will slow as you accelerate and fall closer to that which is creating the gravity well. Your clock, therefore, is determined by speed, as you flow with space or as space flows through you. You are your own reference point. If you do compare your clock to any other location, they can only be the same if your speeds are the same. When traveling with space in any direction, you are not facing any resistance because you are flowing with the wave front of space. This wave is not caused by a unilateral movement of energy like a wave in water. The movement of energy is coming from the center of the wave. It is spacetime emerging out of the Fountain Of God particle/ quanta. This gives space the ability to travel omni-directionally, creating the duality of space. This emergence of the wave from a center point immerses us in an energy matrix which flows in every direction. If you are moving in any direction then space is moving with you. You are surfing in a carrier wave of energy. This carrier wave does not interact with its opposing counterpart. The reason is that energy flows from every point in every direction. Once a direction of travel and a speed are achieved, the carrier wave takes you in that direction. Any speed chosen, up to close to the speed of light, has no opposing interaction. The opposing wave is also traveling in the opposite direction, but from behind you. Figuratively, you are surfing on the downward slope of the carrier wave in the direction you are traveling, while the opposing carrier wave is not interacting with you, for the reason that it is behind you on the downward slope in the opposite direction to your travel. Since spacetime emanates from every point, this condition is maintained in every possible speed and direction of travel. Unless you change speed or direction, you will flow effortlessly with space. At a steady speed, spatial pressure from you and through you are equalized. The only time you will actually travel through spacetime is under an acceleration or when you are approaching light speed. When traveling at a steady speed, you are in tune with the replication frequency of that speed. This determines your spatial time zone. As far as space is concerned, you are at rest. Any acceleration takes you out of harmony of frequency, and into contact with the wave opposed to your direction of acceleration. This contact with the flow of energy, from the opposite direction, gives you a gravity response opposed to the direction of acceleration. At close to the speed of light, the wave front of spacetime that is traveling in opposition to you, overlaps the wave traveling with you. This contact with the flow of energy from the opposite direction, gives you an ever-growing gravity response (under continued acceleration) opposed to the direction of travel. This overlapping wave is essential in the growth of space. This growth is responsible for the spatial pressure and the expansion rate. The overlap of the two wave fronts of spacetime are not found at a measurable distance, but rather, at a 'speed'. The equilibrium of these fronts is found at light speed. Light speed, then, is determined not by light but by the replication of space. In turn, the universal replication rate is dictated by spatial pressure prevailing in the universe at any given time. Even though light speed changes throughout time, we who are within spacetime cannot sense any difference. This is because light speed is tied to spatial replication. Space replicates along with time, giving us spacetime. Light is nestled in the equilibrium point of the opposing wave fronts of spacetime. This explains why light sees no time, and the fact that spacetime governs the travel of light. This is why spacetime flow stops light from traveling out of the event horizon in a black hole. At the event horizon, spacetime equilibrium is traveling inward due to an increase of inward flow as compared to the outward flow.

I really enjoyed writing this chapter. This is why it's one of the longest. I hope you understood and enjoyed its contents. I could have written much more, but once one understands the concept, more information could crowd out of your mind the information I deem more important. Do not be concerned. There are a lot more adventures in the remaining seven chapters.

CHAPTER 14

Earth, the Center of the Universe

THIS IS ONE of the most mystifying things about the universe. We sit within something believed to be 93 billion light years in size. And that, only in its observable size, not in its entirety. We can only imagine its actual vastness, and yet, we have a center ring seat. It makes no sense how, from Earth, which is not even half the age of the universe, we can see from its center. If that was not enough, listen to the full story. If I could materialize you, at any point in space, no matter where, within those 93 billion light years, you would still be looking out from the center. But wait. We are not done. If I could send you back in time, you would still be at the center of the visible universe. But wait there is even more. I could send a group of people to different places and times; each one would see from the center of the universe. "No way", a reader just said. It also seemed impossible to me too. I deduced it while thinking, "What are the implications of a self-replicating spacetime, starting from a single spec?" Yes, I now know. Science already knew that, but I did not. I realized it's a must, if spacetime is truly replicating. Envision the beginning in that small spec. It begins replicating outward, in all directions, its replication creating an energy web, creating spacetime, and reality, itself. At this point, you need to stretch your mind in order to imagine the implications of something replicating from a center point. Can you envision that since each new spec is new, it also replicates from its beginning? I hope I have not lost you. Each spec is the center of its own universe, and each is its own point of reference. Each spec of space is born in a time and space, unique to itself. No matter where that spec is pushed to, by replicating space, it maintains its centeredness.

Since all observers in the universe see spherically, do they all see the same thing? Yes and no. The best I have been able to decipher from science, is that they believe it is linked to location. This belief can be illustrated by a bunch of circles drawn at random on a sheet of paper. Some intersect and share parts of themselves, while others don't touch at all. I don't believe that at all. We only have Earth from which to view the universe. Clearly, Earth is not in the middle of time. And it's very unlikely that it's in the middle of space. Yet, we see to the beginning in every direction. To me, location is irrelevant. The deciding factor is time. Each observer observes from their location in time. If you were looking out from a planet, before Earth existed, you would still be looking from the center, clear back to the beginning. However, you could only see what had become visible, up to that point in time. So, in this case, location is not important. I would say the three important things are time, time and time. Let's draw circles on a sheet of paper to illustrate the influence of replicating spacetime theory on what we see. Start with a circle one inch in diameter. Draw 13 concentric circles around that circle, increasing the radius of each by one inch. Now let's walk through this. We have 14 circles, each representing 1 billion years of the age of the universe. The innermost circle would be a very young universe. Looking outward from the center of the first circle, you would only see what existed when the universe was 1 billion years old. The second circle is equivalent to 2 billion years of age. Again, from the center of the circle, you would see what the first observer sees, plus an additional 1 billion years. This continues until time advances to our vantage point, 14 billion years from the beginning. Still observing from the center, we see everything that was seen by the previous 13 observers plus the last circle, covering the latest billion years of the universe's history.

One thing is a sure bet, when talking about the universe. Its almost unlimited size gives us almost unlimited questions. The 14 circles we used above are great, giving us 14 snapshots of the universe. But clearly, the universe is in constant flow. How does the growth of the universe manifest? Well let's recap what you learned in Chapter 3: Expansion Rate Made Simple. The universe is in constant growth. It grows by replicating existing space, and by creating new space and matter at its outer edge. I know. You do not have to remind me. Science says the universe does not have an edge. I have no doubt that the universe has an edge, and that the edge is that which was once the beginning. This beginning, having no time, is still doing what it started doing, 13.8 billion years ago. It is expanding the sphere of the universe into the nothingness which is outside of created space. This means that each of those 14 circles we mentioned is expanding and giving the observers within them a larger and more populated universe. The growth does not manifest itself beyond what any observer sees as the edge. All growth happens between the observer and the outer rim. No matter how old the universe gets, there can be nothing older than what we see at the outer rim. Those bodies were the first to materialize. They will always be the oldest. Everything else, being younger, must then come into view between the observer at the center, and those things that propagated the universe in the beginning.

Now that you think you have a handle on Earth centeredness, let me shake that handle. See if you can hold on. The visible is obviously limited by light speed. Each observer would see the distance from the center of the universe to the edge of the universe, according to the age of their respective universe, but each would not share the same snapshot. They would share the same snapshot, if they share the same time. The obvious question is how is this possible? Because time is not fixed. It is tied to space. Allow me to illustrate. Let's pick that galaxy, GN-z11, which we identified as the farthest from us. Currently, we see it 13.4 billion years in the past. If I had the power to instantly materialize you at the point where we see that galaxy, you would be in for a shock. Upon arriving there, you will not find the target galaxy. You might find empty space, or a completely different galaxy there, instead. In order to transport you to where we currently see GN-z11, I would have to place you at the location, and at the correct time when our galaxy was there. But it gets even more interesting. The location and the time from where the light was emitted is not where we see the galaxy, now. "Ok, time out" you say. "Follow my specific instructions. Place me at the exact time and place I'm seeing right now through this telescope." OK, you got it. There you are right now. What are you seeing? You are in a very young universe, in one of the first galaxies (GN-z11). Your vantage point is still the center of the universe, but your spherical universe is very small and young. You are so close to the beginning that all you can see are the first few galaxies which existed back then. The rest of what you see, is the darkness of the opaque region, some 370,000 years or so from the beginning.

In the Old Country, we have an expression, "You left me stranded". How is it that what we see furthest away is not older? Well, spacetime, furthest away from us, is older, but what we're looking at is a mirror image. So, light that is reaching us now, was emitted in the past, much closer to where we are (in space and time). The duality of space is giving us a mirror image. When we look into deep space, we see spacetime headed, not away from us, but toward us. We do not see the future; we see the past. This is why I call it a mirage of lights. We are seeing a bygone era. So, where is our actual future? Our future is emanating from within us continually. The future of what we see in the past, is on the other side of what we're looking at, further ahead than our field of view. "Whoa," someone said, "I thought what extends in front of us, is our future." Yes, indeed, our future is in front of us. But we don't see the future, mostly we see the past of our future. If that were not enough, sometimes we see things far away which existed before our time, but we can also see things closer to us that came after us. Now I've done it. Some of you are pulling out your hair. Wait. Please let me explain. The problem is the duality of spacetime that works in conjunction with relativity. If you look at something far away, then you are looking at the past of its past. You know that it took time for that reflected (mirror) image of the item's past, to travel to you. Yet, once you see the item, you realize that the object is no longer there. It is much further ahead in its future. So, you are seeing the object's past of its past, while at the same time seeing the object's past of its present. Let me give you another example using your day-to-day experiences. If someone is walking in front of you, do you see his past, or his future? You see his past, where he has been. But, at the moment that you see his past, it is the past of the past, because it took time for light to travel to your eyes. Where is his future? His future is in front of him. It's the next place he will be stepping. You see his past coming to you, because it is a reflection of light. It is a mirror image. Great. The hair pulling has stopped. That is good news. Some of us don't have much hair to spare. As a friend of mine says, "I have wavy hair and its waving goodbye". Everyone is back. Let's check whether you really have that handle gripped tightly. What will you see when the person turns around, faces you, and then walks toward you? If you say his future, you are partly right. The space you see between you and him, is his future. The reflected image coming back to you is the past. One last question. Where is the present? His present is emanating from him, just like your present is emanating from you. Each is its own reference point. The closest to a shared present, is when you both come together and embrace each other.

The fact that we see clearly back to the beginning of the universe, is very revealing to me. This leaves me no doubt that the universe is spherical. If it isn't a sphere, you could not see back to its beginning. It is no accident that the circle is so prevalent in nature. A sphere is preferred because, that is the result of a universe that is replicating and doing so in all directions. It also tells me that space is expanding (actually replicating) from every location in a 360-degree manor. If it was merely expanding, then you would create different views from different places. The reality is that we see it as a sphere, from anywhere in space. However, we don't all see the same time. This, obviously, is because not everything began simultaneously. Each spec in the universe created its own time reference in relation to the rest of the universe. This, of course, is because the emergence of space creates time. It's also clear to me that, if we reverse the process, we would end up as a single spec, in the beginning. Because the universe is expanding spherically, that which began at the center, is now at the edge. We can also be sure that light speed has been constant and reliable, since it began. If there had been any anomalies, then there would be patches of sky with no light or information. As we have previously discussed, nothing in the macro world can travel at, or faster than, the speed of light. If something ever did, then it would become invisible. I remind you, again, that there are examples of celestial bodies moving away from us, at speeds faster than light, and this due to the expansion of the universe. Each object is its own reference point. Only those things which move from themselves, at or faster than light speed, become invisible. As any object reaches light speed, no longer can its reflection travel away from itself. However, this is not the case when two objects are moving away from each other, with a cumulative speed exceeding that of the speed of light. While at sub-light speed, all objects can emit or reflect light. Any object at sub-light speed, within the observable universe, will remain visible unless it is blocked by a newly formed galaxy or body.

We have an issue restricted to those with great reading comprehension. I want you to understand that none of us ever understand everything we read. I dare to say that the most brilliant of us can pick up perhaps sixty percent of any complex concept we read. The advantage of a book is that you can camp-out on a passage, until you get it right. Of course, the biggest problem is that most of the time, we do not realize that we did not understand. If we did understand, then we could not be ignorant. Genius is best shown by recognizing your ignorance. Perhaps it was said best in Plato's Socrates, "I know that I know nothing." This should be the ultimate statement on this matter. Unfortunately, ignorance also reins here. You see, the experts cannot agree if either Plato or Socrates said it.

If the beginning is what we see today, then what will we see tomorrow? We will see the same thing we see today. That did it, many are exasperated. They are asking. "How can we see tomorrow the same beginning that we see today"? The explanation is so easy, that it's almost impossible to understand. Allow me to explain how the picture of the beginning is always the same. Think of it this way. Time is indeed passing, but space is growing. So, the beginning is receding from us, and it gains time as it does so. This means that it is like a still picture. We are looking at the same thing: the beginning. This has been the same since the beginning, and it will never change. A trillion years from now, we will still see the exact picture that we see today. The only difference is that it will be a trillion years older. There could be differences in resolution, but the content of the beginning is frozen in time. You could say that it is a picture in now-time. But it is a picture of a past now-time.

In Chapter 8, I told you that there was one missing clue about the CMB. But I could not tell you about it, because it was pivotal to the concepts in Chapter 14. Well, here is the final piece of the CMB puzzle. There is no echo at work in the CMB. The same occurrence that causes us to see a static picture of the beginning, is responsible for a static picture of the CMB. This signal of the first light of the universe did occur in the beginning. But what is reaching us right now is, indeed, the signal from the beginning of the beginning. Why? For the same reason that the rest of what we see, is also a snapshot. There is nothing older, and as we look into the past, it is the oldest picture of that past. It is the end of the line. This picture is moving away from us as the universe ages. Since our view of the beginning is ruled by the age of the universe, this is all we can ever see. When we look into space, we see the past. Clearly, if you look into the past, the last thing you see must be the beginning of the past.

I know that some of you who have been waiting for the final clue (since Chapter 8) to make sense of the CMB, are not impressed. The paragraph, above, may be a good argument, but it does not really disclose the mechanism at work. Allow me to shed some more light on this topic of first light. The CMB we see at the current time is indeed the earliest light. How is this possible? Well, you already know that I believe the universe is still making space, matter and time, as it did in the beginning. This should tell you that we will always see the Creation's first light, no matter the age of the universe, whether it be the very first occurrence, or a much later version of that light. But it goes beyond that concept. In reality, that first light began in the beginning. But let's say for argument's sake, that it lasted one second. One second in the beginning, seen from our vantage point 13.8 billion years in the future, is equivalent to 13.8 billion years. Can't you see this fact? How old is the beginning today? 13.8 billion years. How old will the beginning be, one billion years from today? It will be 14.8 billion years old. It can only be the same thing we had seen, a billion years earlier, seemingly older, due to redshift.

The universe had a beginning in time. How long did the beginning last, as seen from down range in time? That beginning is eternal. It just keeps stretching with spacetime. When you look into space, you do not see the present, you see the past, and that past had a beginning.

So, what you see as first, is the end of your view. That view can never change, because there was nothing before it. It is a mirrored picture. We are seeing the universe turned inside out. What you see as the outer most edge, is really the beginning that took place in the center, in the beginning. Can we ever see the current beginning, creating space, time and matter? Of course, not. We cannot see the present, we can only see the past. Where is that current beginning located, right now? It is much further ahead than the beginning which we see right now. What we see right now is the beginning of the beginning, not the current beginning. The current beginning, by some estimates, could be 250 thousand times further ahead than the 46.5 billion light year radius of the universe we see right now. All you need to understand the CMB (according to RST), is found within the three paragraphs above. Camp on them until you understand them.

For those of you who think the universe is infinite, you must accept that the universe is eternal. I remind you of spacetime. If you tell me that you have infinite space, then you must have infinite time. Have you forgotten that space and time are inseparable? An eternal universe would not give us a view from the center. If you don't agree, then you don't believe that we live in a relative universe. Entropy would have no part in an eternal universe. For one thing, if it is eternal, then how can it still be here, since it has had an eternity to decline into disorder? It also leaves you with the problem of explaining just how such a process could begin in infinity, and yet, be so symmetrical. Even the beginning would be an impossibility. Something that begins, cannot be eternal. Neither can it be infinite. And, of course, you would be left with no explanation as to why we see a younger universe, at its edges with smaller galaxies. One last thing: how can something be infinite, and yet be expanding. To where can it expand, that it hasn't already been? It takes more willful ignorance to believe in an infinite universe, than it does to believe that the Earth is flat.

The view of the universe from its center, is very intriguing. I can only hope you have understood the concept of looking through time, not through space. Because, if our view was through space, instead of through time, then our view would be from that quadrant of the universe in which we were located. But, because we see through time, we see from the age of our particular locale, all the way back to the beginning. If you get it, then your understanding of the universe will leap forward. It's really easy, if you accept that the universe started replicating from a single spec, each spec being its own reference point in time, and by default, the center of its own universe. Someone has said "That is not possible, because then our vision would be impaired by what is in existence in our quadrant". Not at all. We see the past, so only those items which are old enough for their light to have reached us, will be visible. This view, governed by time, can only be from the center of the universe, because you are not governed by space, but by time. Question: if what we see is the past, then where are those heavenly bodies now? Yes, indeed. They are in their own present time, much further away from where we see them in the past. Just as yesterday is only a remembrance in our brain, the things we see far into space are a remembrance in the form of light. Lights are a reflection, or a picture-show of things gone by in time, which may or may not still exist. Some, or everything we see in the past, might have flown apart, or have come to an end by now, and it could still be billions of years before we are able to see it. The universe could have already started its demise, billions of years ago, and we would be none the wiser.

This time and place business is wild. We have gone back in time. What if we were to go to where GZ-n11 is, right now? Let's go... We're here... but where is here? We've gone very far in time and distance. The universe is much older, and much larger. Your view of the universe would still be spherical, but the longer time results in a much larger sphere. How is it that GZ-n11 is in the center, through time? It's simple: spacetime regenerates from every point.

If we are where GZ-n11 is, we are no longer talking about what we see, which is the past. We are in the future, and very far away from where we started. From wherever you look, a time is associated with your location. From that time and location, spacetime has expanded equally in every direction. Even though it is not possible for you to see the entire universe, you would see equally in every direction. The distance you will be able to see, will be governed by the speed of light. The expansion rate, as we have already discussed, is a factor of light speed. Light speed also governs the travel of information. Granted, the expansion rate that we see is not reality. It is the visible reality.

I need to explain how modern telescopes are able to see the older rim galaxies, while looking right through the newer galaxies. We are actually looking right through the location where the newer galaxy would one day be. "Wait, just a minute. If they are between us and those rim galaxies, then they already exist". Yes, you are right. They already exist, but they are between us and those rim galaxies, in Newtonian time. Everything that is between us and the Rim, is in existence at this moment. But our view of the universe is not Newtonian. It is Einsteinian (relativistic). The only thing that is yet to be, is that which will be materialized at the Creation Rim. Every second, at the Rim of Creation, there is another light second of spacetime, in every direction, along with the matter being made. We cannot see all of space. We can only see that space, which is old enough for its emitted, or reflected light to reach us. We see an image of the past. What we see is not where we see it. As time goes by, our universe grows. Those things which are already in existence, will appear between us and those first galaxies in the rim. Don't worry, they will not collide. The image is only light, while the galaxies are real matter (more on this in Chapter 19). A long time ago, the old galaxies were in the place into which these newer galaxies are presently emerging. These newer galaxies might eventually block our view of those older galaxies. The newer galaxies will materialize, within our current view, as the Arrow Of Time lifts the shadow created by relativity.

In the Old Country, we have an expression, "You left me stranded". Well, I think a great many readers are still stranded. They can't understand how every point in space could be its own reference point, and the center of its universe. Allow me one last try to illuminate the subject. Just a few paragraphs ago, we imagined a series of 14 concentric circles. If you are a child of radio (and there are few of us left) use your imagination, and draw 14 circles using the same center, with each additional circle increasing its radius by one inch. If you are a child of TV, you'll need a large sheet of paper and a compass, to draw out this example. I'm not saying that the TV generations are dumber. It's just that in radio, you had to exercise your imagination to draw a picture of what was being described by the announcer. With TV, no imagination is required. You are given the image that supports the words you are hearing. Now that both groups have drawn their circles, put one dot anywhere but not in the center of the circle. Now, take your physical or mental compass. Extend your compass from the dot you made to the nearest point on the largest, outer circle. Now, using the dot as a new center, draw another circle. Your dot marks a time and location. The distance from the dot to the Rim of the universe, is associated with a measurement of the age of the universe. In any direction you peer, there is a limit to the distance your telescope can see. The speed of light limits your ability to see outside of the sphere (circle) inscribed around your dot.

Please keep in mind that in this illustration, when you draw a dot away from the center of the universe, you are choosing a point closer to the edge of the largest circle. This corresponds to a point closer to the beginning. You have travelled back in time to when that point in space (your dot) was at the center of the universe. So, you see, no matter your location, you are looking out from a particular time, when that location was in the center of the universe. Remember, everything we see, is light from the past. It no longer exists. It is a mirror image coming back to us. By moving the dot closer to the border of the circle, we are, actually, reversing The Arrow Of Time, from our current frame of reference on Earth. In my opinion, this is only possible in our imagination. When we look out into space, we see the past. When we travel into space, we travel into the future. We see the past, when observing outer space, because light is coming back to us. This reflection is in the form of a mirror image. That is the past. I hope everyone has understood. Let me test you. Where would you have to place your dot in order to be able to view the maximum distance to the edge of the universe? No hurry, this is a book. You can take as much time as you need. I will give you a hint: radius of largest circle. OK, are you ready? Great, you got it. The position of the dot to afford a view of the entire age of the universe, would be the center of the largest sphere (circle). Extra credit question. Can you tell me why the center of this sphere gives you the oldest viewpoint? Wow! You all got it. Yes indeed, this center 'was' the epicenter of the beginning. The beginning 'is' now The Creation Rim. Congratulations! You are now so knowledgeable, that you have regressed to what humanity believed in the Dark Ages: SUB The Earth is believed to be the Center Of the universe.

We have pealed back the layers of the mysteries of Space, like those of an onion. My readership has split into three groups. There is a small group of rebellious skeptics who know there is a problem with my take on "the beginning". And another group has a nagging feeling that something is wrong with the picture I've painstakingly painted for you. And another group sees nothing wrong. This reminds me of three commonalities within humanity. The first group makes things happen, the second group watches things happen, and the third group says, "what happened?" Well, you are all right.

To all of you, there is indeed a problem. Allow me to clearly identify the problem, and define the terms used. Then I will give you the solution. It has become clear to me that if you do not understand there is a problem, then you are like the last group above. You ask,

"What happened?". Once you understand the problem, you will have the capacity and the desire to hear the solution. Like any good salesman, it is imperative that the customer understands the terms used in the sales pitch. Equally important, if I fail to show a problem, I cannot get you interested in buying a solution.

The problem is this "What we observe with our newest telescopes, doesn't seem right". Our observations show us the past. At the end of that view into the past, is a static frozen-in-time beginning. But I tell you that the beginning has not stopped. It is still creating at the outer edge of the universe. Then, how can we see a static beginning, if the beginning is still creating and expanding the universe outward? So, our observation shows one thing, and our reason tells us it is wrong.

The terms used to discuss this problem are numerous. But the pivotal ones are three. Two of the terms are used to describe the same event. The event is 'the beginning'. The reason why we need two terms to describe one event is that the event is ongoing and remains unchanged through time. 'The beginning', then, is described by the term 'the beginning', in addition to the ongoing 'beginning' at the Rim of Creation. The third term, 'A view', as used here, is a revealing snapshot which can zoom (given today's technology), to reveal galaxies 14 billion years ago.

The solution: Our telescopes are not lying to us. They are, indeed, showing us the beginning. But being that it is a mirror image, we see the past, and it is obvious that, if looking into the past, the end of that view would be when the beginning began. The current ongoing beginning cannot be seen through telescopes. Telescopes cannot see past the end of the view of the past which is the beginning of all things. Our telescopes are limited to viewing into the past. The view of the past is limited by the age of the universe. Everything that is close enough to us, for its light to get back to us, is visible between us and those first galaxies, in the beginning. Everything that is in existence, and that which is being created now, at the Creation Rim, will be seen by us (if humanity lasts that long), when time allows its light to travel back to us. All the new things will appear over time, between us and the old galaxies we currently see as closest to the beginning.

There you have it, the solution to the biggest crisis in my Replicating Spacetime Theory. We see the past when peering into space. The only way to see the present, where the Rim of Creation is still creating in the ongoing beginning, is to travel there.

Chapter 14 Bonus material

Have you ever wondered what ends up in the editing floor? In books, like in movies, some material gets cut or re-written. That material never makes it into public knowledge. Well, I for one would love to have access to the discarded material of my favorite books and movies. Just in case some of you share the same curiosity, here are the endings for Chapter 14 that did not make the cut. This is the only chapter that I had any significant trouble with, from my editor. These endings were deemed too long, complicated, or difficult to read.

First discarded ending to Chapter 14.

We have peeled back the layers of the mysteries of Space, like those of an onion. My readership has split into three groups. There is a small group of rebellious skeptics who know there is a problem with my take on "the beginning". And another group has a nagging feeling that something is wrong with the picture I've painstakingly painted. And another group sees nothing wrong. This reminds me of three commonalities within humanity. The first group makes things happen, the second group watches things happen, and the third group says, "what happened?" Well, you are all right.

I have explained and demonstrated through illustrations, how the Earth is the center of the universe. I have explained that the universe is expanding through replication. This replication makes every point in space its own reference point, and the center of its own universe. More importantly, replicating space creates this view from the center.

But there is one aspect which has not been demystified. I have told you that space grows at its edge. How, then, can we see a static picture of the beginning? The growth at the edge turns this static view of the past on its head. The edge is changing with growth. Why can't we see that change at the edge? I truly hope you are ready for this mind-bending concept. What we observe through our telescopes never happened. Not in the order we see it. It is a mirror image. We see back to the beginning, that beginning no longer exists. We still see it because, being a mirror image, we see from young near us to old far away. It stands to reason, then, that we now see the beginning far at the end of our view. What else could we see at the end of our view if not the beginning? We obviously can't see further than the beginning while looking back in time. Bottom line: when we look out into space, we see the past. If you want to see the present, which is where the creation rim is currently creating new space, you need to travel there. That future cannot be seen from our vantage point because we see the past, not the future.

Some of you overcomplicate your thinking of the beginning. No, I do not mean that the beginning is a simple matter. What I mean is that you try to deal with too many variables, to understand what we see as the beginning. Clear your mind. Now just follow my lead. What do you see when you look back in time at any process? Let's take one thing in particular. Your schooling. What is your last degree? Now, think back in time, regress to your first day in school. Has your first day always been your first day? Can there be any way in which you could see a day in school before that first day? OK, that is settled. Now, look out into the night sky. What do you see? Light from stars emitted long ago. If you had access to the world's best telescopes, what would you see? That's right, the further you see, the further back in time you see. How far is the furthest you could ever see into the past? To the beginning of the past. Voila! It's simple. We see a fixed picture of the beginning because that is when time began. There is nothing older, therefore the furthest view seen in the past, present, and future can only be the beginning of the beginning of time. I do realize that some of you are thinking that is wrong: a finite event in time emitted a finite reflection. This means that the reflection should have gone past us. You would be completely right, if we did not have relativity. The oldest galaxy we see right now is 13.4 billion years, which means that we see the light it emitted 13.4 billion years ago. As this galaxy gets older, it is receding from us at faster than light speed. Time cannot be seen past the beginning. As the beginning recedes, we always see the same snapshot. I'm so happy for you who finally 'get it'. We are seeing the universe in its entirety. We just see all of time, not all of space. Everything that exists, right now, is between us and the beginning that we see. Most of it is just not old enough for its light or reflection to make it back to us. Once more, the end of the view of the past is now, and will always be the beginning. VOILA! Eureka! And WOW!

Second ending to Chapter 14.

I hope you remember that the 14 circles cover the entire age of the universe (from our frame of reference). Time, like beauty, is in the eye of the beholder. If you could inquire of light, emitted in the beginning and traveling for almost 14 billion years, "how long have you been traveling", it would tell you "No time". Likewise, if you could ask a dot in space "how old are you" it would tell you "I just emerged here". If you could ask someone beyond the event horizon on the first black hole in the universe "how old is the universe?", He would say "it just started". If a monitoring probe was placed at true rest in deep space in the beginning, its time log would show at least 14 billion years, and probably more. So, where is the center of the universe? Everywhere. If there is a center, could it be found? That is not possible because we cannot measure to the actual ends.

We have peeled back the layers of the mysteries of Space, like those of an onion. My readership has split into three groups. There is a small group of rebellious skeptics who know there is a problem with my take on "the beginning". And another group has a nagging feeling that something is wrong with the picture I've painstakingly painted for you. And another group sees nothing wrong. This reminds me of three commonalities within humanity. The first group makes things happen, the second group watches things happen, and the third group says, "what happened?" Well, you are all right. You have been told and shown through illustrations how the Earth is the center of the universe. But there is one aspect that has not been demystified. I have told you the universe is both expanding (through replication) and growing at its edge. The expansion does not create a problem for the concept that every point in space is its own reference point and the center of its own universe. More importantly, it does not create any issue with our snapshot view of the universe. The growth at the edge, however, turns this static view of the past on its head. If the universe is indeed growing at the edge, how is it that we see the beginning? The edge is changing with growth. Why can't we see that change at the edge? I truly hope you are ready for this mind bending concept. The universe is governed by the duality of spacetime. This duality is tied to the duality of time. The duality of time is the concept that the universe is both Newtonian and Einsteinian. There are two basic times, not to be confused with the many time zones in relativity. Newtonian time is a 'time with no time', meaning time is the same everywhere in the universe. Einsteinian time means relativistic time composed of all the time zones in the universe. Under Newtonian time, the universe is doing its thing everywhere at once, with no time difference, no matter the distance. If this 'time with no time' could be seen in real time we would see the edge maintain its youthful appearance, since all that is made at that edge is indeed younger. But the view of the edge would change with time. It would progress from the edge inward with time all the while experiencing entropy.

Of course, as it ages, all the galaxies evolve through time. The stars within these young galaxies are born and die all the while picking up the materials appropriate to their age. In turn, the normal view of the universe is Einsteinian, meaning it is ruled by linear time. Since it is a mirror image, it shows a static beginning. Remember, I keep telling you that we see the past, a mere mirage of light, or a reflection of a bygone era? Well, these are all clues as to how we see the beginning frozen in time. We do not see space. We see space through time. It is a mirrored image. In a mirrored image you are not merely seeing things inverted, you are seeing things turned inside out. If you turn time inside out, then you always see the beginning and everything that comes after that beginning will be seen emerging through time, between you and the beginning. This means that our view is a snapshot of space through time. Since we see the past, we cannot see what happens as time moves forward in real time. We can only see time moving forward from the beginning. Since there was nothing prior to the beginning, the beginning is the furthest we can see back in time. Whoa! (Stop) VOILA! (There it is) Eureka! (I have found it) And WOW! (Wonder of wonders)

Third ending to Chapter 14

We have peeled back the layers of the mysteries of Space, like those of an onion. My readership has split into three groups. There is a small group of rebellious skeptics who know there is a problem with my take on "the beginning". And another group has a nagging feeling that something is wrong with the picture I've painstakingly painted for you. And another group sees nothing wrong. This reminds me of three commonalities within humanity. The first group makes things happen, the second group watches things happen, and the third group says, "what happened?" Well, you are all right.

This is the third attempt to get the ending of this chapter past my good friend and Editor Jeffrey Sterling. The first two were long-winded paragraphs that, to me, seemed the best thing since sliced bread, and so easy to understand that I thought everyone would scream out "Eureka!". Then it came to me. My test audience (my editor) can't understand the solution because he does not see a problem.

I must start with stating the problem and defining our terms. Then I will give you the solution. It has become clear to me that, if you do not understand there is a problem, then you are like the last in the group above. You ask, "What happened". Once you understand the problem, then you will have the capacity and the desire to hear the solution. The problem is this: In our observations we see the past, and that past stops with the beginning. But I tell you that the beginning has not stopped: it is still creating in the outer edge of the universe. Then how can we see a static beginning if the beginning is still creating and expanding the universe, outward. After all, we are looking outward to where this is occurring. It is imperative for you to understand that the beginning is continuous through time. It refers to that point in space and time where the universe is made. But clearly a continuous beginning, in this case the beginning of everything, goes back in time to a place where itself began. Prior to that, nothing physical existed, so no view is possible of anything before the start of the beginning. Please don't miss this distinction. Science says the beginning was a fraction of a second where all we have in the universe suddenly materialized. I do not believe such thing. The beginning did have a split second in time where it began. But once having begun, it has and will never stop creating. I make a distinction from "the beginning" and the continuation of that beginning which I have called "the edge, or the Creation Rim". If you do not understand the problem, how can you understand its solution? Like any good salesman, it is imperative that the customer understands the terms used. Equally important, if I fail to show a problem, I cannot get you interested in buying a solution. Do not move from this paragraph until you fully comprehend the problem and the terms used.

'We see'. That is the key when looking into outer space. We see time into the past. This past is a mirror image. Please don't forget that a mirror image is not what you see from your location. It is what the mirror sees reflected back to you and now seen by you. In a mirrored image, you are not merely seeing things inverted. You are seeing things turned inside out. If you could see without this mirrored image of time, you would see what is actually happening. If you saw the beginning, you would see an ever growing universe at the edge. We actually see time in the past and getting older. If we could see in real time we would see the present and getting younger. But we cannot see the present or the future. We can only see the past in linear time because it takes time for light to travel back to us. If what we see is the time of an object, namely the past, then we are limited to only seeing time and that time only in the past. The further we see, the more in the past we see, so obviously, the furthest we can see is the beginning, because there is nothing further in the past than the beginning. The duality of time makes the mirror image. It is a mirage of lights.

Perhaps there is an easier way to walk you through what we see when looking into outer space. Again, please realize that everything we see is the past. It is light coming back to us from an object's present. This means that no matter the distance, far or near, all we see is in the past. That is clear, so why has the frontier always been beyond our capacity to see? Because the frontier exists in the present. When looking out into space the further we look the farther back in time we see. The edge or frontier of the universe is then on the other side of our view of the beginning. We can never get a view of the entire universe because when you factor in expansion the present is continually racing in front and getting further ahead of our view. Due to the limitation of our optics we could never see the edge (frontier) at this stage of universal age. It is just too far. But even if the frontier of the universe was close enough for us to see with the naked eye, we would never see the edge creating new space because it does so in the present, not in the past. Light taking time to come back to us only gives us a view of the past, and that past stops at the oldest point in the universe, 'THE BEGINNING'.

Fourth ending to Chapter 14

Allow me to finish this chapter with a tale of two realities. These two realities come about by the duality of spacetime and the fact that the universe is home to two types of time. This universe functions under Newtonian now time and Einsteinian relativistic time. Newtonian time is easy to understand: 'time is the same everywhere in the universe'. Einsteinian time is relativistic and harder to understand. Relativity gives us time zones based on the speed you flow with space, or the speed space flows through you.

First let's deal with Newtonian time. This time is only available to things that travel at or faster than light speed. Light for instance is under Newtonian time. It does not see time passing from its frame of reference. This 'time with no time' we cannot experience since nothing in the macro world can travel at light speed. But that does not make this type of time less real. This 'now time' is responsible for the entire field of quantum mechanics. Once you accept that there is a 'time with no time' operating in the universe, quantum mechanics is no longer a mystery. I will leave the rest of the story for Chapter 18 Cat and Cats. I do want you to know that this 'time with no time' sees the universe carry out all its functions in now time. It supports reality by allowing the entire universe to be 'on the same page' sort of speak. Right this instant, as you read this book for instance, the universe is creating new space at its border. I know science says there is no border. But they can't prove it. I, in turn, have plenty of evidence to show that the universe is a sphere and that the border is a Creation Rim. This rim continues and will never stop making new space, time, and matter.

Einsteinian or relativistic time is a lot more complicated. This time varies with an observer's frame of reference. Any variation in your speed as you travel with spacetime or as spacetime travels through you, will give you a different clock speed. I have called it a time zone. Let's jump right into the dilemma of what we see when we look toward the end of the universe. First, the end of the universe is what I have called the Creation Rim. This is the outer border of the universe. It is now composed of what was, at one time, the beginning. This beginning is now the outer Rim. How far away is this Rim right now? No one knows. We can be sure it exists because we see it as it was 13.8 billion years ago. As we look into outer space, we see its mirror image coming back to us from the past.

We don't really see anything. Rather, 'we witness' the past. To 'see' sounds to me like looking and pulling in a view. We do not pull on anything. We witness what is already reaching us, which is a view of the past. You may think that when you train your eyes on an object far away your sight reaches out and you see the object. This is why we mistakenly think that we see the present. But in reality, that reflection of the past is striking you whether you look at it or not. You cannot pull anything into view. You expose your eyes to the reflection of objects in the past. You could never pull anything into view because pulling is bringing something in from where it does not exist. Spacetime pushes light to you from everywhere. You are your own reference point.

We will never witness the current ongoing beginning. We forever see the beginning of the beginning. By the time we see the ongoing beginning that is creating spacetime right now, it will be beginning between us and the beginning of the beginning, those first galaxies we see in the beginning of the past. The very end of our view. You could think that something that is ongoing would emerge into our view over time. But you must realize that what we see is light and matter, even if the creation rim was slow enough for us to see it, it would be an area with nothing in it.

The explanation why we see things like quasars close to the beginning is that we see things that are emerging into our view that had previously formed. They are just becoming visible because the shadow of the beginning is just clearing them and those items that already exist are revealed.

As we view the past, our view would never include the ongoing beginning because the ongoing beginning will always be beyond what we see in the past. This is because the universe is expanding at the speed of light plus the speed that space is expanding, so it will always stay ahead of our view.

When we look into outer space and see the past, we only see a small fraction of what actually is currently in existence. Between us and those small young galaxies we see in the beginning there are many more times the number of items than those that we see. Use your imagination. We see only what emitted its light much closer than 14 billion light years from us. Now imagine what has materialized in the area between where the light we currently see and the 45 billion light year radius we see. Now this 45 billion is the radius of the observable universe. No one believes that that is the total current size. It could be as much as 250 thousand times larger than that. Science thinks that all matter was created in the beginning, but Replicating Space Theory tells us that matter creation is still ongoing. So, our incredibly huge current view of the universe is a miniscule fraction of what really exists.

CHAPTER 15

The Duality of Spacetime

T HE DUALITY OF spacetime, seemed to me, to be one of the simplest concepts of my original work. To my surprise, many readers had questions. What do you mean? Why do you see it as important? Perhaps most troubling, there is no such thing! Well, this duality is key to reality. Our vision is unidirectional. We do not experience this duality because our eyes, although twins, are tied at the hip. They are located on one side of our face and can only look in one of the two opposing directions of spacetime. You could spin in a merry-go-round, but no matter how fast you went, you would only see one side of your world at a time. Have you ever considered that your eyes and your feet face the same direction? Oops, maybe too simplistic for some, and too deep for others. For those who think it is simplistic, you do not understand the question's complexity. Your feet carry you toward the ongoing beginning, while your eyes give you a report of the past, coming back from the same direction that your feet are taking you. The great difference, then, is this. Your feet carry you to the future, where the beginning is ongoing. Your eyes are seeing the past, which ultimately ends with the end of the beginning, or should we say, the beginning of the beginning. All creatures within the physical universe are linear creatures. We can only travel in one direction, or bead of time, at a given time. We are unidirectional beings. We cannot detach any part of ourselves. If you separate any part of the physical body, it dies. There is a list of vital organs we can't live without. Even if it were possible to make two live bodies out of one, we can't divide our consciousness. Likewise, in the animal kingdom. Most creatures are actually well suited to travel forward. There is only one exception that I'm familiar with. It is a bird, of all creatures. It is the hummingbird. This tiny creature is as graceful flying forward as backward. I, myself, think it is even more graceful flying in reverse. I guess it's the moon-walk effect. It is worth mentioning that the world's smallest bird is native to my old country of Cuba. The Zunzuncito, a.k.a. the bee hummingbird, which comes in at a minute 0.092 ounces. Not impressed? Consider that its weigh is about that of a penny. If you are fortunate enough to see one, you will have witnessed one of the great wonders of the world.

I wonder what man could learn, if he could see in a 360° panorama. From the land animals, I believe the closest to see in a 360 degree panorama, is the chameleon. Their eyes can move independently on a 180° arc. However, they have to rotate their eyes and refocus. They also cannot see the field of view covered by their own bodies. In the water world, there is a creature that gets pretty close to seeing in a 360° panorama. Can you guess? You guessed it, the jellyfish. Their eyes' field of view is not interrupted by their bodies, since they are transparent. Their two eyes, along with 20 clusters of light sensing ocelli (simple eyes) give this creature almost 360° field of view. I would love to experience this for a few minutes.

Back to duality. The one thing that reveals duality best is a mirror. I really enjoyed our excursion into the shenanigans of mirrors. If for no other reason, you should read my first book. I'm not here to rewrite that first work, but let's lightly touch on it. When you look in a mirror, you are looking at both horizontal planes, simultaneously. But even then, you are experiencing them in your vision, at different times. Where is the present? The present is at your center, your belly button. This is where 'the present' emerges. If you accept that the brain is where reality becomes real, then we would say that zero hour of reality is your brain. Back to the mirror, what do we see? You are looking at two very distinct things. You are experiencing a short horizontal plain in one direction, from your eyes to the mirror. The reflection in the mirror is reality, or sight, from the mirror back to you. This explains the mirror image effects. Your right arm becomes your reflected left, because you are seeing what the mirror sees, but from your vantage point. You should know that a mirror image is not merely an inverted image, it is an image turned inside out. This is why, when we look into outer space, we see the past all around us. The mirror effect of light, coming back to us, prevents us from seeing what is going on in the present. It only allows us to see what has already happened in the past. Since we are encapsulated in a sphere of time, we are limited to a view that is limited to the total age of the universe. This is why we cannot see the present size of the universe. We are seeing a view of the past, and that view only extends to the beginning of the universe. The key to understanding is in the words "WE SEE". If you remember, we can only see the past. The present has no end, because it keeps expanding before us. But the past only goes back to where it began. I wish we were in a time when we humans will have data ports attached to our brains. I find it very frustrating that these concepts are as plain to me as my name. Yet, I can talk to people smarter than I, till I'm blue in the face, and all I get back is a blank stare. The mirror's view is not short. You could say it sees all the way back to the beginning, if it is aimed into space. But what happens when you are between two mirrors? Then your view is limited by the distance between the mirrors. How many times do you see yourself? Limitless, but why? You are actually witnessing yourself, through time. Each bounce of your reflection on the mirror, is older than the previous one. You are, in a sense, watching yourself, or should I say, your image is time-traveling. You will notice that you cannot see yourself in the mirror until you get in front of it. Don't dismiss this statement. It defines reality. The movement of spacetime and information, at the speed of light, makes our reality.

If you are not fascinated by mirrors and their effects, then you either ignorant of their shenanigans, or you have no imagination. The mirror is the best tool with which to learn the effects of the duality of space, on our universe. Have you truly thought why it is that light bounces back from a mirror? Is it bouncing back like a rubber ball hitting a wall? Of course not. The mirror has no flexibility to store the energy of the light, and to then release it in the other direction. Neither does the light photon. It is easy to just say that it is a good reflective surface, so it gets reflected. But wait, if it does not get reflected, it is because it is absorbed. So the deciding factor is not that it is reflective, but that it is, or it's not absorbent of light. How does the mirror propel the light into a different trajectory? Where does the power come from to launch light's mass, in what can be a completely opposed direction? Please do not go into denial again. Light does have mass. Light is energy. Einstein proved that mass is energy and energy is mass. We could argue that light was launched out of a star, by the huge energy output of a star. But, the mirror has no such huge energy output. As a matter of fact, a mirror has no power emanating from itself. We definitely are seeing a manifestation of energy pushing the light in the other direction. Notice that light does not slow down when it bounces. It hits the mirror at 186000 miles a second and bounces back in the other direction at that speed with no slow down. If it was a bounce we would see a loss of speed after the bounce. Have you ever seen a ball get bounced off the floor? Did you notice that each bounce is smaller until the ball stops bouncing? This fact is true of every bounce. Energy is lost in each bounce, and it shows up as a loss in speed. But light does not lose any speed. It does lose energy. Some photons are absorbed by the glass and turned into heat energy. But the speed of the bounced light remains the same.

Here is the answer that Replicating Space Theory provides for us. Light does not travel through space. Light travels with space. When light hits an obstruction, if it is not absorbed it comes to a stop. At the point at which it comes to a stop in one direction, it is still in the gap between the duality of time. It can no longer travel in the direction of its original trajectory, nor can it sit still. It is now subjected to only a flow of spacetime away from the glass. Being housed within the gap between the duality of spacetime, it is propelled by the outrushing spacetime in the corresponding opposite direction. If it hit straight into the mirror, it bounces straight back. If it hits the mirror at an angle, it bounces back at the exact same angle, but in a mirror image of that angle. I do not know if any of you notice a rabbit trail leading away from this mirror. Let's explore that trail. If light is stopped by the mirror, and it's propelled in the opposite direction, does it loose time in that stop and reversal? My opinion is yes, it must. Do we have the ability to measure such a small difference in time? I think we do. We have cameras that can take a snapshot of a photon of light. If we set the camera, let's say, ten feet away from the mirror, we can see the photon travel in and out. The total amount of travel is 20 feet. Since we have clocks that can deal with such minute bits of time, we can measure how long the light stood still.

I hold, as undeniable truth, that everything physical in the universe is energy. It is no less true that replicating space is responsible for the generation, distribution and movement of all of the energy in the universe. This replication, from everywhere in created space, creates the duality of space. This duality, in all its manifestations, is created by the movement of space, in 3D, from everywhere. The creation of this duality also has a third occurrence. If you have equal opposites, then the point where they join or split from, is a place of neutrality. Here you have equilibrium. Because replicating space creates the

Arrow Of Time, this place, if in equilibrium, has no time. If it sees no time, anything which resides here, has no time.

What is so important about this duality? Duality comes from replicating spacetime. It is replicating from each point in the universe, expanding outward in 3D. I dare say, without this, our universe would not function. All movement within the universe is made possible by replicating space. No matter where you are headed, space is also headed there. This gives us the ability to travel in every direction. The replicating space gives us the ability to travel in any direction, not occupied by other matter. Spacetime, therefore, is made omnidirectional by replicating space. Without this ability to travel in any direction with space, we would be trapped and isolated within our own bubble. We interact with each other, and with the rest of the universe because spacetime is in constant movement. It moves from everywhere, to everywhere at all times. Duality, or 3D expansion, is at the heart of our experience in cosmology. We see in a circle clear back to the beginning. How is that possible, if we are not in the middle of the universe? Actually, we are. Every point in the universe is its own middle. It started from a single point, and expands out, replicating itself as single points. It is governed by a relative clock. This means that no matter where that dot is located it shares the characteristics of the one first dot. It is its own reference, and it is at the center of its own expanding observable universe.

CHAPTER 16

Shape and Size of the Universe

WHAT IS THE shape and size of the universe? There are so many different opinions on this, that I will refrain from telling you everyone else's opinion, and just give you my own. I hope you don't think I'm being conceited. I truly do not have a problem with telling you any of the choices out there. If you would like to explore the different theories or opinions out there, then use any search engine. A search on what is the shape of the universe will give you about one hundred million hits. A search on what is the size of the universe, several hundred million hits. Money is time and time is money. Interestingly, space is to time, as time is to money. With money, you can hire someone to do work for you, so that you won't have to do it yourself. If you need money you get a job where you trade hours of your life, for money. So, both your time and your money are valuable. If you have seen it fit to buy this book, and invest your precious time reading it, then I must conclude that you would like to hear my take on this story. So here goes.

What is the shape of the universe? It is said to be flat, with 99.6 percent certainty. This, according to all of our modern scientific observations. It has been the consensus for some time. That was certainly the case when my first book 'Let there be light' went to print, in early 2019. As I write this book just a few months later, things have begun to change. There seems to be a chink in the armor. The CMB is being gravitationally distorted, beyond what should happen in a flat universe. This is based on data from the European Space Agency's Planck satellite. It's all over the internet. Just do a search for "the universe is a sphere according to Planck satellite data". I don't give you a link, because this book will outlive any link I can give you. Even if this data is wrong, or if our interpretation is wrong, I have no doubt that the universe is a sphere. I can see no other shape, than a sphere. Here are my reasons. I whole heartedly believe that the universe started from a single spec. The reason is quite simple. The universe is expanding. No one doubts that. We see equally in every direction, back in time, to the beginning. If the universe was not a sphere, then we would see different times in different directions.

What I call the actual flatness problem is a problem born out of the nonsensical belief that space warps. It is irrefutable that everything in space moves in straight lines. It is a very powerful argument to say that if the universe was a sphere, then you could not close a square of equal sides in space. Or, that all sides of a triangle would equal more than 180 degrees. This belief in a flat universe would be correct if we were on the surface of what we call "the universe". We are not on the surface of the sphere; we are within the sphere. Imagine, if you will, that the Earth was not solid, and that we humans lived within Earth. Could you then close a square within Earth? Likewise, could you not draw out a triangle with its three inside angles equal to 180 degrees? Of course, within the volume of a sphere, the geometry would seem flat. According to RST, the universe has, is, and will always be a sphere.

There is also another very powerful reason. Everything else in the heavens is round. The planets are round, the moons are round, the stars are round the galaxies are round, the black holes are round. All explosions propagate outwardly in every direction. On Earth, almost all fruits are a form of round, or at least tubular. Blood cells and other cells are round, some viruses are round, hurricanes and tornados.... We humans begin in the womb, round. Our heads and eyes are round, our bodies and extremities are tubular, a form of round. Our industries pump out millions of products, in many cases round, or at the very least tubular. Our transportation cannot function without the round wheel. No round components equal no planes, trains, cars or motor boats. Whether air, sea or land, you cannot have modern transportation without round components.

Air transportation did not become safe and profitable until airplanes became round. Do a search for Ford Trimotor, one of the first airliners. It was square. Then, do a search for the DC3, the world's first profitable airliner. The greatest difference is that the DC3 had a round fuselage. Round is the strongest form of structure. You see it time and time again. Look at architecture, at the arch. Look at the honeybees with their modified hex, round honeycomb. Do you think it is a coincidence that a bubble, blown out of soapy water, is round? How about blowing a bubble with bubble gum? Even when blowing glassware, the unworked initial shape is a bubble. Have you ever had a crack in any material that just keeps getting bigger? Drill a small hole at the end of the crack, and it will crack no further. Even in sports, take away round balls, and you lose baseball, softball, cricket, soccer, basketball, polo, water polo, ping pong, croquet, pinball, golf, tennis, volleyball, rugby, racket ball, badminton, squash, jai alai, miniature golf, hockey (round puck), bowling, marbles, billiards, Frisbee, and the hula hoop. Take away the round wheel and gears and we lose cycling, automobile racing, and motorcycles. I will stop here, but I'm sure you can keep adding to this list. This strange occurrence begs the question: why are things round?

the universe prefers round, because that is the way it grows. Replicating spacetime is emerging from every location. This, coupled with gravity and other forces, favors round. If most of the physical things within the universe favor round, why wouldn't the universe be round? I personally have no doubt that the universe is a sphere. How sure, you may ask? More sure than being alive. Mind you, this concept will always be outside of our reach, to prove. Between us and the edge of the universe, is the light speed barrier. This barrier is not only a barrier to sight, but to all other forms of information. Even if we could somehow see to the beginning, how could we see past that point? When we look out, we are looking into the past. What we see as a beginning, is the first light traveling back to us. If we could see past the point where light began, we would see the beginning. The beginning was the beginning of the physical world. There was nothing physical past that point. I smile when I read that we can't see the shape of the universe. It is true, we can't see its current shape. But we do see its shape. 13.4 billion Years ago, it was round, then. It is round, now.

Why would all of our instruments and observations lead scientist astray, as to the shape of the universe? Well, scientists do not consider it possible that a beam of light can travel straight unless the universe is flat. They see the universe as a given mass, stretching ever larger. To them, no matter its shape, the universe is closed. To them, that's all there is. Whatever its shape, it will bend all light beams to match it. Even now, they are saying that there must be curvature, if it is a sphere. Then, they say, if it's a closed sphere, then a beam of light would come back to where it started from. How can we explain that a spherical universe has the characteristics of a flat universe? Due to everything traveling in a straight line, from a common beginning, I see everything traveling with space in straight lines. If you could shine a laser far enough to reach the end of the universe, then it would never curve back to us. Instead, it would become part of the energy making matter, at the end of the universe. Replicating space demands that the beginning is ongoing, at the edge of the universe. This is an ever growing sphere at the edge, growing in all directions, making space, matter and time, as it goes.

When you look out, you see the past. When you look into the past, you are actually looking back to the time of the beginning. Here's where things take a wild turn. While looking into the past and the beginning, are you not looking into a smaller universe? Yes, you are looking at a time when the universe was only 13.8 billion years in size. What will we see when the universe is 20 billion years old? We will see a sphere, 20 billion years in every direction. We will still see to the beginning. I know. You don't have to remind me. Science says that in about 19 billion years, we will stop seeing what we currently see at the edge. I think they are wrong. The expansion rate is fixed in space, but not through time. The rate of expansion is the result of a fixed light speed and a relative time. As space doubles, time halves, but light speed remains constant. That is, if constant even makes sense with something governed by a relative clock. So, as space doubles, the expansion rate halves.

The size of the universe, for all practical purposes, is infinite. We can see back in time 13.4 billion light years. However, what we see, at that point, is most likely 46.5 billion light years from us, now. The total observable universe is believed to be a total of 93 billion light years in diameter. I don't think there is anyone who believes, that is all there is. Why is it impossible to know the size of the universe? The problem is caused by time. If time did not exist, then we would see all there is. But the universe is ruled by time. Time is relativistic since it emerges with space, as spacetime replicates out of God's Fountain. In a nutshell, we look into the past. But, since the past gives way to the present, the further we look out, the further back in time we see. Let me drive home the implications of what I'm describing. Let's say we look out and see a galaxy 13.4 billion years in the past.

Is that light which we see giving us an accurate report of where that galaxy is right now? No way. The light which we see was emitted much closer in space and time, to us. So, it is no longer where the light was emitted, nor where the light says it is. That galaxy is much further in space from us and much further in the future from where we see it. I personally believe the universe is unbelievably larger than that which we can observe. If asked to pin a size on it, in light years, the best answer is "all of them". For one, once you get over trillions of miles, distance is meaningless to us. There is another more practical side. However many trillions or googolplex miles or light years it encompasses, those would be all the light years there are. Since there is no distance outside of the physical universe, that which is in it, is all there is.

Here is the reason why. Once you have accepted replicating space, the universe is no longer constrained to a fathomable size. What we observe of the universe, is governed strictly by light speed. We can be fairly certain that, for a time, at least, in the beginning, spacetime expanded at a speed much faster than light speed. Do to the duality of spacetime, this means that from its beginning, it expanded in all directions. At the very least, this would make the universe much bigger than that which we will ever observe. Let's forge ahead. The concept of replicating space results in the same extraordinary expansion at the edge of the universe, since its beginning. How can we fathom the size of something if we have no idea how much it has been growing per unit of time? Logically, the fact that it is growing, tells us it was once smaller. Taking it all the way back to the beginning leads us to a very small speck. How small? Again, possibly infinitely small. The guestimates run the gamut from one city block, to the size of an electron, or all the way down to one hundred billionth the size of a proton. You thought I had a vivid imagination? How does anyone begin to calculate something so small? But if it existed, it was measurable.

There seems to be a resurgence of the infinite universe concept. Logically, it is impossible for the universe to be infinite, in the true sense of the word. If it began from a point it cannot be infinite. I'm familiar with the concept that the universe started in infinity and expands everywhere. Then we have the problem of us looking back in time. We can look all the way back to the time when younger galaxies were smaller. Beyond that point, which is the beginning, the universe is opaque. If the universe was infinite, all observations would have one thing in common. No matter how far back in time we would look, we would see more of the same universe, with no age difference. The fact that there is a spherical vantage of time and space around the Earth, is very compelling. It is finite. We see, in a sphere, all the way back to the beginning. This fact, that the beginning surrounds us, is insurmountable evidence of a finite universe.

There are other bits of evidence. For instance, look up the discovery of quasars. They are only found at gigaparsec distances from Earth. This means that they were common in the distant past. This proves that the universe is not homogeneous. How can an infinite universe show signs of difference in age, when it started in every place, in one moment in time? This is proof positive that it is finite. We, indeed, see all of time, but we will never see all of space. There is more space than the speed of light can report to us in the time that has transpired. Common sense tells us that an expanding universe is finite. How can something expand into a place, if it's already there?

To those of you in the camp that believes in an eternal universe, please reconsider. It is a nonsensical argument. I have already put before you several strong arguments against the concept. Now, I will bring your eyes and mind against you. If the universe is eternal, then it must also be infinite. I remind you that time and space are inseparable, they are spacetime. If the universe was eternal, then what would we see when we looked into a telescope? Logically, we would see no discernible age difference, no matter in which direction, or how far back in time we peer. As most of you already know, that is not what we see. We see in a circle, all the way back 13.8 billion years, to the beginning. Please stop denying logic, common sense and the report of your own eyes.

We are at a great disadvantage in our quest to prove the size and shape of the universe. It would be an easier quest if we could shed our existence in linear time. We would step outside of time and the physical universe and witness the sphere of Creation from outside itself. Well, thankfully, we do have a vehicle within ourselves to do just that. It is our imagination. In this magical realm, we can transcend the physical limitations, and imagine what we cannot see.

Allow me to be your guide into a fantastic trip, outside of the realm of reality. Imagine yourself with the power to travel through time, space, dimensions, and reality itself. Follow me as we leave the confines of the physical world and travel to a point outside of the universe. Good, we are all here. But where is here? We are outside the universe in the nothingness outside of creation. We are here through the power of imagination for the purpose of seeing the universe in its entirety. Our first observation is that of a sphere. We see this sphere suspended in nothingness, and it's composed of everything that is physical. Because we are outside of physicality, we are not in any particular time. We, therefore, see the universe in its entirety. Not only in space, but in time. First question. How big is it? Because it is composed of everything there is, it is infinite. Is there a center? Since it encompasses all the time there is, and it is relative, then every point within it is a time that marks the center of the universe, at that time. Where is the beginning? The beginning is everywhere, because every spot had been the beginning, at one time. If we turn on time, at our vantage point, what do we see? We see the current universe getting older. Starting from the center, we see a uniform universe. As we shift our view to the outer rim, we see the universe growing at light speed, at the edge. This ongoing beginning shares the characteristics of the beginning. The galaxies are smaller and the stars are younger. The iron content is less within the stars, since that is the beginning. As we move our gaze further to the center, we see the galaxies merging and growing. We see the stars dying and their replacements showing the appropriate content of an older universe.

So what is the shape of our universe? It is a sphere! What is the size of our universe? It is not static. Therefore, at every point in its existence, it is infinite, since infinite can only mean "all there is".

CHAPTER 17

Information, Is It Eternal?

I HAVE PURPOSELY STAYED away from quantum mechanics. I don't mean just in this book. I mean in my progression of self-learning. The explanation, I would guess, at the end of the day, is fear. Fear of getting into a subject that is beyond what I can assimilate. Possibly, it is also fear that, again, I will revert to an earlier time in my life, when the universe made no sense. We humans are peculiar creations. What makes me fall into deep thought, makes the next man just laugh and walk away. No, I will not fully open quantum mechanics, and the contents of that can of worms. Can of worms? Interesting. The worms must be coming from Schrodinger's dead cats. There is, however, an intrusion into our common everyday world that I cannot ignore. This intrusion is the commonly accepted belief that information cannot be lost. The best area to debate this topic is in the effects of a black hole. First, we should introduce this monster from the point of view of replicating space. A black hole is a super low-pressure area in space. It is the equivalent of a super cyclone in space. Beyond the event horizon, not even light can escape. Do you see a problem with this picture under the warp space idea? Of course you do. Space can't be merely warped, space has got to be flowing in. Think of a vacuum cleaner. Does a vacuum suck or push stuff in? A vac pushes stuff into its nozzle. Let me tell you how it works. You push air out of the canister with a fan. This creates a low pressure area in the canister. The atmospheric pressure then pushes the dirt into the vac nozzle. I know, some of you still think that a vacuum cleaner sucks or pulls stuff in. Here's the coup de grace for your argument. Will a vac work in the vacuum of space? It is not warped space, but space flowing into a black hole that carries light in with it. Proof positive that nothing travels through space, everything travels with space. It also proves that the fastest thing in the universe is not light. It is spacetime which is the medium. More importantly, the information barrier is governed, not by light speed, but by space speed.

Back to information. Supposedly, a black hole will hold onto the matter that falls into it, forever. But, it also is supposed to hold onto information. Enter Stephen Hawking, and Hawking radiation. The belief is that black holes do not live forever but dissipate by emitting radiation. This radiation is random. If random, then, what happened to the information? Again, I'm almost 100 percent ignorant on the topic, but since I don't know that there is a box, I can truly think outside the box. I can think freely without even acknowledging that there is a box. I don't think black holes store matter or information. I think all that they store are the basic building blocks of the universe. The ultimate God particle. God's fountain. Once matter falls into a black hole, the immense gravitational field disassembles it. If matter was indeed made from energy, then, if you reverse the process, it stands to reason that it reverts back to what it once was.

There is a large elephant in our midst. What in the universe could this Hawking radiation be made of? It's simple. If we accept that a black hole stores only energy, then what comes out of it must be energy. If it is basic energy, then it must be the Fountain of God. This is energy flow out of the black hole. But wait, if energy is flowing out, why can't light also escape? Eureka, this is the same energy creating spacetime. This energy is capable of faster than light travel. There is one huge nugget in this line of thought. If a non-feeding black hole can dissipate, then more energy is flowing out than is flowing in. Now, I can truly comprehend why black holes can have matter circling them without falling into the hole. The immense gravitational pull is being offset by an outflow. Of course, this outflow is greater at its equator, if you will. At the area where the poles would be, (analogous to a planet), the lack of rotation cannot offer as much outflow. All that approaches the black hole, from the direction of its poles, is swallowed up. I imagine this is why we see some black holes with accretion disks.

We have made the case that a black hole does not store matter or information. It only stores energy. The energy in a black hole, I theorize, is the Fountain of God, which is not reducible. From this arise several questions. How can this energy exist in such a barbaric gravity field, without compressing itself into matter? What is the core of a black hole made of? What is the distance between a black hole event horizon, and its core? Let me give you my take on these questions. First, why does the energy not compress into matter, in a black hole? Get ready to think outside the box. Once inside the event horizon, gravity is normal to that within deep space. That did it. I lost the last of the learned ones. How can any sane person believe that, just to the outside of the event horizon, gravity is insanely strong? While just inside the border of the event horizon, gravity is normal? Here is why I believe such an unbelievable thing. Science says that a black hole is an area of compressed space. But I believe you cannot compress space: you can only compress time. Let's say you survived the trip through the event horizon. What would you find inside? I think you would find an unbelievably huge volume of space. But wait, how can there be less area in the outer circumference than the inner perimeter? This is so, because the event horizon is not a break in space, but rather, it is a break in time. As you approach the event horizon, time dilation increases. At the event horizon, spacetime is traveling in such a unilateral direction that not even light can travel out. At the event horizon, time is so dilated that you could travel untold distances in the equivalent of seconds, had you been in normal deep space.

I thought that all the learned ones had left us. But I heard one say, "You got it backwards. If we could see an object at, or beyond, the event horizon, then we would see it standing still." Yes, from your vantage point, you would see it at a standstill, or with very slight movement. But in the place where the object resides, the distance is so vast, that it could travel a trillion miles and you could not tell that it has even moved. So where does the immense gravity of a black hole come from? It comes from the vast amount of spacetime that is encompassed within a small sphere. Remember, adding energy to an object increases its mass. So, concentrated energy increases mass in a given area. However, once you are within the frontier, or the event horizon, you are in a different time. We see, then how a black hole can dissipate. If it does not feed, it gradually dissipates, as spacetime leaks out of it. Next question: What is at the core of a black hole? I believe, that the sudden collapse that makes a black hole, reverts matter back to energy, in its most basic form. This would mean that the collapse is so fast, that the outer circumference collapses inward, as matter turns back to energy. Given a strong enough collapse, the event horizon remains stable. It can even grow, if the hole feeds on matter. Lastly, what is the distance between the black hole event horizon, and its core? These distances are vast. Sagittarius A, the black hole at the center of our galaxy, is approximately 2.6 million solar masses. If Sagittarius A reverted back to spacetime energy, what would be the resulting size of new space? I think it would be larger than the galaxy.

Let's try to put it in a nutshell. The rapid collapse of a massive star creates a super time-dense area in space. All of this area is filled by spacetime. If it feeds on matter, then it grows. If not, its dissipation is greater than its inrushing spacetime volume. It will eventually dissipate.

Have you heard information is power? Well, get ready to learn how true that statement really is. Remember the old vinyl records? You youngsters, like me, who have a lot of accumulated youth, we all remember. The information on those records was cut into a vinyl disk. Hence, the phrase, let's cut a record. The information on the disk was a type of energy, was it not? I know we used amplifiers to make the sounds. But we really were not making the sounds, were we? We were amplifying the sounds. The sounds are created by the vibrations of the needle, following the cut groove. Some of you have seen the old phonographs, where they used a funnel to amplify the vibrations. Would it be a stretch for us to say that the information was stored energy? How about stone tablets? Did it not take energy to chisel the information onto them? OK, let's go into the modern era. Who remembers reel to reel, 8 track or cassette tapes? How about computer floppies or tape backups? I can hear the laughter of the millennials. You millennials think that you are in the modern era. All those things are useless, antiquated things, right? You are past all of that, right? Well, how do you think a computer hard drive works? It's recording information in the form of magnetic energy. Yes, I heard you, hard drives are no longer magnetic. They are solid state. What do you think is the information stored in those hard drives? Yes, it's in the form of energy. Power is used and by default, stored, as the actual nuclear arrangement of the medium is modified to record the data. Here we can come to a conclusion. Information is power. Literally.

Do you have a headache yet, because I do? Wait, hold on there is more. Gravity at the event horizon of a black hole is stronger than at the surface of the biggest star. Then, how can matter loose cohesion? Matter should be compressed to the density beyond that of a neutron star. Here is where things get really strange. There should be a core that was formed by the collapse of the star that created the black hole. But, is the event horizon its beginning? Is there an area between the event horizon and the core? There must be space between the event horizon and the core. Not only does logic dictate it, but so does relativity. At the event horizon, light travels inward unilaterally. This means that time stops, or at the very least, time seems to stop. If time almost stops, then how long does it take to get from the event horizon to the core? Possibly, billions of years. So, if you travel at almost light speed for billions of years, what would be the distance between the event horizon and the core? Stop, please. Let's take a break. Take a sip of your drink. Maybe get a snack, and allow your brain to cool. I will do the same.

OK, we are back. I hope everyone made it back. I contend that spacetime is relative, but it is also unbreakable. Once it emerges from itself, it can no longer be undone. It is, I believe, the smallest particle or entity in the universe. It is the building ingredient for everything there is in the universe. As spacetime is drawn into a black hole, it enlarges the area within, by decreasing the time to space ratio. This would mean that the event horizon is a horizon, or a border, between spacetime. This is why it is invisible to us. At the event horizon, the speed of light and information is broken. Think of it this way. Each second before the event horizon, light travels 186,000 miles, but inside the black hole spacetime would travel faster than light. It would be like witnessing a plane breaking the sound barrier on Earth, and all of a sudden, the plane is no longer where its sound places it. But we're talking about light-sight-information. The image and information of everything which passes through that barrier, becomes invisible to us. If you could survive the passage into a black hole, would you disappear to yourself? Of course not. You are your own reference point. You would see yourself, and everyone around you, sharing the same speed. You, however, should not be able see past the event horizon, to the place that you just came from. What does this have to do with information? Well, black holes emit Hawking radiation. If something comes out, and if it can eventually dissipate, then what happens to all the information that went in? Everything that went in, is shredded into the lowest form of its original existence: namely energy. But wait a minute. That would be a free lunch? Doesn't the process of disassembly, or erasing information, expend energy? Yes, it does. But the same process releases information, which is recorded as matter, into its lowest form. This erasure, therefore, creates a lot more energy than it consumes.

What do information, universal expansion, and time have in common? When you begin the study of a subject, how do you go about it? Do you ignore the history of the subject? Do you start from its beginning, and expand outward, mimicking universal expansion? Do you take it as a monolith, and build on top of it, as you study? Do you not start from the beginning, and as you research, you co-mingle what is known, with your own opinions? This is one of those thoughts that is not 100 percent real. This fits the bill for a fragment of dreamland. Why would I even think that information, universal expansion and time are related? Let's delve into it before my waking mind dismisses it as silly. All three of these are important parts of this book. We will discuss these relationships. What is information? We must conclude that information is the story of energy in the universe. As you may remember, my argument is that information is energy. Its creation, recording, storage and playback are all governed by the use of energy. OK, the skeptics among you are frowning. Let's add a little more evidence to the scale. I type these thoughts on a computer, and it consumes electric energy. My brain was overtaxed, using a lot of energy in making these thoughts. Energy was used to record the info into the computer's hard drive. After editing, it was sent to the publisher. Sending it electronically, through the net, used more energy. The publisher got the download, using more energy to process it into book form. The information was sent numerous times between author and publisher for confirmation. When everyone involved was satisfied, it was sent to the printer, where more energy was used to print it. It was printed on paper (matter equals energy) produced by a tree. The ink used was formulated using energy. It was shipped to you using more energy. You are now reading it, using what? Energy. There are many steps I left out, which you probably thought about, while reading. All the while, using what? That's right, more energy. Again, why is information energy? Because that is all there is in the universe.

Now let's deal with information as it deals with universal expansion. Just like expansion, info has a beginning from a central point. Yes, I heard those of you who believe in an infinite universe. Information can begin simultaneously in many places. But I could interject that infinity requires not many places, but all places at once. Let's continue. I argue that information propagates from a central location, in all directions at once. All your knowledge, experiences, and beliefs are put together in order to elaborate upon a new idea. It could be argued that, at least for me, I carry a thought outward on a single path, but not all at once. But you would be wrong. It is true that I will pick up a thought and expand upon it until it ends. Then, I will pick up my mind's eye, to begin again at the center, to go back in its past. This does not mean that the process does not go in every direction, eventually. I just work in a linear fashion, not globally. You could say I take the clearest paths, first. But I do explore everything that remotely applies. My conclusion is that information is a picture of expansion. As far as relating to time, we don't need to get into that. I don't think any of you will argue that information is so close to time that they co-mingle.

There seems to be a problem with the concept of loss of information within a black hole. I really don't see the significance of the loss of information. Some believe that, upon our death, all we are, and what we have learned and experienced, is gone. Why would there be a concern that we preserve information within a black hole? We are the self-aware beings who are rationalizing this information loss. If we, who we are, what we have learned, disappears, why would anything matter? But let's play along with the more scientific types. How do we rationalize what happens to information upon encountering a black hole? The problem is: why can't Hawking radiation carry information out? What is this radiation made of? Is it not replicating space energy? Yes, I believe that the radiation coming from black holes, is composed of the real God particle: God's Fountain. But wait. If it is coming out of the event horizon, then why does it not bring light with it? Clearly, spacetime is the only entity that can flow out of the event horizon. I think it flows out at greater than light speed. It sheds everything else as it emerges. Can matter be dragged along by this outflow? Yes, I think it can. It would have the ability to be pushed out at close-to-light speed. What would it look like? A fireball. Matter traveling at close to light speed would ignite like gasoline in our atmosphere. The friction between it and inward flowing spacetime would mimic an immense atom smasher. Here is the last question related to black holes. If the flow of spacetime into a black hole is greater than the flow of spacetime going out, why does it dissipate? I think that the energy lost by outflow and the consumption of energy for its internal processes, result in a net loss of energy and the dissipation of the black hole. The only way to sustain itself, is to continue to feed on matter, the protein, if you will, of the universe.

CHAPTER 18

Cat and Cats

I 'M TRULY SORRY. I meant what I said about staying away from quantum mechanics. But I had to dip my toe in it, to give answers to some problems. These problems arose out of the concept of replicating space. I cannot finish this book without discussing cats. The cat in quantum mechanics is Schrodinger's cat. Being a farmer, I'm well versed in animal husbandry. I think this cat needs help. Is the cat dead or is it alive? It is both. If you are not familiar with the subject, you'll want to search on the internet for Schrodinger's thought experiment. Here are my thoughts on the cat mortality problem. First, I feel shortchanged by this 'felineticide'. Why only one cat, if we are entangled in entanglement? I see the two inferred particles in the 'dead or alive' scenario. I just wish two cats had been used. For the benefit of simpler minds like mine, we will use two cats in our cat-shenanigans. I call your attention to this one fact. The luminaries who argued about this felineticide, willfully or otherwise, ignored a basic component. The device that kills the cat is triggered by a timer. A random timer, but a timer, nonetheless. How could a timer work if you were in a 'time with no time'? If you notice, I specify no mechanism to make my tag team of two felines alternate, between dead and alive. After all, if you are going to imagine something fantastical, then why would you try to make it conform to reality? Perhaps they were so brilliant, that they were making it more fantastical by implying that a timer could work in a 'time with no time'. I would like to ask the reader, Is it only me, or do you, also, wonder what defines an observer? What level of intelligence is required? Isn't the cat, at least the live one, an observer? Perhaps the observer is disqualified because he is part of the quantum world. This reminds me of the assertion 'Christopher Columbus discovered America in 1492'. Wait, there were people already here. How can we claim to discover a place that already had a population? I guess the alternative was not very appealing. What did Columbus actually do? He removed the ignorance from which the other side of the world was suffering. In the interest of moving forward in our discussion, let us agree that the observer has to be self-aware, and cannot be part of the quantum system. There seems to be an even higher problem (net search Copenhagen interpretation). If, up to a few years ago relatively speaking, we were unaware of the cat, then did he exist? Prior to Hubble's discoveries, we thought our galaxy was the only one. How can reality exist, without an observer? How can an observer observe all there is to observe? You will only get the answer to some of these questions in Chapter 20. Let's go back and pounce on our cats.

We should first ask what makes reality. Does ignorance make reality? Does knowledge/observation make reality? Reality has only one ingredient. Existence. Did the microorganisms exist, prior to our observance of them? Of course, they existed. We have written accounts of disease and death, caused by them, prior to our discovery of them. Was the new world new, or was it only new to the Europeans? Was it new, when the first inhabitants, the so called Indians, settled it? The new world was a reality, and was very old before a single man ever set eyes or foot upon it. This, to say that the cat is either dead or alive before being observed. What the observer does, is to reveal the cat in his spatial time zone. The cat, up to that time, is not in any given time. We still have the problem of entanglement. Once one particle is observed, how can the other particle be its opposite, regardless of distance? The problem is not distance, the problem is time. We are in linear time. The particle is not. They never leave close proximity to each other, unless you open Schrodinger's box. When you open the box, in linear time, you observe the cat in eternity. To us, they can appear billions of light years from each other. But to the cats, they are in close proximity to each other, and if one is dead, then the other is obviously alive. For those who are familiar with quantum tunneling, this is cat tunneling. They can't both be dead or alive. If one is alive, then the other is dead, and vice versa. Now, if the cats alternate between dead and alive, then the answer is still the same. We are in linear time. If we open the box within linear time, then we have revealed our cat to be alive or dead. Whatever our cat is, the other must be the opposite. Why? Being copies and not governed by time, if they alternate, then, once viewed in time, they are identified to that time. At the same moment, the counterpart is also revealed. But wait, time is relative, is it not? Yes, relativism gave rise to this cat conundrum, in the first place.

This cat problem was not an issue within a Newtonian universe. To us, time has meaning. To the particle (symbolized by the cat), time and space have no meaning. They remain in whichever state they began. "Wow, do you mean to tell me that the one cat is dead from the beginning, and its counterpart is alive from the beginning? Is this true, even if they alternate?" Yes, if we are to believe that these particles travel at the speed of light, then they are in suspended time. For us, they are alternating. For them, they never change. Why? They have no time to alternate. They are in the boundary between duality. They are in the region of a 'time with no time'. Get over it. Accept that the universe is both Newtonian and Einsteinian. Whether they alternate or not, it is irrelevant. We cannot prove that they alternate between dead or alive, because as soon as it is observed, you have identified it to a time. It's like taking a reading in an electrical circuit. Once I place my meter across the two wires, the meter changes the resistance in the circuit, so whatever I read is the new reality. I can theorize the original circuit's voltage or resistance, but I can never know, because as soon as I know, I've changed its true value. Referring to the cats, you have taken them out of a 'time with no time', and placed them in linear time.

I see some light bulbs flickering above my reader's heads. "Does the live and dead cat reveal that the universe is both Newtonian and relativistic"? Yes, I'm so glad some of you have seen, in your own mind, that the theory of everything is already known. Relativity is definitely part of it, but so are Newton's laws. The rest of linear reality is in the other theories. Currently, String theory and Quantum theory. Think of our reality as a bridge. The two shores are eternity, and the distance in between, is linear time. Eternity is not without time, but it is without end. As temporal beings, we live within linear time. We see ourselves in the present. The past is behind us. The future is before us. This linear time saw its beginning from infinity, in time and space. The further back in time, the smaller the physical size, and the shorter the time. If we play time backwards, we reach singularity in space and eternity in time, or a time when there was no time. The further forward in time, the larger the universe, and the more time. "Eureka!" Someone screamed. "Time and space are tied at the hip". Particles see no time, because they are too small and fast to be seen in time, or to be part of observable time. Once you are capable of seeing the cat, it becomes part of our reality, emerging out of timeless time, stepping into relative linear time. This, then, seals their reality within linear time. Given the laws of Conservation Of Energy, if one particle is spinning up, then the other must be spinning down. Having just emerged out of eternity, or a 'time with no time', they are manifested in whichever state they began, whether they are capable of alternating or not. We contemplate the probability that the cat is alive or dead from linear time. Without our observation, the cat is both alive and dead. We have crude examples, all around us. To us, anything going real fast in a circle, seems to be solid. Most of us have seen the propeller on a plane or helicopter. Who has not used a rotary lawnmower? It has a single blade, yet it cuts a circular path. Why? Because as far as the grass is concerned, the lawnmower has a circular blade, like that on a circular saw.

What is the purpose for this apparent duality in the universe? Why can't the universe just be relativistic? Why must it also be Newtonian? First, let me say, a 'time with no time' is also part of relativity. All of our observations show that we cannot reverse The Arrow Of Time. So then, can we stop time altogether? No, I believe not. But let's say I told you that a trillion years on Earth is equivalent to a trillionth of a second, in some other place. Would you not consider that other place to be in a place with no time? I think that difference is enough to make them opposites.

I think it is time to shine some light on this subject. A photon of light experiences no time from the furthest reach of the universe. When it is stopped, at any point along its travel, it emerges into linear time, but it has not seen any time elapse. This is why, from the perspective of a linear temporal being, the photon seems to be in a 'time with no time'. If it were true that it was in a 'time with no time', then several observers could observe it at different points, at the same time. But clearly, only a single observer can be the one to observe it. The question becomes, if several observers look at the same time, then who sees it first? The answer is, 'whoever sees it first'. This tells us that there is a base time, almost infinitely slower than our linear time. At this moment in time, we have no way to compare 'No Time' to 'linear time'. We are left with a question. For what reason and purpose does the world of the minute reside within this 'time with no time'? Here, I think, we see the backdrop, or the support, for reality itself. Although it's true that relativity makes reality, 'time with no time' maintains the cohesion of reality, throughout the universe. What cohesion could exist, if there was no communication across the universe? Would the universe not fracture each time it reached a point where information could no longer be seen, from one point to another? But wait, if we are to accept that each point in space is its own reference point, then what? Any point in space marks a distance to some other point, from which information cannot reach us. Without a 'time with no time', wouldn't spacetime fracture at every point in the universe? Yes, there can be no cohesion without 'time with no time'. Let me give you an example. Can there be a living creature, so large that its blood could not circulate to its furthest limb? No, if a creature was so large that blood could not reach its longest limb, that creature would die. At the very least, his limb would die. If you will allow the analogy, the life blood of the universe is information. This means that the universe could not exist further than the distance from which information could travel. We can then safely conclude that entanglement is vital to the existence of reality. Reality is unsustainable without the universe connecting in real time, that is, in now time or in a 'time with no time', aka, Newtonian time.

You may be wondering how we can have a stable, seemingly smooth functioning universe without a rigid value of time. Let's bring it all together. We have two distinct types of time: Newtonian and Einsteinian. These two are the basic concepts of time. Neither one is without variations. Newtonian 'no time' must include some basic level of time. This, for the reason listed above. If several observers, of some distance apart, were to try to observe a light photon at the same time, then only one would see it. It would be the observer closest to the source. This requires that there be some level of time, even at light speed. The observation, of course, would cause a collapse of the wave, because you have stopped the wave of probability, in linear time. This wave of probability is caused by this 'time with no time'.

Do not be misled into thinking that a particle truly exists in more than one place at a time. If you collapsed a wave and a single particle was revealed, then that was all there ever was. The wave is a blurry image on steroids. You were simply seeing the effect of a particle in a 'time with no time', from linear time. Not being governed by time, it does all that is possible for it to do, in 'no time'. This makes it look to us as if it was a wave. It just means that we see it in many places, at once.

We still have a loose end. Why would we see a wave? Why not a whole sea, if it's true that it's doing all that it can do? This wave is no different than a wave in the ocean. In linear time, we only see the waves in our vicinity. We could never see all of the ocean, or the entire life of a single wave. The wave is the only glimpse we can detect, from our point in linear time. Why do we see this wave? Because it is the most probable point for the location of this particle. This is yet more evidence that a 'time with no time' does have a base time. The equivalency between a 'time with no time' and linear time might never be found. But one thing is for certain. The ratio is ludicrous. I should point out that this ratio is so great that it creates the illusion that an effect can precede a cause. It has been experimentally proven that we can seemingly cause an effect before the cause. If you would like to see proof, then look up 'delayed-Choice Quantum Eraser'. The solution to this illogical issue is quite simple. At a 'time with no time', chronological space is scarcely linked to chronological time. In the absence of time, the 'cause' cannot be determined by position in space. Settle down, did you already forget that a particle in a 'time with no time', does all it can do, within no time? If you have no time, then cause and effect happen in the same 'no time'. Upon being manifested in linear time, they will be arranged in the proper chronology demanded by spacetime.

Allow me to elaborate on the cause-and-effect violation-fix that I proposed, above. I know most of you get it. You would not have read this far into the book if you were incapable of grasping the difficult ideas. But, I think this particular concept is beyond difficult. I have just told you that chronology, within linear time, demands that effect comes before cause, in order to keep 'cause and effect' from being violated. Let's imagine that we would not see this seemingly wrong image of 'effect before cause'. What would this mean to the nature of the universe? If the 'delayed-Choice Quantum Eraser' had shown that linear time is the rule within the quantum world, then the universe would cease to exist. I have already explained that the universe cannot exist without real time communication throughout its entirety. This real time communication is made possible within a 'time with no time'. Here is the key to understanding that this experiment does not violate the laws of the micro and macro worlds. The observer is in linear time, observing what happens in a 'time with no time'. From this frame of reference, he sees space and time together as spacetime. This frame of reference demands that space and time be arranged chronologically. But the experiment also demands that the result of a 'time with no time' be manifested. This realm of 'no time' has particles doing all they can do, in 'no time'. When seen from our vantage point, they appear simultaneously. Let me see if I can distil it to its most basic level, even if it's not scientifically accurate. The particle does come through the experiment as a wave. But then, it gets drawn out into linear time, and is revealed as a particle. But since linear time demands that whichever is seen first is chronologically first, then the 'effect' is manifested before the 'cause'. The Arrow Of Time is honored in linear time, but so is the requirement of Newtonian time, or 'time with no time'. I hope you see it clearly, now. The photon must be seen as a particle from linear time, because it was revealed as such. But, by the same token, the nature of a 'time with no time' must also be revealed. That is, everything that happens to a particle at light speed, happens at the same time, if seen from linear time. Linear time demands that The Arrow Of Time be respected. Well, this is why the wave is seen to collapse before the 'effect' of the experiment. The experiment covers linear time and space: spacetime. But it is showing what happens in a time where space and time are not linked. We, then, must see the 'effect' and the 'cause', not bound by chronology, but by space. Which space comes first, in the 'delayed-choice quantum eraser'? The wave detector. Which space comes last? The eraser. We do not see one happening before the other. We see both parts of the test simultaneously. The 'delayed-choice quantum eraser' is not showing 'cause' before 'effect'. It is proving one of the pillars of Replicating Space Theory. At the point in speed, where replicating space is replicating, there is 'no time'. This is exactly what our experiment confirms.

Einsteinian time is a whole lot more complex. It is so complex that it covers more 'times' than Newtonian time, yet it is encompassed by a 'time with no time'. This heading has an almost infinite number of time zones under it. Due to the difference between the micro and macro world, these variations in time are a must. Think this through. Let's say we observed GN-z11 from Earth, right now. How old is its light? 13.4 billion years old. And let's say that beyond us, another one billion light years away, there is another planet. This planet is an exact copy of Earth, so it shares Earth's time zone. How old is the light that this other planet will observe from GN-z11? Intuitively, we might say it is 14.4 billion years, give or take, after allowing for expansion. But this is wrong. The planet must see the light (if it is observed at the same moment as Earth's observation) from GN-z11 as 13.4 billion years old. Why? Because the light was emitted relationally to that location at the same ratio as the light hitting Earth. Well, it looks like I left most of you stranded. How can we both see the same aged light from different locations, when we are ruled by relativity? Because we are all looking back into time, not into space. The universe, being 13.8 billion years old, governs everyone's view to that maximum age. Bottom line: we must conform to both Newtonian and Einsteinian times. The age of the universe is manifested by Newtonian time, or a 'time with no time'. But this age was created by Einsteinian relativistic time. Fascinating. We see in time what was created in 'no time'.

Perhaps nothing I can ever say will convince you that the universe is both Newtonian and Einsteinian. But that does not mean that I can't tie your brain into a pretzel, even if you are adamant that only relativity rules the universe. Allow me to ask you some questions. How old is the light emitted from a flashlight, if I turn one on right now? That is correct. The light is brand new. How old is the light we see currently from GN-z11? That is correct. 13.4 billion years old. All good so far. How about from the frame of reference of the light itself? How old is the light from the flashlight? It just began. How old is the light from GN-z11, using its frame of reference? It just began. Both lights are ageless, yet if examined in linear time, we can tell their age by their redshift. Up to this point, no one should have any objections. So, how long will it take the light from our flashlight to travel the same distance as the light we see from GN-z11? The same 13.4 billion years it took the light from GN-z11 to reach us. How old will the light actually be to itself? Zero years. How old will the light be to the observer in linear time? 13.4 billion years old. If you still believe that the universe is only relativistic, then I give up. Let me just leave you with a question to ponder. Imagine that you were running with the light from our flashlight. Could you communicate with someone on GN-z11, in Morse code, by turning the light on and off? Whatever your answer is, can you justify it in a solely relativistic universe?

It is not that, when at light speed, a photon can be in many places at once. Rather, it is that when a 'time with no time' is viewed from linear time, it gives the impression that the photon travels in a wave. But, there are no multiple photons. If brought into linear time, only one photon will emerge. We must conclude that if two observers try to view the same photon, then only one will be successful. There is, indeed, a time element governing existence. For instance, a light photon could be said to be in more than one place at once. But it would only be viewable from Earth at the linear time corresponding to the time it takes to get here. Do not assume that this gives you issues with a 'time with no time'. There is no doubt it is real. The photon is traveling with spacetime. From its frame of reference it sees no time. But, to an observer watching the photon travel, the spacetime which it inhabits is, indeed, associated with a time. It is space, and not time that gives a 'time with no time' its semblance of time. "Wait a minute! Are you telling me that the photon is timeless until it is brought into linear time?" Yes, think of it this way. If the light photon was never brought into linear time, would it ever age? No. The light from the farthest reaches of the universe is ageless, unless observed. Observation, of course, demands bringing it into linear time. "Wrong, Mister Farmer. When we see the light, it will show its age, due to the redshift". Sorry. You did not realize that redshift is caused, not by time, but by space. It is the expansion of space (actually it's growing) that causes the redshift. The photon is zero years, regardless of how far it traveled. The perception of age is only real to the observer in linear time. In order to see the redshift of a photon, it must be observed in linear time. The real interesting question is the following. Does the photon 'redshift' to its corresponding level in the split second that it is brought into linear time? This takes preference over 'spooky action at a distance'. This is 'spooky action with no distance'. If, somehow, you could view the photon sharing its frame of reference, the photon would be exactly the same age as when it was emitted. Furthermore, the photon will be the same age when viewed from other locations. Every location is associated with every other location, because replicating spacetime and relativity create time zones correlating with speed.

I was going to leave the above paragraph as the complete explanation of what happens when a photon emerges out of 'no time' into linear time. I could not. If I leave this topic open it could mean a third book. At this time I don't want to consider another book. So let's explore this materializing of a photon into linear time. Upon being forced out of a 'time-with-no-time' into linear time, how old is the photon? If it had stayed in its place of no-time, it would be zero years. Once brought into linear time, it has all the characteristics of that time. But the question remains. How old is it? Wow, we are stuck. It looks like it's old, but its age only started when it was brought into linear time. The photon was not experiencing time as it moved in a wave with spacetime. The inside of this wave is timeless. The spacetime, itself, on the outside (if there is such a thing), is associated with a time. We can all agree that every particle is real. It physically exists. We have no absolute proof, but everything seems to point to the supposition, that at light speed, time stops, or at the very least, it almost stops. Particles traveling at light speed, therefore, exist in a 'time-with-no-time'. This tells us that existence is not predicated on time. There is existence without time. We must also admit that, if these particles exist outside of time, then space can exist without time. I claim in this book that space began in a place that has no time. Having no time, this place can never end, because you can only have an end, if you have time. To conclude, the photon shows redshift. It was not caused by time, but by space. The photon is ageless unless it is brought into linear time. I think the only way to give light age, is to stop its travel. This has already been done. Do a net search for 'light stopped for a minute inside a crystal'. This stopped light will definitely get older. Light can now be observed using modern high-speed cameras. The observer is in linear time, and the photon remains at the speed of light, in no-time. I would love to be able to place one of these cameras before the double slit experiment, to see if taking the picture causes the collapse of the wave. I don't see how a picture can interfere with the wave function. If the wave does collapse, then I must conclude that taking the picture interfered with the speed of the photon. A follow up experiment might be to set up multiple cameras. We can then determine whether taking pictures of the traveling photon affects its speed. If the photon drops out of light speed, then we have solved the measurement problem. If the photon remains at light speed, then refer to Chapter 20 to resolve the issue.

I'm surprised that none of you have raised an objection about the camera mentioned above. The issue is this. I have repeatedly told you that something at light speed cannot be seen. This is because, at light speed, there is no time to emit or reflect light. But wait. A camera captures light. So how can this camera capture an image of a light photon traveling at light speed? The answer is in the speed. Can your phone's camera capture a single light photon, in its travel? Of course, not. Your camera is not fast enough. This seems to mean that the camera which is capable of capturing a photon in mid-travel, must have a shutter speed equal to or greater than light speed. But we know that is impossible. Perhaps, it is the angle at which it captures the image. Maybe it is not capturing an image in one spot. The answer could lie in capturing the picture of the photon covering some distance. The picture could then be computer assembled at the point where it is believed to have been when the picture was taken.

You guys are sharp as tacks. Some are asking, "Wait Mister Farmer, you have said that, at light speed, there is no time. But you also say that where there is no time, there is no light. These statements cancel each other". Glad to see that you are using your head for more than a hat rack. Yes, your statement is worded correctly, but is catastrophically incorrect. Timeless light cannot travel within a median that has no time. But timeless light can and does travel within a medium under the influence of time. In either case, from the frame of reference of light, there is no time. But from a frame of reference outside of light, if in a space governed by time, then light is visible and is perceived as if ruled by time. If, within a place where there is no time, then light is not visible because time is revealed by light, and light is revealed in time. In a place with no light, can you accurately measure time? Imagine yourself in a room with absolutely no light. How could you tell the passage of time? How would you know when to sleep? There is actually a sleep disorder among the totally blind, called non-entrained circadian rhythm. Known as Non-24. They have no way of telling day from night, so their sleep rhythm becomes disrupted, resulting in insomnia and many other life disrupting disorders.

By now, there are various states of mind, among my readership. Some are glued to the pages, some are tempted to put the book down because they are lost, and some are begging me to answer a very important question. Let's answer the question. I think it will serve all the groups mentioned. How wide is a 'time with no time'? A 'time with no time' is place in speed, not a place in time. This place exists at light speed. It has nothing to do with light. It just happens that light resides there, because it is the place of equilibrium. There, spacetime is clashing with itself, forming a place where time stands still. Think of it as a place from which time emerges. If you are at its center, there is no movement for you, so there is no time. OK, but that does not answer the question at hand. How big is this place? It is both infinitely small, and infinitely large. I told you, it is a speed, not a place. If you speed past it, (or slow past it) it is infinitely small. But what happens if you match its speed? How far does this place extend? If you are traveling at light speed, then a place with no time extends forever. You can travel within it from one side of the universe to the other. All of you are familiar with a hurricane. What would you say if I told you that I can travel in an old cloth-winged biplane, in a cat-5 hurricane, for as long as I wished, in complete safety? All I need to do is to take my airplane out of a bunker, when the eye of the storm comes overhead. I can then take off and fly for as long as my fuel holds out, in complete safety. Of course, I must stay within the eye of the storm. But in the case of time, it's not the lack of wind, but the lack of time, that makes this no-time zone. Clearly, a 'time with no time' is also a time with no spatial limitations. Don't you see that we have space, but we have no time? So how many times can I go to the end of the universe and back again, in the time that it takes someone in linear time to blink? There is no limit to how many times I can travel to and fro. This, in essence, is the wave function.

It is an item, in a 'time with no time', doing all that is possible for it to do, in no time.

Perhaps I could be accused of being fixated on matter. I cannot deny it. The matter of matter matters very much to me. But really, what's the matter with matter? I'm sorry I could not help myself. Let's explore it a bit more. Matter is 99 percent empty. So how empty is that? Imagine an atom being the size of a baseball stadium. Now, how much space would occupy the solid parts of that atom? Would you be surprised to learn that it would occupy home plate? And here is the shocker. It would really be the size of a single black bean, not home plate. Consider that the next time you think of yourself as being substantial. Some of you are really sharp. Someone just said, "Mister Farmer you forgot your own concept. There is nothing empty. All of created space is permeated with spacetime". You are absolutely right, nothing within created space is truly empty, and spacetime permeates every nook and cranny of the universe. I merely wanted to highlight the actual solid matter in a body. Just how much matter is in a body? A person is composed of less solids, than the volume of a dust particle. It is likely that you could fit all of humanity in one small truck. Of course, it would possess the weight of all humanity. It would create strong gravity around it. If you held one person in your hand, it would punch a hole through your hand. Just think how little effort it takes to pierce your skin with a needle. Now imagine 200 pounds concentrated in less area than the point of a needle. Are things becoming more clear? When you cut something with a knife, are you cutting or are you really dividing? The logical answer is: dividing. Why, then, will a sharper knife 'cut' easier? Because you are making contact with less matter. You are pushing less matter out of the way. Have you ever seen a nail gun shooting nails into concrete? Imagine if the nail were blunt. It's the same thing with a dull knife. You end up pushing, rather than dividing.

Interestingly, speed facilitates cutting or penetrating anything. The question to us laymen, is why? Is it the so-called kinetic energy?

Or, is there something more fundamental at work? I doubt that any of you have witnessed what I'm about to tell you. I have noticed numerous times, fine copper wires driven into solid, hard rubber tires on lawnmowers. These fine wires came off of electrical cables which were chopped up by the lawnmower blades. I have tried to pull the wires out of the tires, only to have the wire break flush with the rubber. I have also tried to insert the leftover piece back into the tire. There is no way that soft wire can be pushed into that hard rubber. I can envision how the wire was propelled by the blade at tremendous speed. Then it struck the tire. Replicating space delivers a push to each atom of the wire, equivalent to the same energy that was imparted by the blade when it struck the wire. As the rubber material tries to accelerate the wire to a stop, the force of gravity pushing the wire drives it deep into the hard rubber tire. But to untrained minds such as mine, we wonder the following: does speed allow this occurrence? Does speed aid this thin wire to find the empty space in atoms? Is this an intuitable thought? I must say yes. Is it true? I really don't know. This reminds me of the history of aerial dog fights, dating back to World War 1. Early biplanes could not mount the guns directly in front of the pilot, because that is where the propeller was placed. If my memory serves me, a pilot put a gun right in front of him so he could take better aim. He fitted metal wedges to the propeller to keep the bullets from cutting off the blades. After some success, not surprisingly he developed engine trouble and came down behind enemy lines. The Germans saw his idea but went one better. A mechanism was devised to time the firing of the bullets when the prop blades were not in the line of fire. That was a complete success. Afterwards, the pilot could more accurately aim at his target. When we apply this idea to cutting or penetrating, if we shoot a projectile at great speed through matter, then it is less likely to encounter the solid parts of the atoms. Interesting.

The preceding paragraph brings to light a thought that is prevalent in unlearned minds like mine. If matter is so empty, then why does it seem so solid? We are told that matter is not solid. It seems solid, because of the nuclear force. But it makes more sense to the lay person that matter seems solid because it may not be solid in the atomic realm, but it is solid for us in linear time. If a particle seems to be in every place at once, then what about a colony of particles? To a layman, it makes sense that matter is a solid, because electrons don't really orbit. They pop in and out around the nucleus so fast that, for us, it makes a solid surface in linear time. Unlike the propeller example, there is no real movement, and so, no travel or shifting is felt when making contact with it. If it was like the movement of a propeller, where the matter and your body are made of the same thing, then instead of sensing the feel of a solid, both you and the object would blend. Both are 99 percent empty and are moving at the same rate. It would be like two propellers facing each other, rotating at the same speed and direction. If brought into contact, they would not strike each other, since they are standing still, in relation to each other. Here is an example. Can a man stand barefoot on water? Yes, I have seen it done. A boat can pull a skier barefoot on water. Most of us have felt water as a solid, when we belly flopped on a failed dive. Matter, then, is a manifestation of energy in the form of particles in their wave function. The manifestation of the wave function in particles creates the illusion of solid matter.

It's not hard to imagine the next question. What happens, in our cat conundrum, if I open the box and find the cat alive? I know that, if there is another box entangled with this one, then it has a dead cat. How about if I kill the live cat? Mustn't the other cat come to life? Of course not. If you were to kill the cat, then you have taken an action in the matter. By adding energy to the system, you broke entanglement. The situation arose, because, when you have two particles split from one, they must be equal and opposite. If one spins up, the other spins down. No, particles don't spin. And up or down has no meaning in this realm. Please search the internet for the 'Gerlach experiment'. If you are unfamiliar with particle spin, there is no real need to fully understand the concept. Suffice it to say, that they are equal opposites. By adding to the system, the conservation of energy is no longer in force. Equally important is that bringing the cat to life would be reversing time. If we brought the other cat to life, then we would reverse The Arrow Of Time. Someone just got it. "You can't reverse The Arrow Of Time, because as soon as you reverse the arrow, there is no time".

Another issue is that the cats are entangled, but far away from each other. How can the one know it must be opposite to the other, upon being observed? I believe that they are not far away from each other, as seen from their point of reference. They are in a 'time with no time'. To us, there has been a movement of time, but to the two cats (or particles), no time has elapsed since they became entangled. When you open the box, in present time, one will be dead, and one is alive. Now, that satisfies entanglement, and the information problem. But what about the light speed barrier, and the location problem. How can the other cat (or particle) materialize far away, seemingly breaking the light speed barrier? The cat never breaks the light speed barrier. The cat travels far away in the blink of our eye, but in a 'time with no time' from its frame of reference. Is there a distance limit, to where the second cat can materialize? There is no limit. We waited within linear time, to open our box with the cat. Meanwhile, the cats in both boxes were free of time. For them, all of linear time went by, and no linear time went by. In other words, our split second is the cat's eternity. For a temporally short-lived being, eternity is not an easily conceived concept. It is difficult to imagine that our split-second could be as long as eternity for something else. Harder yet, is to conceive that our entire life may amount to less than a split second, for something with a different frame of reference. Think of how many things we do in our lives, how many paces we walk, how many places we see, how many times we blink, how many times we breathe. Yet, to the cat or the particle, everything happened in no time. In other words, if time is standing still for the cat, then all of the places to which the cat could have traveled, were so travelled. All the possible states he could have been in, he has been in. He also never left and is entangled, yet he left an infinite number of times. If it is possible for the cat to travel to the top of Mount Everest, we could go and find him there. It is not that your observation created reality, per se, it's that you brought the cat into your time. Once he is observed, he can be no place else, because he is now in linear time. The bottom line is that at any given time (our time, of course), the cat is everywhere he can possibly be.

Much of what you read in this chapter would be equally at home here, as it would in the chapter on time. Perhaps nothing has caused more mental conundrums for me than trying to make sense of time. I think some of you have already realized that my position on 'time with no time' seems to be flawed. I will explain for those who I have been able to convince, by keeping them in the dark. Logically, in a place with no time, things should not happen. As you travel faster, your clock is slower in comparison to the clock at your starting point. If going really fast, as seen from your starting point, you would seem frozen in time. But this is not what I claim happens with the particle/wave paradox. I claim that, at the speed of light, you do all that can be done simultaneously. This, as seen from a slow frame of reference. Logically, if you can see someone in this 'time with no time', you should see them frozen in time. This last sentence has the answer to our conundrum. I wrote "if you could see them". That's just it. You cannot see them. If you force the issue, and see them, then you must force them into your time. This immediately negates your ability to see what the thing can do, in a time where there is no time. Let me give you an example. All of us have seen propeller-driven airplanes, at least in movies. Let's take a comic break. Do you know the purpose of a propeller on a plane? No, most of you were wrong. The purpose of a propeller is not to propel a plane through the air. The real purpose of a propeller is to keep the pilot cool. You can ask anyone who has been in a plane where the propeller stopped. In every case the pilot starts sweating. Hope you enjoyed that.

Spinning propellers, because of their high speed, appear to us as a disk. In other words, it seems that a two or four bladed prop turns into a solid disk. Why, because at high speeds, we, from our slow frame of reference, can't see it at any given point in time. But wait, there is a way to see it at whichever point you care to see it. The propeller is only capable of rotating in a circle. We can't go look for it, at the tail of the plane. It's just not within its capacity to be there (in a stationary plane of course). We can be sure that it will be within its circular travel area. But where? Let's deal with a two bladed prop. Let's label one blade A and the other B. We already know that we can only be 50 % correct, as to which blade we choose to observe. So how can we see a blade with the naked eye? Simple. We make a device to slide two blocks of wood, on opposite sides, in the path of the prop. We cover one side, to see only one prop blade. At the appointed time, from our frame of reference, we move the blocks into position. They are spring loaded to move fast enough to get in the way of the prop. Wham, a loud collision is heard. Right before us, is blade A. Don't get ahead of me now. Follow my analysis. Can you still see the prop in everyplace at once, within the circle? Of course not. You have stopped it, and in so doing, brought it within your spatial time zone, governed by your speed, (or lack of it). Now it's time to go where some of you were headed, earlier. We can only see one blade: blade A. Do we know with certainty which blade is covered, and out of our sight? Of course, if we have A in sight, then B is the one shielded from our view. Here is where this example ties in to the universe, beautifully. If blade A is down, where is blade B? You've got it. If A is down, B is up. If A is to the right, then where is B? That's right. B is left. At what point does A become B? That's right. At the center of the shaft. This corresponds to the point in space from where time emerges. This is the division of the duality of time. This makes both sides of the blade, equal opposites. In this example, the blade alternates on one side from A to B, so what will we see if we do the test 100 times? We will see the A blade about 50 times and the B blade about 50 times.

But wait. There is more. Where can we find the blade? Wherever we look for it. The blade will emerge wherever we look for it, by sticking the block of wood in its path. At the same time, the blade is no longer seen everywhere at once. No longer rotating, the blades now reside in our visible time. Does this mean that there are alternate realities where the blades reside, when they are not in one place within our time frame? Don't be ridiculous. As with a particle, you can mathematically calculate the probability of finding the blade at a particular place in its ark of travel. No, I will not do the math but I will walk you through it, logically.

Let's start at the tip of a sixty-inch, two bladed prop, with 6 inch blade width. The rpm is at 3000. What is the probability of seeing the blade, at any given second along its arc of travel? We can divide the total circumference into seconds, factoring blade width and rpm. But there is no need for that. Just run your mind's eye from the tip of the blade to the center of the shaft. Can't you see how probability improves toward the center? The closer you get to the center, the more it is probable that you will find the blade in any given fraction of a second. What happens at three inches from the center? That's right. If the blade is 6 inches wide, then, at 3 inches from center it is present 100 percent of the time. We see the blade everywhere along its circular path, but it is actually in only one place, at any given time. Just as the blade is in one place at a given moment, so are particles. There is no wave function problem. There is only an observational problem.

How many of you realized there is a problem with the analogy of the propeller above? That would be most of you. I keep forgetting how sharp you guys are. Yes indeed, the increase in the chances of finding the prop closer to the center is not influenced by probability. The main factor influencing the probability is prop width. The real interesting question is why? Yes, I'm waiting for an answer... Just as I thought, you guys are as sharp as tacks. Indeed, the prop is not a replacement for a particle. Particles prefer to move in a straight line, as does everything else in the universe. A prop rotates in a circle. This is abnormal. That's why it is subjected to a gravity response, known up to the writing of this book as centrifugal force. Agreed, the prop analogy is not 100 percent accurate, but it does have its uses. Allow me to use something we are all familiar with to bring the point home. You remember an ice skater spinning on the ice? Do you remember what happens as he brings his arms closer to his body? Yes, he picks up speed. If he were to keep his fists closed and equal distance to his body, we would get a clear picture. Do you see that the closer he brings his hands in, the faster he spins? As he spins faster his fists create a circle. Do you see how the chances of finding his fist at any given second in one place of the circle improves as his circle gets tighter, and he picks up speed? Do you think this is just a coincidence? Of course, not. The skater must pick up speed to conserve the time zone that the moving arms have achieved. In the case of the skater, he loses speed due to friction on the ice and air resistance. But if in space and zero gravity, then this change in rotation can be done indefinitely because there are no friction losses.

I think we can glean more from this propeller analogy. Until now, we have been dealing with a stationary airplane. What happens if we put this plane in motion? And, while in motion, where can we find its propeller? Can we find it on the tail? How about the fuselage? Better yet, the wings? Yes, indeed, now the picture is complete. What emerges is a wave of probability. You see, as the plane stands still, no matter the speed of the prop, it can only be found within its arc of travel. But when the plane is in motion, other locations become possible. For instance, a wing. An airplane in motion has the ability to turn or bank. If you look for the prop on the left wing, while the plane is banking right, can you find it? Isn't it more probable that you will find it on the wing, but closer to the fuselage? Would it be less likely found in the direction of the wing tip? How about the tail? As the plane moves forward, is the prop not where the tail was, only a second ago? From the frame of reference of a stationary observer, the prop can be found at the tail. The closer to the tail, the less probable. But because the plane moves so fast, it is probable. You see, the prop is not only rotating, but it's also moving. Could we find the prop far away from the plane itself? Well, it's rare but props have been known to come off of their engines. So yes, we could find it far away, or even within the fuselage, on rare occasions. This analogy only goes so far. Our prop driven plane is fast and serves to give us a taste of the probability wave. But as fast as our plane moves, its speed is nothing, compared to the speed of light. Each of the above scenarios would be possible, if the airplane was traveling at the speed of light, and if we observed it in linear time.

Now put on your best thinking cap. How does our propeller illustration apply to relativity? Here it goes. Imagine that you were an ant, at the tip of a propeller blade. And, that there was another ant on the same propeller blade, one inch from the center of the blade. Let's say the blade was 120 inches long. Each time you, the ant at the outer tip, complete one rotation of the propeller, the ant who is standing one inch away from the center, has travelled only 1/60th of the length of the outer circumference scribed by the propeller tip. So, if turns are equated to time, then the ant at the center will age 60 times slower than the one at the tip. Each ant's clock would still have the same 60 seconds in an hour. But their time, in comparison to each other, cannot be the same. Why? Because, if they both travelled the same distance in the same amount of time, then they could not be on the same solid straight propeller. If the ants shared one clock, it could not be one universe. They both share the same existence or reality. That is, they can look down the blade and see each other. But they cannot be in the same time. Why? Because space replicates for both, at the same time. This makes their clocks uniform, from their point of reference, but relative across distance or speed. If you understood this paragraph, then you now know more than Einstein knew. He knew relativity. After all, he discovered it. But from his writings, we can't say that he knew what caused it. Relativity is a result of replicating spacetime, the ever-growing reticulation that makes the universe possible. The luminiferous ether of old, the construct, the venue, the backdrop, the locus, the medium, the plexus or matrix, is an energy fabric.

There is one last thing we can glean from our propeller analogy. What happens when the ant closest to the center, steps backwards, across the center of the shaft? That's right. She will be traveling backwards. If we equate turns to time, then she is going back in time. You see, the center is equal to a 'time with no time', that is, light speed. The other side is faster than time, which should equal reversing time. I contend that time is not circular, but linear. So, what happens in the real world, is that the ant near the center is rotated around, and is found facing in the direction of travel, close to the center, which represents the beginning of light speed. Now, can both ants still see each other? No. Between them is the shaft that holds the propeller, or in terms of light speed, the 'time with no time', which would render visibility impossible. It's like the sound barrier, except this is sight. With sight, anything travelling at light speed cannot be seen, by anything traveling at sub-light speed. These two ants were sharing the same spacetime. Suddenly, one went faster than light. This is not the same as if they remained on the same side of the blade, and the blade had stretched. Space stretches enough, at great distances, to make two objects recede (from each other) at greater than light speed. Notice that these ants were in visible range, until one went faster than light, within the same locality or time.

I can sense that some of you are not satisfied with the previous paragraphs. You don't have a clear understanding of 'time with no time'. Let me ask you, what is the furthest day from Sunday? Saturday, right? No, the furthest day away from Sunday is Thursday (12:00am). Why, because Sunday is preceded by Saturday. This is the case, because the days of the week repeat themselves. It's like the prop on the plane. Is time circular? Time is a straight arrow, time never repeats. Time emerges from a time where there is no time. If you think for a moment about the propeller, it is easy to see this time paradox. If you are a microbe at the very center of the shaft, are you moving as it spins? Very little, if any. This is the division between the duality of spacetime. Spacetime travels from every point in every direction. The point of emergence has no time. What follows the point of emergence is not the shortest time zone, but the longest. That center point is a real place, not governed by our linear time. This is from where reality emerges. This is why everything that can happen, does happen, simultaneously, as seen in linear time. This is a place where time does not correspond to our linear existence. It is more a speed, than a place. Spacetime is being grown, in each minuscule point in space. It is an exact replica of the beginning. There is irrefutable proof of this in cosmology, once you understand it. Every point in the universe is the center of an observable sphere. This is not merely the result of being able to see in every direction, as the Earth spins. It is also not the result of light speed. If it were merely light speed, we would not see back to the early universe, in every direction.

Let me bring this home, with the double slit experiment. For those not familiar, please do a search for "double slit experiment". When the photon, or particle, is sent through the double slits, it is sent in a 'time with no time'. To an observer in linear time, we see the particle in a wave. But why? Because we are watching the big picture. We are observing a single particle in motion, from linear time. Being in a 'time with no time', the particle seems to be moving in a wave: a wave of probability. Which means that you could find it anywhere it could possibly be, governed by how probable it is, that it could be there. This means, for instance, that in the double slit experiment, you would never look for the particle to land on the back side of the collection screen.

Yes, I heard your objection, you are still not convinced that the photon travels in no-time. "If it moves through space, then how can it do so using no-time". Your point is rooted in sound linear-time logic. But, you forgot one very important detail. Nothing travels through space. Everything travels with space. Light, and other particles flow with space. From their point of reference, they are not moving. They see no time. This makes them ageless, unless they are brought into linear time.

The wave seen in particles is the result of viewing all of its travel, simultaneously. When we add a detector before the slits, we see only a single particle cross one slit. It's as if the universe tells the particle, "the gig is up, they're onto us, drop the wave, be a particle". "Easy", I heard a reader say. "It is before the slit, so the observation caused the collapse of the wave". Not so fast. We get the same result when we put the detector on the other side. How can the particle know beforehand how to behave? I believe this is an anomaly caused by our shortcomings. Uncertainty in quantum mechanics comes not from the answer being uncertain. More likely, I think it is due to our observational limits. Limitations in our test instruments, and our limits of knowledge, produce uncertainty by simply not asking the right questions. It's a case of not seeing the whole picture or not being able to measure 'cause and effect' properly. We, in linear time, experience cause before effect. In a 'time with no time', particles correct their action, in what seems to us to be in the future. This makes us think that the reaction precedes the action. But it's like looking at a blurry picture. The particles are in a 'time with no time'. This change is correct within their frame of reference. To us, it looks as if the correction came before the problem, out of chronological order.

Eureka, eureka, eureka. I see that some of you have learned well what I have been trying to teach. No matter how, when or where you observe the particle, you, in linear time, can only see one particle. You could say that we have narrowed our observation, from a wave, of all possibilities in eternity, to the one particle in linear time. What's that I heard? A reader just asked, "But wait, all the observers present no longer see the wave, and see only a single particle, right?" That's right. One or many observers, it matters not. Welcome to relativity at its maximum expression. For me, the greatest mystery about the wave and particle problem, is not that we can force a wave to become a particle, but that we can glean that a particle is acting as a wave. Do not dismiss this huge evidence of relativity. This is the best example I can think of, that proves there always was, there always is and there will always be, a 'time with no time'.

CHAPTER 19

Concepts Almost Beyond Imagination

T HIS CHAPTER COVERS some speculations that I don't believe, and things that aren't what they seem, but it is fun to think about them. In the previous chapters, I have placed concepts before you, which are foreign to you. You must know that those concepts are a certainty to me. All my life, I could not understand the universe. Things like relativity, speed of light and the explanation of gravity made absolutely no sense. We are all wired differently. I, myself, think in what seems to me, a time-line type of thought. I take the present, and imagine whatever process I see, until the end of time. At the very least, to the logical conclusion of said process. Then I start in my mind's eye from the present and think back to see where that process began.

Here is a natural progression of replicating space. Does light really mark the barrier of travel or merely the travel of information? Could we, if we developed the technology, go past the speed of light?

It may seem ludicrous to you. But the reality is, that there are many unknowns. You already saw in the previous chapter how clueless we are about certain things. I think nothing can exist that does not make sense. If you find something that is proven true, yet makes no sense, then everyone is ignorant. All that is true is logical, and understandable. Just because no one in the world can understand, we cannot say it is not understandable. It just means we have not reached that level of technology needed to understand such complexity. Perhaps the right person who has the capacity to understand, is not aware of the conundrum's existence. The problem can be in physics, and the only person with the right mental pathways to understand it, could be a janitor or perhaps a farmer.

I would like to explore with you the age of the universe and its effects on vantage points. It is reasonable and well-accepted that from every vantage point, you would see in a circle. The circle, of course, is caused by the speed of light. Light, traveling at the speed of light, will travel back to you from an equal distance from every direction. Up to now it's easy going. Now, let's start throwing monkey wrenches into the works. Science claims that this is the case, because light travels back to meet us at a perceived center. There is a huge problem with this. It is true that in a universe of great size we only see as far as light can travel back to us. Here comes a monkey wrench. Why don't we merely see back to a uniform universe? Why do we see back to the beginning, in every direction? We know we are looking into the beginning. The galaxies we see at the end of our view, in every direction, are smaller and younger. Unless the Earth is smack dab in the middle of the universe, we should not see the beginning in every directions. By the way, not only would we have to be in the middle of space but of time, too. The Earth would have had to materialize in the middle of space at the middle of time.

We have touched on how the universe grows, and how we view that growth. The conclusion of the other chapters is that the universe grows from every point in space. It grows through replication, and grows at light speed at the Edge. Well, some of you may not accept the actual end of Chapter 14. You might also reject the other alternative endings. The problem we are trying to solve is the following. If the universe grows at its edge, along the Rim of Creation, then how is it that we see the edge as the first to appear, chronologically? As the growth at the edge materializes, it should assume the place of the early universe. This would constantly change as it grows outward. Yet, what we see is the very beginning in every direction. Here are three more (although far-out) alternatives, to solve this conundrum. We can imagine that my supposition of how it grows at the edge is correct. Please understand that what we see when looking out into space, is indeed the past. That past is just a reflection of what has already happened. But that reflection is accurate to the last detail of how things did happen. So, let's endeavor to explain what we see. It is easy to understand that the reflection grows with spacetime between us and the edge. After all, this is just a reflection. But how can the edge be unchanged through time if there is continual growth?

Firstly, we could explain the steady unchanging view through quantum tunneling. The edge is creating the growth and that growth quantum tunnels through spacetime, to take its rightful place chronologically, within the sphere that makes up the universe.

A second choice would be one of aging. The edge could maintain its young appearance, since all that is made at that edge is indeed younger. Then, as time progresses, it takes its chronological place in the sphere of the universe. Of course, as it ages, all of the galaxies evolve through time. The stars within these young galaxies are born and die, all the while picking up the appropriate materials appropriate to their age.

The third option is the weirdest of all. All of the universe exists in a 'time with no time'. Therefore, it exists in its entirety. Time only reveals to us that portion, which its age allows us to experience, in linear time. I will leave it at these three. But you are qualified, at this point, in the book, to come up with other choices. Why don't you use the margins on this, and the following pages, to list your own ideas? It will be a great addition for posterity.

What would a man see if he was at the edge of the universe, right now? Yes, at the Rim of Creation. I have already made the case that, if the universe started from a single speck, and is expanding, then it is finite, and if it's finite, then there is an edge. The alternative would be that an infinite universe started in infinity everywhere at once. This would mean that the younger universe that we see as we look out, backward in time, was never real. All of the universe would have to share the same age. The other problem we have already discussed is, how can an infinite universe expand? Where can it expand to, that it's not already there? Most are convinced that it started from a very small place. If it started from a center finite place and expanded, then it can't be infinite. I realize that it is believed that it started from a singularity. This entity is infinitely small and infinitely dense. So, you could say it started infinite, so it must be infinite. You, of course, would be wrong. The beginning would have seen that singularity give way to inflation, or expansion. Once that happened, it became finite. It had a measurable size. If we can measure something, it is no longer infinite. If something is, or becomes finite, then it could never again become infinite. Expansion and relativity demand a finite universe. To those of you who are not yet convinced, let's agree to disagree. For the purpose of this excursion into lunacy, imagine that the universe is finite. If finite, it has an edge. If we are at that edge, what would we see? We are in a real pickle, are we not? Do you still see in a circle? Or do you only see half a circle? Here's a wild thought. How old is that space you occupy? Since it was just made a short time ago, isn't it new? But if it's new, then how can it be part of a universe that is billions of years old? This would mean that each location within the universe has its own age. If this were the case, that each bit of space has its own age, then it makes sense that we see in a circle, in every direction we look. The circle seen at the edge of space, would be very small, since you are close to the beginning of the universe.

We can imagine that only matter has an age. The universe is all the same age. What would be the implications of a universe with a set age, but in which matter has a variable age? Within that type of universe, we would always see in the same circle, no matter our location within it. In other words, you could only exist within the center. The edges would be visible, but only as light. It would be like Schrodinger's cat, on a grand scale. In this case, reality would only materialize if we were present.

Now get ready for an escalation of this lunacy. Are you ready? Here it goes. We cannot travel to a different time from our own, except at faster than light speed. The edge of the universe is very far away in space, but it is also very far away in the future. "wait a minute." I heard someone say, "You have said, as we look out, it's the past." Yes, indeed, as you look out, you see the past, but as you travel, it is actually the past of your future. We are, indeed, traveling into an area that is younger than where we came from, but the time it took us to get there, made it older than the place from where we started. If we were to travel at greater than light speed, then it should take us back to the past. At any speed below light speed, a lot of time would elapse as we traveled to the edge of the universe. The universe, expanding before us, would deny us ever making headway. The only way to travel to the edge, then, would be at faster than light speed. If we travelled at many times the speed of light, then we would eventually get there. But when we finally get there, would we not be very far in the past? Yes, indeed. We would be very far in the past. Our vantage point would again be a circle. This circle would be very small, covering only the age of the universe at that time in the past. Therefore, we only have access to the edge of the universe, if we go into the past. The outer edge is still creating and expanding faster than light. This is the exact description of the beginning. The edge of the universe is, therefore, the beginning.

It would seem that we are done with this Edge of the universe, and time travel business. After all, we have arrived back at the beginning.

But wait, there is more! If we have arrived at the beginning, then what has happened to where we came from? Here, we have a few choices. If we say that our old past exists, then we are faced with multiverses or multiple realities. If, on the other hand, we say that the past does not exist yet, then that presents a whole new set of problems. If that past has not existed, then how can you remember something, which has not existed? If it exists, then how can it be, that you, a former member of it, are no longer there, when clearly, you were there before. If you were not there before, you could not have traveled into the past. Mind you, I do not think it is possible to travel into the past. But if it's possible, I only see one possibility. You get on your ship and travel many times faster than light. As you travel you are traveling back in time. As you travel back in time, the past becomes your present, and the future is erased. The circular vantage point becomes smaller in every direction. Question. Do we have to travel in a specific direction? No, not at all. Remember, the past is seen in every direction, in a circle around you. This is another feature of the duality of spacetime. Just as a clock is affected by your speed, the reality is also affected. You travel further and further into the past, until you reach the edge, where the first galaxies are seen. At that point, the universe is young and small. You still see in a circle, only as far as light can travel in that time frame of universal existence. I truly hope I did not lose you. I got lost there, myself, a few times.

Let's approach time travel, with replicating space as the only reality in the universe. In other words, let's ignore all of the other possibilities. Let's get into our imaginary spaceship. With its star drive, we are capable of breaking the light barrier thousands of times over. A while ago, I came across an imaginary friend who I had not seen in several decades. When he asked me how well I had done in business, I told him I was on my fourth million dollars. He said "Wow, how does it feel to have that much money?" I told him I had no idea. The first three were too hard to amass. So, I quit on those, and started trying to amass the fourth million. Why the joke? To get you in the mindset to understand the following: Each multiple of the speed of light is a barrier. But once you break through it, I believe that replicating space seems to favor that you are again facing no barrier until you approach the next multiple of the speed of light. In other words, a barrier is only encountered when a multiple of 186,000 miles a second is reached. If we were talking about the sound barrier, within the atmosphere, it would only happen once. A missile capable of Mach 3 only experiences one barrier. After Mach 1 it has already left sound behind so it will not create another sound boom at Mach 2 or 3. But when dealing with multiples of the speed of light, I think you enter a new realm each time you break through the next light barrier. The barriers in front and behind you, would limit your view to that which is between those two points.

Interesting question: how far is one light barrier from the next? Just like the sound barrier, it depends on the rate of acceleration of the craft. Here's an interesting wild thought. When we reach the light barrier, we are facing all of spacetime, flowing in one direction against us. Would this not dissolve matter? How can our existence continue, if we are being bombarded by spacetime at light speed? Would time not cease to exist for us? As soon as we cross the barrier, wouldn't we be at a time when we did not exist? If I'm right, and the fastest time in the universe is just past each multiple of light speed, then what happens to sight? At light speed there is no time, so your reflection can't be seen by a sub-light observer. But once beyond light speed, you are, again, in the fastest time zone. There is a reflection coming from you. But who can see it? As weird as it sounds, only those who are traveling close to your same speed. You are ruled by time, but your speed prevents you from reflecting enough photons to be seen by someone traveling at sub-light speed. We are born, live, and die within the confines of light speed. If you break the light barrier, you would eventually reach a time where information of your existence does not exist. If there is no news of your existence, and you are not visible, do you exist? If you exist, are you in another dimension? It is likely that, at the light speed barrier, we cease to exist. What would cause our dematerialization? Can we exist in a time before the existence of our own matter? We can argue that the barrier is not one of light, space, and matter, but of time. It's all very interesting, but I believe we are forever ruled by linear time.

Here's a wild thought. Is space the only thing that is growing? Or does everything in the universe grow over time? Remember this, we judge distances in feet or in meters. Both are measurements derived from physical entities. The foot was originally based on the human body, while the meter was based on Earth's measurements. Nowadays, the meter is based on light speed. And the foot is now based on the meter. But the newer measurement for the meter, based on light speed, is governed by time. What is speed, if not distance traveled per unit of time? If everything is growing, then can time remain the same? No, I don't believe that time is immutable throughout time. How would we know whether measurements had changed over time, had there been no immutable standard? Both the Earth and a man's foot, or any other standard we used, could have grown proportionally. The same thing can be said of our weight measurements. Weight measurements are based on physical things within our experiences. Whether everything has grown proportionally and constantly, we will never be the wiser. If found to exist, we could call this marvel spatial- imperceptibility. In my mind, there is only one way to tell if we are indeed facing this phenomenon. This would be a time jump. Imagine if we could jump 1,000 years into the future, where humans are 100 feet tall. Remember this is Chapter 19. I don't believe matter grows along with spacetime. The best argument against this growth is the fact that a larger Earth would have a greater gravity. This, along with a man's greater height, would eventually render our cardiovascular system inadequate. It would have put an end to mankind.

Black holes. Could they be a rupture in the space time continuum? Where would the energy, flowing in the form of matter and spacetime, flow to? Could it create a wormhole? Just what is a black hole? A black hole is a super low-pressure area within spacetime. This entity supports the concept of replicating space, like nothing else in the universe. Picture the nozzle on your vacuum cleaner. Can you see the air rushing into the nozzle? Now picture a black hole. You can picture spacetime flowing into a black hole, pushing everything with it. Even light cannot outrun its inward flow. Here's an odd question. Is it flow, or is it the absence of time which is holding back the light? If we could stand in a black hole, and shine a flashlight straight out, what would happen? At the very least, time would stand still after the event horizon. It might even run backward. If it was standing still, then light would never move out of the flashlight. How about if time is going backward? Well, if it is really moving backward, it would immediately reverse your course and spit you back out. But wait, there is more. As soon as you cleared the event horizon, time would again flow forward. You would be pulled in again, and stay in this loop, forever. Then again, you might be in this loop only long enough to be shredded into basic energy.

I don't believe that there is no time, or a reversal of time, anywhere within created space. I cannot accept that there is no time (in its true sense), or space beyond the event horizon. If you have no space or no time, then where and when is it located? Once spacetime is created, that region will never again revert to nothingness. The notion of a wormhole is nonsense to me. Matter does not survive in its form when entering a black hole. If you revert matter back to its basic component, energy is what you end up with. There is no information left. Therefore, past the event horizon everything seems to be lost, except for energy. The conditions past the event horizon, although extreme, are still governed by the laws of nature. Although laws cannot be broken, they can be bent. You must wonder how things actually function. I think that as we learn more about the universe, we will be able to understand the possibilities within this wondrous phenomenon. But like a woman, to us men, they will always remain deliciously mysterious and a thing of awe.

We have discussed the expansion rate, at length. You may remember that I believe the universe is slowing down, but that it will never stop expanding. This chapter covers the 'what if'. So, what if the universe did come to a standstill. What if it stopped its expansion? What would happen within it? What would happen at the outer edge? I think we would not notice any difference within the universe. The spatial pressure would increase, and time would slow. To the observer within the physical world, everything would seem to remain normal. The real change would happen at the edge of the universe. I have speculated earlier that antimatter is expelled out of the universe during the expansion. If this is true, and if expansion stops, then antimatter is left to invade the universe. That would cause an explosive destruction of the universe, not just its matter content. Even space, itself, would start exploding. I imagine the speed of its progression would be light speed. Then this would be a fourth possible end to the universe. You could say it would end with fire. We could call this end "The Great Burn Off". If antimatter does not bring the universe to an end, then the stopping of expansion would create a rim of concentrated matter. There would be an increase in gravity within this region. We would see galaxies racing toward this rim of concentrated matter. The formation of stars would increase. Larger and larger stars would form, creating, upon their death, larger and larger black holes. These black holes would eventually come together to form a rim of huge gravitational force. This would force all of the outer matter comprising the Rim of Creation, to collapse inward. The contents of the universe would then be pulled to the Rim. When all of the matter in the universe feeds the Rim, and the Rim is composed of black holes, then what? Unmanageable gravitational forces would cause the entire universe to collapse into itself. That would be a really big crunch. It would also give us a really bad hair day.

Let's explore reality. What is real and what is not and where is the line? We live in a universe of energy. What we see as solid is actually 99% empty. Our greatest test of reality is sight, yet what we see is always the past. We see our own Sun eight minutes in the past. It takes eight minutes for its light to reach us. This, of course, is our nearest star. We could say it's touching us as far as cosmic distances are concerned. At 12:00 noon tomorrow, a time traveling black hole could swallow it, and we would not know it until 12:08. Both the loss of the Sun and the gravitational effects of the loss of the Sun would reach us at the same time. This is because light and gravity share the same speed. For those who say that seeing is believing, you could not utter a more foolish statement. Since we see the past, you can never be sure if what you see is still in existence. Factor in our brains creating reality by filling in the blanks, and the delusion is complete. We see only a portion of any given image. Then, using what it has already seen in the past, our brain draws out the rest of the picture. This is how we are easily fooled by movie makers. You can film a Western in a town, using nothing but building facades. On film, from the front, a facade is indistinguishable from the real thing. A magician gives you a glimpse of what he is doing, from a point of view where you get the impression of the illusion. Of course, what they show you is what will lead you to believe their illusion. The magician does not trick you. You are tricked by a conspiracy between your own eyes and your mind. We live in the past, interpreting that which we see. This leads to a very troubling question. If we don't see reality as it happens, then who determines reality? If the uncertainty principle holds true in the quantum realm, does it not apply to the larger picture? Is not everything in the universe made of the same thing, namely energy? If it's all made of the same stuff, then it shares the same fate. Who, then, makes reality? Answer to follow in the next chapter.

I would like to give a certain few of you my most heartfelt apology. These few are the string theorists. I have mostly ignored String theory. I must confess my ignorance and bias against string theory. I made a conscious effort to stay away from this topic because I unequivocally reject the multiverse. But, late in this book, only days away from going to print, something changed. A reader of my previous book asked if I was familiar with string theory. I told him I did not pay much attention to it, because I don't consider it even remotely possible that there could be other universes. He said Don't get hung up on just one facet of the theory. So, I dipped my toe into string theory. To my amazement, I realized that the so-called strings are what I have called God's Fountain, the most basic building block of everything in the universe. I truly regret that I ignored this theory. It looks as if String Theory and My Replicating Spacetime Theory have many things in common. I will immerse myself in string theory. If these, my first two books, become a trilogy, then String Theory (according to Replicating Spacetime Theory) will probably be prominent in the third book.

CHAPTER 20

Spiritual Implications

IT IS MY hope that everyone who began reading this book has made it to this chapter. I truly hope that the universe has come alive before you, in its pages. Most important is not to know the universe, but to know He Who created it (1). I have purposely refrained from making Bible references through the first 19 chapters. My purpose was not to mislead anyone, but to allow the reader, regardless of his level of spirituality, to continue reading. Believe me, it has not been an easy task. I believe that the universe can only be truly understood, if you know it's Creator (2). There is, however, a method to my madness. Our brains are said to best remember the beginning, the middle, and the end of anything we read. This is why I gave credit to my God, in the beginning. I wooed you through the book, with His creation, and now I will try my best to reveal who He is (3).

First, I would like to say why, from the many gods which humanity has imagined, I believe only the God of the Bible is real

(4). Humanity, wherever it is found on Earth, has a god. That, in itself, is proof that a true God must exist. How can entire empires, or small remote villages, each have the same ingrained thought? We have yet to find a people group who are atheist in their common belief. Mind you, we live in the age of worldwide communication, and most of the world is aware of the God of the Bible. But centuries ago, wherever explorers went, they found new gods. Here is a common question I'm asked, whenever I debate an atheist. Which god do you believe in, and what makes you so sure He is the right one? Let's answer this question first.

I was 7 years old, and playing in the dirt, putting together a little toy crane, made from a spool of copper wire from a starter solenoid and a few sticks. We were at my paternal grandfather's farm, in my birth country of Cuba. I was making this little toy, because in their Machiavellian wisdom, the socialist/communist government deemed toys to be optional. A child was given the right, by the government, to buy only three toys a year. The toys were categorized as follows: Toy 1 is termed 'Basic': for example, a little windup toy car. Yes, perhaps you could get a bicycle, but they only sent one to our country store, and it was always taken by the first in line. A mom or dad or perhaps an uncle of the lucky child would camp out for months in the line (la cola) for the upcoming toy sale. Toy 2 was termed non-basic: for example, a bag with a few marbles. Toy 3 was termed 'Directed': for example, a deck of cards or perhaps a few stickers. These toys were not available at Christmas, since the system was atheistic, and Christmas was outlawed. The toys were distributed around June. I can't remember the date I built my toy, but I imagine it was around August. As an active youngster, a couple of months of use was all I could get from the government-sold toys. Upon finishing my little crane and moving around my first load (a few twigs), I had an epiphany. Looking around in a circle at the trees, birds and farm animals, I said to myself, I built this toy, but who built all of that (5)?

We were blessed when, in 1971, we were able to leave the country in exile, for the USA. When arriving in our new country, for reasons explained under "the proximity paradox" in my first book, we searched out our own kind. We joined a church of the Christian and Missionary Alliance, pastored by Rev. Eugenio Castaneda and his wife, Germania. There, upon hearing the Bible, what I now know as the word of the only true God (6), I asked Jesus Christ, the Messiah, into my heart and have walked with Him ever since (7). What could have convinced a young boy of 11, to trust that the God of the Bible was that Creator who revealed Himself through His creation, years before? The answer is very simple. I realized that the Bible proves itself as God's word (8). Going through school, I was taught that the universe and life, itself, was explained through a series of fortunate accidents and coincidence. But it just did not hold water. Every time I saw an accident, it was always bad. I never saw a car with a bent fender get into an accident and emerge fully restored, or as good as new. I always saw things go from good to bad, unless acted upon by intelligence. We can only understand creation from a point of view of intelligent design. If you only accept the 'physical', then you could never understand your existence. No one has any doubt that there was a beginning. If there was a beginning, then there was a time where the 'physical' did not exist. If nothing could exist, then nothing could come from it. But just like zero, multiplied by any number is zero, nothing from nothing is nothing. Then, there was the fact that the book begins at the beginning. I would expect the book given to an intelligent creation by its Creator, to start at the beginning and end 'happily ever after'. It is the way things made sense to me. Indeed, it is the way things make sense to all of us.

Think of any good movie. All movies worth watching follow the same plot. It generally starts with a time long ago, a simpler time where innocence reigned. Then evil shows up, and kills or at least symbolically kills, the existing good. Good, or protagonist dies, or at best, said protagonist forfeits his life for the sake of his loved one.

There is a period where evil seems to reign. Then, the restored or reborn protagonist reenters the scene. This time he is no longer the martyr, but the victor. He vanquishes evil, saves and gets the girl. They are seen walking away to eternity, happily ever after. Why is this the plot that best tickles our psyche? It seems to be ingrained in us. It follows the biblical theme. The story begins in the garden, in the time of innocence. The devil/evil shows up, destroys things, death enters, kills the first Adam, and evil and death seem to reign for a period. The savior, our Lord Christ, the second Adam, makes his entry, is killed and resurrects. There is a period where He goes to prepare a place. He returns, destroys evil, rescues His bride, the church, and His people, and they live happily ever after. So here it was. A book that is said to be from the Creator himself, that follows the format I would expect to see. Then there are the nuggets of scientific knowledge. Allow me to give you all that I'm familiar with, of things that are common knowledge now, which seemed gibberish just a few decades or centuries ago. The following will be a long list, with knowledge from the Bible, which preceded discoveries and events. Sorry, it will not be an enjoyable read but it is very informative. All verses quoted KJV.

Genesis 1:1. That there was a beginning is confirmed by the discovery of the echo of the Big Bang (Penzias and Wilson 1964), by the COBE data, by the WMAP mission, and by the European space agency Planck satellite.

Genesis 1:1 "In the beginning" (time) "God" (force) "created" (energy) "the heavens" (space) "and the Earth" (matter). Time, force, energy, space, matter. In 1820, Hubert Spencer gave the world these five principles, useful to study the unknown.

Genesis 1:2 science agrees, the universe began dark.

Genesis 1:2 Thermodynamics Second Law confirmed. Earth was organized to start its decay.

Genesis 1:2 There is enough water to cover the surface of the Earth. Many deep-water aquifers have been found. One of these aquifers, under the USA, has enough water to equal all of the world's oceans. In Russia, the Kola Superdeep Borehole is the deepest man-made hole on Earth, with one branch coincidently called SG3, the name to my third spaceship (if I christen a third ship). In this bore hole, at a depth of several miles, flowing water was found.

Genesis 1:2. Water is as old as the Earth. Confirmed by science in 2019 by the NASA probe Osiris Rex.

Genesis 1:3 Light preceded the stars. It is the consensus of science that the beginning of the universe was so chaotic and dense, that, initially, there was no light. After this period of darkness, light preceded the formation of stars.

Genesis 1:4. In the beginning, God separated light from darkness. Science agrees that light emerged out of the darkness.

Genesis 1:7 Initially, water vapor and clouds were at ground level, and were present when Earth was forming. God divided the waters below and above the firmament.

Genesis 1:9 Earth was a water world before God organized it. Many deep-water aquifers have since been found. One under the USA has enough water to equal all of the world's oceans. The Kola Superdeep Borehole is the deepest man-made hole on Earth, with one branch coincidently called SG3, the name to my third spaceship (if I christen a third ship). In this bore hole, at a depth of several miles, flowing water was found.

Genesis 1:11 Vegetation precedes herbivores.

Genesis 1:11-12, 21 Living things reproduce according to their own kind. Genetic sequences were mapped in the 20th century.

Genesis 1:16 Stars did not appear at the beginning. The oldest galaxy we have observed is GN-z11, which is 13.4 billion years in the past, just 400 million years after the beginning.

Genesis 1:20 Animal life exploded out of the waters, during the epoch which science calls the Cambrian explosion.

Genesis 1:24 Animal life appeared last on land, after there was vegetation.

Genesis 1:24 and 2:7 God makes animal and human life from Earth-based matter. Science concurs that all of the ingredients for our physical bodies are found on Earth.

Genesis 1:24-25 Complex animals exploded onto the scene. Science calls it the Cambrian explosion. All phyla date back to this era.

Genesis 1:26 God gives man dominion over the Earth and its creatures on the land, in the air, and in the sea. Early on, man conquers the land. The Wright brothers took flight in 1903, and we have explored even the depth of the sea.

Genesis 1:27 God created man after the animals, both male and female.

Genesis 2:21 God uses anesthesia to do surgery. Dr. Morton and surgeon John Collins Warren are credited with the first successful surgery with anesthesia on October 16, 1846.

Genesis 2:22 God uses cloning and chromosome/gene manipulation to make Eve from Adam. The first cloned mammal, Dolly the Sheep, was cloned by man on July 5 1996.

Genesis 3:18 Earth was cursed. Weeds will rule.

Genesis 7:11 Great reservoirs of water exist deep in the Earth. Many deep-water aquifers are recently found, one under the USA has enough water to equal all the world's oceans. The Russian Kola Superdeep Borehole is the deepest man-made hole on Earth, with one branch coincidently called SG3, the name to my third spaceship (if I christen a third ship). In this bore hole, at a depth of several miles, flowing water was found.

Genesis 17:12 God ordered newborns to be circumcised on the eighth day. In the 20th century modern medicine discovered that the 8th day is indeed the best day for circumcision. Due to several key factors, the 8th is the only day in a male's life in which prothrombin, a protein produced by the liver, key in blood clotting, is above 100 percent.

Exodus 10:21 "darkness which may be felt". A place where light does not travel would feel abnormal. With the advent of the theory of The Big Bang in the 20th century, science holds that in the beginning, space was so different that there was no light.

Exodus 10:23 (paraphrasing) the Egyptians were in total darkness, while the Israelites had light. Light in the absence of an incandescent source (not from the Sun nor from fire). Peter Cooper Hewitt patented the world's first mercury vapor lamp in 1901. This is the grandpa of today's fluorescent lights. In 1968, the first commercial LED lamps were commercialized in Hewlett-Packard's LED display. We can only imagine that the light mentioned in Exodus 10:23 was created by God ordering energy to emit light. In a more spiritual sense, God is light. Those who have God, have light. This light was only present in

Goshen, where the Egyptians permitted the Israelites to live. While during the same three days, the Egyptians were in complete and utter darkness. You have to love God's sense of humor. I find it hilarious that the Egyptian's chief god was Ra the sun god.

Leviticus 14:8 Quarantine. It was not until the 14th century, when this practice was recognized as beneficial. It was instituted to protect port cities from ships offloading epidemic contagion.

Leviticus 15:11 Washing of hands to prevent contamination. In 1847 a Hungarian obstetrician Ignaz Semmelweis began advising his fellow doctors to wash their hands before working with their patients. This was to stem the tide of childbirth mortality in the hospitals, which suffered a rate as high as 20% greater than at home births.

Leviticus. 17:11 The life of the flesh is in the blood. In the 20th century, medicine learned to test blood for a diagnostic report on the entire body.

Job 25:5 (written 1800 B.C.) Moon has no light of its own, Anaxagoras (500 BCE–428 BCE) was first to explain that the Moon shines through reflected sunlight.

Job 26:7 the universe is expanding, as confirmed by Hubble in 1929.

Job 26:7 That Earth is hung on nothing was visually confirmed by Soviet cosmonaut Yuri Gagarin 1961.

Job 26:8 There is a surprising amount of water in clouds. We now know that one large thunderhead can hold 2 billion pounds of water. Even a moderate cloud holds water equal to the weight of a 747 jumbo jet.

Job 28:25 Air has weight. In 1640, Evangelista Torricelli discovered that air has weight.

Job 30:5, 6 The existence of Cave man, as described, became common knowledge in the 20th century.

Job 38:33 Man is powerless against God's laws which govern creation. We have discovered many of these laws and agree they are laws.

Job 37:7 Unique fingerprints. In 1858 Englishmen Sir William Herschel started using fingerprints to deter fraud in India.

Job 38:7 Stars sing, as confirmed by Nasa Tess satellite star data (launched April 18, 2018).

Job 38:16 Hydrothermal vents were confirmed by science in 1977.

Job 38:19, 20 Light travels. The speed of light was measured in 1676 by Danish astronomer Ole Roemer.

Job 38:22 Treasures of the snow. The uniqueness of snowflakes was only discovered after the microscope was invented. Do a net search for snowflake pics. They are true treasures.

Job 38:24-30 God maintains the universe, even where man is absent. Speaking in terms of the Copenhagen interpretation, this makes God the ever-present observer.

Job 38:31 That heavenly bodies are gravitationally bound was discovered by Sir Isaac Newton in 1680.

Job 38:35 Light can carry information. Fiber optics, was discovered in 1956 by Narinder Singh Kapany, said to be the "Father of Fiber Optics".

Job 40:15-19 Who killed the dinosaurs?

Psalm 8:8 The oceans have paths, as confirmed by Matthew Maury, in the 19th Century, after reading of them in the Bible.

Psalm 19:4-6 The Sun orbits. Harlow Shapley found that the Sun was not in the center of our galaxy. Using Kepler's Third Law, it was estimated that it takes the Sun 230 million Earth years to complete one orbit.

Psalms 90:4 Time is relative. The Theory Of Relativity was published by Albert Einstein in 1905.

Psalms 102:25, 26 The Law of Entropy was confirmed by William Thomson in the 19th century.

Psalm 103:12 "as far as east is from the west" given as immeasurable distance, infers the existence of a North and South Pole, the Earth's axis and its spherical nature.

PSALMS 104:6-8 Mountains rise and fall and were once under water.

Psalms 104:6-8 Plate tectonics were first proposed in 1912, by Alfred Wegener, as continental drift.

Psalm 135:7 That lightning fixes nitrogen was confirmed, by man, after the discovery of electricity.

Proverbs 8:27-29 Formation of continents.

Proverbs 17:22 That mood affects physical well-being was confirmed by modern psychiatry and psychology.

Ecclesiastes 1:6 That the winds follow a pattern was confirmed by Matthew Fontaine Maury, in the 19th century.

Ecclesiastes 1:7 The water cycle was gradually confirmed by man, starting in the 16ᵗʰ century.

Isaiah 40:22 That the Earth is a sphere was theorized through the centuries, but only visibly confirmed by the first human in space, Yuri Gagarin 1961.

Jeremiah 5:22 God set boundaries for the ocean. Recent discoveries show that the ocean floor is sinking. Due to sea level rise, it will self-balance

Jeremiah 33:22 Stars, like grains of sand, can't be counted. Even today, we can't count stars. Nor can we count the grains of sand on the beach. We can't even reach a consensus on the length of the coastline in the USA. Likewise, how far the beach extends on either side of the water.

Jeremiah 33:25 God established laws for nature. Man has gradually discovered the Laws of Nature.

Daniel 12:4 As the end nears, there will be ease of transportation and knowledge will increase. It is self-evident that we are there.

Jonah 2:5, 6 Mountains under the sea were confirmed with sonar in the 20ᵗʰ century.

Luke 17:33-36 At any given time, there is day and night on the face of the Earth. This may have been theorized for centuries but was confirmed with communications and space exploration.

Heb. 11:3 Creation is made of invisible elements. The atom was confirmed by JJ Thomson in the 1800's.

1 Corinthians 15:41 That each star is different was confirmed by modern astronomy.

2 Timothy 1:9 That time had a beginning was accepted by the public only after the Big Bang was accepted by science.

2 Peter 3:10 Nuclear process. Man's first nuclear detonation was in 1945.

Rev. 11:9-11 Satellites. The first satellite TV broadcast occurred in 1962.

Revelation 11:10 Internet and web commerce. The inhabitants of the Earth will communicate and send each other gifts within a three-day window.

Revelation 13:16-17 Personal ID chip, and the control of world commerce by one government. ID chips are already in use worldwide and will control commerce in the near future.

This is by no means a complete list. Use this list as a starter. Study the Bible and add your findings to the list on the margins. The book was written in antiquity by 40 writers. It was written on three continents: Africa; Asia; and Europe. Three different languages were used: Hebrew; Aramaic; and Greek. Given all these differences, how can it fit together as it does? Even more amazing, it contains over 1800 prophecies, some yet to be fulfilled. As you have seen in the list above, it contained important scientific facts, centuries before they were known. The Bible is not just a book, it is a living document. It was written for the entire history of mankind. Its unique style made it as useful to a man 2000 years ago, as to one in the present. The most incredible thing is that there are things within the Good Book that will only be useful to someone not yet born. As the sciences have advanced, it has revealed biblical truths. These truths are there for those who have the level of knowledge needed to understand them. I call your attention to Matthew 16:4 (9). What is the deeper meaning of this sign people were asking of Jesus? It does not seem merely proof of His deity. I think it is the common desire for man to know without doubt. No matter how much we know, we always fall short. The more we know, the more our ignorance is revealed. The men asking for a sign were religious, but would the question be the same if it had been asked by an atheist? Yes, it has remained the same through the millennium. The atheist of today would say "you claim that you are the son of God, prove it!" Nothing has changed.

Our planet Earth is home (10). It is home, not only to you and me, but it is also home to all of humanity that has ever existed. I hold a very controversial view on this matter. Not only do I accept that it is the only home we have had, but I think it is the only home we will ever have, in this physical world. The calls for mankind to explore and colonize other planets is always present. What amazes me more is that very learned men think of colonizing inhospitable places, like the Moon and Mars Please don't fall into that abyss. We are on Earth and stuck on this, our only home. Our physical existence is dependent upon a specific set of circumstances that, up to now, is only known to exist on Earth. We must have breathable air, food, water and warmth. Those are just the basics. The problem is that literally millions of things are needed to make those three things possible. It is obvious that I cannot list, and even less, explore each of those millions of needs. But I would like to explore the more obvious ones.

Let's begin with location. I'm sure you are familiar with the three most important things in real estate: location, location and location. Our planet is in the Goldilocks zone. This means neither too hot, nor too cold, just right. It is very curious that we are actually in our present location, as it is the oddball in our solar system (11). Every planet in our solar system is double the distance from the previous one. Our home is out of order. We are right between Venus and Mars when we should be where Mars is. But that would take us out of the Goldilocks zone. If that were not enough, the two planets that we fall between, have no magnetic shield to speak of. I would love to see a simulation of what would occur if Venus and Mars had an Earth-like shield. How would it interfere with our shield?

We have also been blessed with a proportionally large moon. As far as we know, the only one of its kind in the universe. Our moon is not really 'moon size'. The Moon is larger than the planet Pluto, and almost the size of Mercury. Without this disproportionally large moon, life on Earth might not be possible. Earth is in orbit around the right type of sun of the right age. The size of Earth along with its makeup is just right to sustain life. We have the right strength magnetic field to preserve life. The precision of the size and location of our planets, given that they influence every other planet, must be correct to very close tolerances. If not, then over time orbits would destabilize, and Earth would be out of the Goldilocks zone.

There is an obvious question that fits here. Is Earth our eternal home? We know that our Moon, for instance, is moving away from our planet. The progression is minuscule but relentless. This points to a finite date for Earth to stop hosting life. We also know that our Sun has existed for about 22 solar years. The total expected lifespan for our star is 42 solar years. But at 230 million Earth years per solar year, we have some time left. Make no mistake, this is not our eternal home, neither as individuals nor as a species. Yes, our home is temporary (12). This creation was specifically made for man and him alone. We have no biblical or scientific evidence that there is any physical life outside of Earth. The fate of the entire physical universe is tied to our fate. Along with the declarations of finality, comes the revelation of a new creation (13). Once the era of physicality is over, we will be in a new creation. Both our bodies and our habitat will be, as best as we can describe, multidimensional. Why is the universe so huge, if God made it for a physical being that could never experience all of it (14)? The question should be "Why would an unlimited God create a small, limited universe?" He gave us a new and wondrous creation with no end, regardless of how long we last. Remember, the original plan, which will happen after we resurrect, is for us to be eternal. How can an eternal physical being be housed in a finite small universe? Christ is an example of a resurrected human body. (15). He had a real body that could be touched, and he could do all the things that He could do before death, but without the limitations of a mortal body (16). He could talk (17), walk (18), eat (19), fellowship (20), reason (21), and interact as before (22). But His new existence allowed him to go through walls (23) and travel at the speed of thought (24). We can also deduce from verses, that our knowledge will be altered (25). We will know as we are known. It seems that we will have available to us (to a certain level) the knowledge that resides with our Creator.

Let's compare humanity to a computer network. We are terminals. God is the mainframe. We currently have limited access. This reminds me of a family member who was working in computers, early on. His hard drives did not fit in the palm of your hand. They were carried by forklifts. With those early computers, you were given limited access. The higher your position or authority, the higher your access. This meant that computer power was limited by level. If you were a vital player in the company, then your projects went ahead of the others. Well, we believers have access, though it is currently limited. But upon our physical death, our access will change. We will know, as we are known. We will have access to the knowledge held in the mainframe, if you will. No, we will never be mainframes. We will always be terminals. We will graduate from terminals to e-ternals. Our access will change from limited and temporal to unlimited and eternal.

We can be fairly certain that there was a 'time with no time'. This is a way of saying there was a time where time was eternity. We can imagine time emerging out of eternity. But what we can't imagine is eternity emerging out of anything else. If eternity is not eternal, then the previous state was nothing, nowhere. Nothing begets nothing, so eternity was always, or it never was. The fact that we exist in time, in this physical world, tells me that eternity is eternal. An eternity can only make sense to me if it has an eternal God within it (26). By definition, God, Himself, has to be eternal. I think it goes beyond Him being eternal. I think the only fitting definition for eternal is God. He knows all there is to know (27). If He did not, then He would not be all knowing. That would make Him ignorant. That would disqualify Him as God. The same can be said of immutability (28), love (29), grace (30), Holiness (31), sovereignty (32), Omnipotence (33) and Omnipresence (34). It makes no sense to ask from where God came. There was no place before Him from where He could have come. He could not have had a creator, for then He would not be The Creator. That would just beg the question of where God's creator came from? You can only reason that, at the end of it all, one thing is left. God and His dwelling are eternal. Only from this point, does existence make sense. Not only do things make sense, but you have closure. Not only do you have closure, but you have peace, God's peace, that surpasses all understanding. You accept God's existence, receive His gift of forgiveness of sins, and the guarantee of eternal life with Him. You have everlasting peace and truly live happily ever after.

Let's explore time as it relates to the physical universe and eternity. Within the physical world, if space is static, then so is time. This would be eternity. To keep the Sun from its rotation, you do not have to stop the orbits and rotation. If you stop time, or the emergence of time by spacetime replication, then the Sun would stop in its arc of travel. Likewise, if you reverse time, the Sun will seem to run back in its travel. No physical effects of inertia would be felt since you are not changing space, but time. It would then be possible for all autonomous life to keep moving forward in its progression, independent of what space was doing. In the case of the battle where Joshua defeated the five kings the Sun stopped in the sky (35). When King Hezekiah was given 15 more years of life, time was reversed, the evidence seen by the sun dial reversing by ten degrees (36). So apparently, autonomous self-propelled life need not be tied to The

Arrow Of Time. But The Arrow Of Time responds only to God's command. As physical beings within creation, we are children of the time into which we are born. We can decrease our clocks by fast travel or heavy gravity. But within this physical existence, we cannot time travel. If you try to reverse time, you hit the wall from which time is emerging. If you try to go into the future, you reach the same point due to the duality of space. So, the normal state of The Arrow Of Time is a relentless forward progression, albeit at different speeds, as relativity through replicating spacetime demands. If caught in a God-ordained reversal of time, you would not walk backwards. In other words, there is no biblical evidence that God has ever reversed time in the affairs of men. The time reversals have been in regard to inert matter. All evidence seems to show that God does not allow interference with the timeline.

I listed Exodus 10:21 and 23 in the beginning of this chapter, and highlighted the relevant scientific evidence within those two passages. I will revisit those two passages, because they cannot be covered properly in a short statement. There are four things, found within those two verses that I would like to expound upon: the darkness that could be felt, the immobilizing effect of the darkness, that the Israelites had light, and the significance of the denial of light to the Egyptians. First, darkness that can be felt. How can we say that we could feel the absence of light? For those of you who have truly understood RST, you know the answer. Light travels with space, if spacetime is stopped from replicating, then the resulting darkness can be felt, as if it were a wall. This is consistent with the next point. Secondly, the immobilizing effect of darkness. If light cannot travel, because space is stationary, then it takes effort to move throughout that space. I should point out that the time frame where this took place was ancient Egypt. Their method of starting fires was, we believed, a bow drill. I can tell you from experience that is not an easy way to start a fire. The easiest way they had to light a fire was with a fire. I suspect that each household would keep a fire going all the time. If not, they would have to start a fire to cook each of their meals, and to light torches or lamps to see at night. This begs the question; how could they be in darkness if each house kept a fire burning 24/7? This is the best evidence we have to show that they experienced more than just darkness. They experienced the immobile wall of dark energy of stationary spacetime. Thirdly, the Israelites had light. Well, at first glance, some could say that's no big deal, they are the Israe-lights. That is sharp of you, but their light came not from their name, but from God. If you notice the passage says, "the children of Israel had light in their dwellings". This seems to mean that their dwellings had light-ability, but not their environment. Fourth and lastly is the significance of denying the Egyptians light. The Egyptians were polytheistic. They had many gods. But Ra, the sun god was their chief god. You have to love God's sense of humor. Put the worshippers of the false sun god in darkness. It's hilarious.

Here is another instance where God's sense of humor is evident. I remind you of the epic faceoff between the 450 prophets of Baal (found in 1 Kings 18:16-45) versus the prophet of God, Elijah. This confrontation came after Elijah prayed to God to withhold rain from the land. It did not rain for three- and one-half years. At Mount Carmel, God's prophet tells the false prophets "Let's offer burnt offerings, but each side will have their god provide the fire." Try as they may, the 450 prophets of Baal could not get Baal to send fire to light the dry wood on the altar. Even with the aid of 400 prophets of asherah coming to their aid, not a single spark, nor bolt of lightning made its appearance. Elijah had ordered his altar, along with the wood and the sacrifice, to be drenched with water. The false prophets prayed for hours with no results, and Elijah mocked them. Paraphrasing, 'Cry louder! Perhaps he's talking or sleeping and must be awakened.' At the appointed time, Elijah prayed to God, and God sent fire that consumed everything upon the altar. Here is the hilarious thing. Baal was the god of weather. First, he was powerless to bring rain upon the land. Then, he was proven powerless to bring even a single bolt of lightning to the altar that was manned by his prophets. That's hilarious! A weather god who can't make rain or lightning.

Here's an interesting question. If I saw time stop tomorrow, since I think I know how it is done, would this make its occurrence less an act of God? This premise is at the heart of the atheist interpretation of the "God of the gaps" *. The fact that you understand what needs to happen, or how something can happen, does not remove God from being the God of creation. Take life for instance. An atheist would argue that if man was to make life from its inert components found on Earth, then we would prove that there is no God and we are equal to God. Nothing could be further from the truth. If we make life, we are not proving evolution, we are proving intelligent design. Could a dog develop the tools and the technology to make life? Of course not. Only humanity is capable of acts of creation at this level. I say, "at this level", because we can create new things with existing matter, or better said, from energy. We cannot, nor will we ever be able to make matter, or its basic component energy, from nothing. Being made in His image, we can create new things from existing matter. God said, "let Us make man in Our image (37)". You don't really think it's His physical attributes that we share, do you?

Some could be wondering how theology influences my thoughts on the shape, size, age, and expansion rate of the universe. The shape is the easiest of all. The shape of the universe has, is and will always be, a sphere. I could not add any more to what I have already said on this matter. On the size of the universe, the observable size is currently 93 billion light years across. Some have said it could be 250 thousand times more. My thoughts are that those estimates are but a fraction of reality. The age is, in my opinion, the most elusive of all. Age, I have said throughout the book, is in the eyes of the beholder. So when you ask about the age of the universe, you must specify to whom. Clearly, we specify age using time. The universe is ruled by Newtonian 'now' time, by the many time zones of Einsteinian relativistic time, and most importantly by Earth time, as seen from a perspective outside of time, by our creator. It is my belief that the Creator's perspective is the real and accurate measure of the age of the universe. This age comes in (using my poor math skills) at just under 7 days. The exact number that I calculate, for the true age of the universe, is 6.85 Earth days. As far as expansion rate, again, using whose frame of reference? Also pivotal is the question of size? I think this is one of the most meaningless questions that has ever been asked.

In my first work, I wrote a quote from a family member. His name was Joel Borges. We suffered his loss, this year. As I was in the process of getting ready to write the first book, he paid me a visit. The day he visited he called ahead of time to check if I was home. When he called, I remembered a conversation we had back in 1972. Discussing the Bible, he had told me that he did read the Bible, but did not consider it to be infallible. I asked him why? He said "Look, the Bible says that God will resurrect our bodies. When I die, I will be buried. Let's say there is a mango tree near my grave, and the roots pick up some of my nutrients. Someone picks a mango and when he eats it some of me will be in him. When God resurrects us both, who gets what?" Well, I had no answer for him. Fast forward to 2019 and his impending visit. I prayed and said "God, would it not be great if I could answer that question for him today. Before getting to the gate on the golf cart, the answer came. "Don't be silly, the body is just a vessel for the being inside". God has no need to match the atomic content of our bodies, in order to make us true to form. The arrangement of our atoms will be exact. We will be exactly (with no imperfections) who we are, possibly in an exact re-creation of when we were at our prime. Possibly, at around age 32. But there is no reason to think we will have our original atoms. Atoms have no discernable characteristics. Our bodies do not remain the same through time. The only thing that remains constant are our brain cells. I can see how it would be a problem to replace brain cells without losing our memories. If our bodies change their content over time, then which body gets resurrected? At the end of the day, we are energy. One last thing: we will have glorified bodies. That alone negates the possibility that we will be composed of the same atoms. I believe we will be a fusion of energy and trans-dimensional material, allowing us to do as Christ, to travel at the speed of thought. Also, we'll be able to do all that a physical being can do, but without the limitations of regular matter.

I would like to point out some hard stops, if you will, in the creation of the universe. These are points within creation, which do not have any explanation without direct divine intervention. Why hard stops. Because, without divine intervention, these things would either not start, or not stop. This is, by no means, conjuring up a god of the gaps. I do not subscribe to such a thing. God is the God of all. Without God there would be nothing. He not only made everything but sustains it (38). God can be seen within the Bible, creating Laws of Nature and beginnings having no explanation within those laws (39). For instance, the beginning, itself. There is no way we could ever justify a beginning without God. If there is no eternal God, then where did the energy come from to create the universe? Oh please, do not offend my intelligence by telling me that it is just a gap of knowledge that science will one day resolve. The beginning cannot be scientifically explained. Many attempts have already been made. Curiously, those that make the most sense are a departure from science. They fit more into beliefs, bordering on religion. I will not waste your time, nor mine, discussing all these flights of fancy. But I would like to give you one example. Let's take the recurring universe. This universe is said to be the result of a collapse of a previous universe: a 'Big Crunch'. This immediately brings up a question: Where did the previous universe come from? The answer given is that it came from the one before it, and so on into eternity. You see, at this point they have made a religion or a belief with nothing to support it, other than their imagination. All other explanations are, basically, a combination of things supported only by the imagination, in order to arrive at the inevitable starting point of eternity.

There can be no beginning without it beginning from within eternity. Nothing begets nothing. There can be no creation of a complex system without intelligence. Look at a few rocks on a trail and you don't see intelligence. If we see those same rocks spelling out words, you see intelligence. But if you engage your brain a bit further, you might ask "what are rocks?" I know they are energy, but how did that energy get here, and come together as a rock? Even if that happened, why isn't everything rock? Why did that same energy make the oxygen we breathe and living things, like trees? Then, the biggest question of all: "Whatever possessed energy to make me? How did energy make intelligence?" We are intelligent energy. To what length will man go to deny God? Here I'm afraid there are no limits (40).

Let's venture further into some of these hard stops. The first one: In the beginning, God created the Heavens and the Earth. In the beginning? The beginning of what? Obviously, it was not the beginning of eternity, because He was already there (41). This beginning is the beginning of the universe, the physical world. Prior to this, there was nothing physical. This is why scientific theories all break down at the beginning. Science is the study of the natural world. There are no tools in science's toolbox to go beyond the physical. We can't see past the beginning because nothing physically existed before this point. The only way to peer past the beginning is spiritually, with spiritual eyes (42). There was another very important intervention. God said, "let there be light" (43). One of the most common arguments of Bible critics is that the Bible says God made light without stars. Yes He did. Light preceded stars. But it goes further. He separated light from darkness (44). When He said "Let there be light", light came into existence. I believe this happened outside of time. Prior to the separation of light from darkness there was no time. Spacetime is revealed through light, and light is revealed in spacetime. The division between eternity and the physical and temporal was supernaturally split. From there, the focus shifts from the universe to the Earth (45). You will notice that He orders the universe into existence, but the Earth He orders in person. His attention to the Earth gives us evidence that Earth is the jewel in the universe. Even creation, itself, is described within Earth's time (46). The creation is described within 6 Earth days. There is no doubt that creation encompassed six 24 hour days (47). I would caution you to be mindful of relativity whenever time is expressed. Six days in the beginning looking forward. These same 6 days, for us looking back, are actually billions of years (48). Every time space doubles, time halves. Time, like beauty, is in the eyes of the beholder.

When the attention is focused on Earth, we see many more hard stops, or direct divine interventions. The Earth is said to be 'Formless and empty' (49). This is the normal state of the universe. No other planet has been found organized and filled with life as is Earth. I dare say that none other will ever be found. Could we find a bacterium, or some other basic life form, somewhere else? Yes, I think that is plausible. After all, God made the universe to sustain life. He also had the normal process of creation create the ingredients of life. The universe is, then, capable of sustaining life. Not only is it capable by design, but it has the right ingredients in its matter content (50). I do not think it possible that there is another planet in the entire universe which mimics Earth. Here I would like to tell you about an opinion of my first pastor Eugenio Castaneda. This is something that I personally do not subscribe to, but do not see it as beyond God's capacity or character. My pastor's opinion was that Earth was commanded by God to produce life, and it is still doing so (51). This, of course, is limited to essential components of an ecosystem. In other words, if in a given area a particularly essential form of life is somehow extinguished, it would reappear as it did in the beginning. At first thought it seems ludicrous. I would like to point out to you that there seems to be some evidence of this. Have you ever heard of a living fossil? How many times have you heard of a species declared extinct many years ago, to only see it reemerge? I realize that the Earth is a big place, and we could have just missed them, until one day we find them. But I have to believe that science would be diligent in their search for a species before declaring it extinct. I leave this concept of Earth 'reintroducing life forms' for you to decide if you believe it or not.

While on the subject of creation, I would like to talk about procreation. I think the biggest problem with the theory of evolution is the mystery of procreation. The Bible clearly states that creation was ordered by God to procreate according to its own kind (52). We can't begin to imagine the disaster of procreation across species. Take the bees for instance, as they gather nectar, they also pollinate the flowers. Both the bees that are gathering nectar, and those which are gathering pollen, are pollinating flowers. Even if they only gather nectar from one type of tree at a time, their bodies are never devoid of pollen. They always have the capacity to cross-pollinate. It is the division between types, ordained by God that maintains order (52).

How can we make sense of eternity? The answer is found in how we currently make sense of time. Have you noticed that regardless of the distance you travel on a trip, the first time takes the longest to get there? Why? Does it really vary so much, that your internal chronometer can perceive a difference? If you time yourself the first time you travel to a new place, and subsequent times, you will be surprised. It takes about the same time, each time. Furthermore, what happens if you are used to travelling there at 30 mph, and now the road is made into an expressway and the speed limit is 60 mph? You actually get there in half the time. But what happens to perception. Does it not seem that it is less than half the time? We can easily see that information, or the recording of information, changes our perception of time. I still remember how long it used to take me to get through a school year, just to get to summer vacation. Why did it seem so long? As a young man, I was recording much more information. Each packet of information is a recording point. It's like this book. I have to remember to save every so often. If I forget, all it takes is a power failure or a computer lock up, to lose a portion of what I have written. You computer savvy young people are saying that your word processor saves regularly, so it's recoverable. I know that. But I have a bad memory. Even the small part I lose, I might never recover. Speaking of the young, this ability of the young to record more is exactly why we school the young. All our abilities decline with age. This also explains why, as we age, that time seems to speed up. When you are young, if asked to remember the year you just went through, you are flooded with packets of information. When you are older, not only do you have less recording points, but all the points that share the same information are not seen as separate events. We no longer have the mental or sensory acuity to record similar events, separately.

How do all these happenings in the physical world help us understand eternity? Here it goes. Speed and awareness of information are seen to influence the perception of time. What happens if I make you travel at the speed of thought, all the while being able to experience every inch of the trip? How about if I give you all the knowledge of the universe? If you are aware of everything, how does that affect time? If time is perceived by the volume that you record, plus the separate recording points, then what happens if you know it all, and you see it all? Time for all practical purposes stops. It gives way to eternity. Question. Is there time in eternity? Yes and no. Remember how we discussed that between the number one and zero there is eternity? There is no limit into how many fractions you can divide a minute. If you record at smaller and smaller intervals, then it is easy to see why time would become meaningless. One last thing. Will we be governed by an impending end within eternity? Of course not. This was only life on Earth. On Earth, you knew you were racing toward death. In heaven, we have no such thought. If you are eternal, then you are in eternity. Is this the answer to understanding eternity? I believe not. This is but a taste of what is to come for the Christian (53).

What is to come to the non-Christian? What is their eternity? What will be their experience? I think, in the case of either group, it is impossible to know the mystery of eternity from within a temporal existence. If, as a lost soul, you experience only one second of eternity, then have you not experienced eternity? Personally, I believe that along with the new heavens and the new Earth, everything will be new. The non-believer will cease to exist. I cannot stress enough that this is pure speculation. There is no evidence of this in the Bible. More accurately, it seems to say the opposite. Perhaps, it is just a way for my feeble mind to have closure to such an unfortunate thing, as is a lost soul.

Is time the overall reality, or is there an independent reality, outside of time? The only choice I see is that reality preceded time. If there was no reality before time, then the universe also made reality. If reality is not real and eternal, then it came from nothing. Here again nothing begets nothing. There is existence in eternity, a place that seems to have no time. I think there is eternal time. This is not ruled by physical forces. But it does give eternity existence. It is curious that when the Bible speaks about the Timeless Creator, it does not say that time is meaningless to Him. But it gives us an example of equivalency (54). There is also evidence that human souls, in God's presence, are aware of the passage of time. Remember Revelation 6:10 (middle) "How long, O Lord, holy and true, dost thou not judge and avenge our blood on them that dwell on the Earth (55)?" This seems to mean that there is time within eternity, but without atrophy. This means that it does not rule its inhabitants, as it does in physical space. If you never die, does time have the same meaning it has now? If nothing gets old or wears out, can you put a time to that existence? Can our physical mind comprehend a time with a time that has no time? Where there is no perception of finite time or passage of time, comprehension of time is impossible?

The universe and time are like a wall. On one side is linear time, and on the other is eternity. We do not have the capacity to see into the other side. But God, on the other side of that wall, sees all before him (56). "It is not that God is everywhere. It is that everywhere is in front of God", Pastor Conrad De La Torres. He and His angels can choose to emerge into the physical universe at any given time. Being energy, they cross the barrier at will. This, by no means, says that God has any need to change our past. If He did need to, then it was already done (57). From our frame of reference, God resides in all places. In other words, He is omnipresent. If you live in a 'time with no time', you see all time in front of you. It's like a propeller at full throttle. It may exist in one spot in a given second, but, from our point of view, wherever you stick your finger in its path, you will find it. Furthermore, it does not mean that He does not respect man's God-given free will. There is no need to micromanage a complex system to achieve desired results. You need only tweak certain aspects of the present to alter the future drastically. It's like protecting Earth from an E.L.E (extinction-level event). There is no need to change the path of the comet or asteroid within Earth's view of it. If you nudge it with the touch of a feather, a few years before its arrival, the path would change by millions of miles within a few years' time.

I cannot pass up this opportunity to delve into free will. I have often debated this topic. This single concept is the catalyst for misunderstanding, both to the unbeliever as well as to the faithful believers. To the atheist, they use this topic to discredit the theist, by calling attention to their own belief, that if the future is known by God, then it is already set in stone. If this is the case, they say, then how can you be free to choose when the future cannot be changed. To the believer, this topic is also the source of controversy. At the foot of free will rages one of the oldest and more dividing topics in Christendom: whether salvation is by free will or by irresistible grace? These two choices, Calvinism versus Arminianism, were championed by John Calvin (1509-1564), and Jacobus Arminius

(1560-1609). A lot of you are familiar with this debate. Those who are not, do a quick search on the net, and it will get you up to speed. This topic is important enough that many books have been written about it. Most, if not all, books which discuss theology touch on this subject, and this book is no exception. I actually think that the debate is easily settled by what we have already discussed in the first 19 chapters. To sum up the evidence related to this topic from previous chapters: the future is known and is eternal because linear time resides within eternity. So, God knew who his people were even before the universe was created. Wait. Do not celebrate yet. This, by no means, can be used to prove irresistible grace. I don't believe that we can interpret the Biblical text to support Calvinism. I think that the universe gives us the illusion that Calvin was right. But there is clear evidence in the Bible that man has been given free will to choose. Clearly the two concepts have supporting evidence in both the Bible and in what we have covered in this book. Obviously they can't both be right, because these concepts are completely opposite.

After all I have learned and have written, here is my opinion on this matter. I believe both God and man choose. God chose in eternity, and man chooses in linear time. These two choices might look mutually exclusive, but they are not. Think of them, not as intersecting lines, but as parallel lines. They do not contradict each other. They coexist. It is God's will that none perish, but the Bible specifically says that Matt 7:14 "narrow is the way". Clearly a narrow way is an obstacle. No one who is remotely familiar with the attributes of God would contemplate a narrow way as an obstacle for God. We must, then, conclude that the obstacle is man's to overcome. Does God know the outcome of all the universe? Yes. Does this mean that you are trapped into playing a role you did not choose? Absolutely not. As a parent, many times have I foreseen, in my limited human ability, the negative impact of my children's decisions. Even after warning them, they, at times, proceed with the wrong choice. Respecting their choice (dependent on age and severity of mistake of course), all I have done is to get ready to help them with the consequences. If you allow me, I would like to give you an analogy. Free will, to me, is like the power in a car battery. There is potential between the negative and positive post, but only if a load is placed between the two posts will power flow and work be done. Is the battery power (salvation) available to all? Yes. Who will benefit? Those who choose to benefit from it.

There is evidence that, even in cases where God has announced what will happen, man's free will has changed the outcome. I remind you of Nineveh. I would also like to point you to study Jeremiah 18:7-10. Here, God, himself, tells us that the outcome can be changed based on our actions. In this matter, as in all else, it takes two to tango. Out of the two participants, only one can be sovereign. Of course, that is God. This is why His word states Rom 9:15 For he saith to Moises, I will have mercy on whom I will have mercy, and I will have compassion on whom I will have compassion KJV. Do you have free will to reject salvation? Most certainly. If not, the rich man who asked Jesus what he needed to do to be saved, could not have rejected Jesus. Jesus was all man but also all God. Can God choose a specific individual for a task and force the issue? We would not be honest if we said no, in the light of Paul and the Damascus road experience. Can God choose someone for a non-saved job? Again, we can't claim that God cannot choose someone to do a job that excludes him from salvation. This, in the light of Judas Iscariot. But that being said, does God not know the entire history of the universe? Yes, to God, time is seen from outside. He sees all that will happen because He is in the ultimate place ruled by no-time: eternity. So, at the end of the day, the question is irrelevant, because the answer to all aspects of this question is 'yes'. Did God give man free will? Yes. Can God, as the sovereign He is, predestine an individual? Yes (please note that this is my opinion, and it is highly controversial). Can man choose to reject salvation? Yes. There is one very important aspect of free will that is largely ignored. You have free will, predominantly as it relates to your relationship with God. You are not sovereign. Nowhere is this more clear than in your inability to interfere with God's plans, or others' free will.

We have a saying in my old country, Tanto nadar para morir en la orilla. Translated, (it would be a shame to) swim so far just to drown by the shore. Science has swum for thousands of years in a sea of speculation. When they finally achieve some level of success in any of their endeavors, they find that Bible scholars have been there for eons. The Bible is not a book of science, yet it has many bits of scientific information throughout its pages. There is still much we have not identified as science in the Bible, because it has not been discovered by science, as yet. God has given man free will. Free will implies that believing in God can only be done through faith. Free will is only possible if you have the ability to choose without being coerced. If the Bible contained a list of every star in our galaxy along with its mass, would you be free to believe or reject the word of God? No, I think only the insane could believe that primitive men, without the use of telescopes, could have counted the stars, or much less, could have found their mass. The word of God is coded to allow only those with the right knowledge level to understand its scientific statements. This is the only way that man's free will can be maintained. I have come to the conclusion that even though it is fragmented, the great leaps in science have been leaps inspired by God. Scientific leaps have been developed into theories: for example, Einstein's theory of relativity. These leaps, viewed from the vernacular of the age when they were presented, were not a progression of scientific belief. They were radical departures from the dogma of their time.

Both the atheist and the believer have an eternity problem. Namely, that you cannot explain eternity from within a linear relativistic temporal world. I do believe that the Christian has an edge, and the edge is this. We do not have to prove an eternal God, from within a created universe. He does not reside in our realm. At least, not in a way that can be experienced, scientifically. But, in turn, the non-believer has to fight, tooth and nail, for all that he believes, starting from the standpoint that he has to concede that the universe had a beginning. Yet, the energy from which it came must have preexisted in eternity. There is an argument that the energy came from the collapse of a previous universe, but that begs the question: "where did that other universe come from?" Then, of course, some have suggested that the energy was eternal. In response, I say that I do not have enough faith to believe that eternal non-sentient energy can be the catalyst for everything we see. Lastly, "the energy came from nothing". Not only is this a violation of everything science believes, but it is revolting to logic and common sense. I see only one logical answer. An eternal God is the prime mover. He is the source of energy and intelligence behind the design. Of course, this true God can only be the God of the Bible. I think the entire content of this book can be submitted as evidence to support that the God of the Bible is the one true God.

That which we mortals consider as real is made from the unseen, which is more real than what is seen (58). How can the unseen, or the spiritual, manifest itself in the physical world? The most logical explanation is that the spiritual is also energy. Energy can transcend or trespass energy with no interaction, or if desired, can move, shape, or mold the physical world at will. If this is the case, then why would the devil not destroy Earth and humanity? The answer comes down to authority. Even if he has the power, he lacks the authority to destroy that which God has created (59). Why, then, could he, and did he, manipulate man? He conned man into giving him the authority that had been given to this new creation, man. Man is unlike any other creation. It is seen in the love which God has bestowed upon us. What other creation has prompted God to allow His Son to die for them (60). From this, it becomes clear that the great hate shown by the devil toward humanity is sibling rivalry. Prior to man, the devil was the sum of all beauty and perfection, if you will. But, man was made in God's image, unlike all other creations that were merely utilitarian in nature (61). Even Lucifer was a manifestation of God's sense of beauty and perfection. But man was created in the image of the Creator. How must this have impacted the pride within Satan? He deemed man to be his replacement. The devil's entire existence was dedicated to the destruction of this new creature, his perceived replacement, mankind (62).

The universe is a wonder of wonders (63). There is no end to the incredible things that we can see and experience. Earth is definitely a jewel within creation (64). But no matter how wondrous creation is, there is one jewel that makes all of the rest pale in comparison. Mankind is that jewel (65). I accept man as the only sentient physical creation. I do not accept the existence of extraterrestrials or UFO's.

Mankind is unique. Our physical bodies are beyond wondrous. Each human being is unique. Our fingerprints, brains, cardiovascular system, eyes, DNA, among other things, are unique. Each of us is so unique that we are a species unto ourselves. There has never been, nor will there ever be, one like you. This, if nothing else, should drive home the thought of the sanctity of life. When a person is murdered, the loss is not that of a human being, but of a species. Our physical uniqueness pales in comparison to our spiritual uniqueness. When the Bible says God made man 'male and female He made them', this was a spiritual creation. Their bodies were fashioned later. All physical creation was done in the beginning. Man's body was made from matter which was already in existence. But his spirit was a separate and distinct creation. Animal life came from a command for the Earth to produce life. Man was brought to life by God's breath into our nostrils. No other creation, before or since, has had God's direct hands-on intervention. You are His beloved. He loved you so much that He gave His only son as a sacrifice to redeem you (60).

The uniqueness of the spiritual side of mankind is no mystery. After all, this was a direct creation of God (66). The physical body is another matter. Why would the same species be so different, physically? Man is different for the same reason that a snowflake is different. We are conceived after an act of intimacy between a man and a woman. In the act of intimacy, the man and woman share the same spacetime. We truly become one (67). This is why intimacy and monogamy is considered so sacred by God (68). Once conceived, the child grows in the womb, the woman's center. This explains the special bond between mother and child. The blending of the parent's DNA and the unique spacetime in which the child grows, gives us our uniqueness. This also explains the similarities in identical twins. Interestingly, their mother can tell them apart.

I want you to know that the word of God is not just another book. It is The Book. There is no other, nor will there ever be another like it. It is in its original form, the infallible Word of the Creator of all things (69). It has a literal meaning, but it also has a coded meaning (70). I do not mean just in the physical sense but also in the spiritual sense. I'm no theologian, but I will give you an example that my pastor and I discussed a few months ago. Have you ever wondered why God created male and female spiritually, before the physical body (71)? Then He created the woman's body from the man's body (72)? Here is the reason. The woman could not be a separate creation. She had to come from the man. If both man and woman were created separately, then they would be two species. As it stands, they are one, mankind (73). This allowed Jesus the Christ to be born of a woman, since it is Adam's seed that brings with it the inherited sin (74). A new Adam could be born of a woman but not through a fallen man (75). If they were not one species, then Christ could not save the males. A separate sacrifice would be needed to save the male. We have the evidence that God can procreate, as the male counterpart. This is what happened with Mary. Man, on the other hand, cannot be impregnated. Even if done supernaturally, an offspring coming from a male would be contaminated with inherited sin. Never mind that it would be a union of strange flesh, deemed a sin by God. Coming from a woman and God, Jesus was the second Adam, the only man other than Adam that had life in Him. Being of the right species, and having no sin, he paid the price for our sin: 'death'. Both male and female can be saved through the Blood of Jesus (60).

Allow me to explain why Adam and Jesus were the only two live men that ever lived. Adam, before his fall, was both physically and spiritually alive. After he sinned, he died spiritually immediately, and started the clock to his eventual physical death. The father had declared that the wages of sin is death (76). Jesus, the second Adam, was born spiritually and physically alive. This is why he could pay the price to redeem us from sin. You see, no other man was immortal. The most any other man could do was to give the rest of his life. But Christ, being immortal, could pay the price for our sins. Through one man, sin came into the world. Through one man, redemption is offered to the world (77).

It is only here that we can truly explore the spookiness of the quantum world. I refrained in the previous chapters from introducing the spiritual component ever-present in the natural world (78). According to the Copenhagen interpretation, Schrodinger's cat is not in any real position, until he is observed. Now, in all fairness, there are many other interpretations but being conservative, the original is the one for me. If you have not realized it yet, I'm very conservative by nature. I go so far as generally buying the original version of any product. Even as a youngster, I would always be sitting in gatherings where the elders were. This, I think, has paid off for me. I have learned to learn from those who have been there, who paid the ever-present cost of gathering experience. Our elders, for the most part, did not have the wealth of diagnostic equipment that their modern counterparts enjoy. Nowhere is that more evident than in the medical field. My current doctor, Dr. Salomon Mitrani-Sevy, makes me feel young, and believe me, I'm no spring chicken. I'm so old that when my kids were younger, one of my boys asked "Dad, did you get to see the dinosaurs"? Putting two fingers close together, I told him that I missed them by that much. It is almost magical to see one of these old masters, like my doctor, using modern test equipment, not to diagnose you, but to confirm what they already know. A lot can be said about the atmosphere and the talent that supports the original bedrock interpretation of quantum mechanics. The men and women that had a hand in the birth of these concepts were giants in science. Arguably, today we have equal talent. But I think that we have become too specialized. The further back you go, the broader the knowledge studied by individuals. As a result, they had, I think, a clearer understanding of the big picture. I also hold the view that the mind is similar to a muscle. If you want to be muscle-bound, then exercise, the harder the better. If you want to be more intelligent then read, study and think through all that is before you.

You could have gotten the idea that I do not think that there is anything spooky in quantum mechanics. But you would be very wrong. Allow me to illustrate. How about if, in the double slit experiment, we make a slit in the back screen. One which we can open and close, at will. This way, one photon can be allowed to keep traveling to meet a second double slit. We set up this second test, near, but out of view of the first group of observers. When the backdrop is observed by the second group, what will they see? Will they see a particle or a wave? I think they will see a particle. It has already passed through a filter of time. It belongs to linear time. Impressive follow up question: How about if it was observed at a distance, where light could not travel back to the original test site? If light can't get back, then neither can information, right? That is right. The particle observed, beyond the information horizon of the first test area, should act as a wave. "Are you sure" someone asked. No, but it is a good guess. Besides, you could never prove me wrong. If you did have proof, then your experiment would have failed. You see, we cannot know information from beyond the information horizon.

We could conclude that the information in the paragraph above is spooky enough. But there is an even bigger issue which we have not dealt with yet. The question is the following: How or what causes the actual collapse? What is the mechanism? If it is as I stated before, that taking a picture of a light photon should not interfere with its speed, then what? If the light photon remains at light speed when it goes through the double slits, it should be a wave. If it goes through at light speed and acts as a particle, then we have created reality by our observation. You can never truly understand something, if you cannot consider or view all of its components. The natural world is not eternal. Even science now agrees that there was a beginning. You cannot comprehend the physical world unless you can consider that it emerged out of eternity (79). This is clearly taught by the Bible. We could say that the biggest oxymoron is to call the universe natural. The most unnatural and foreign thing known to man, by far, is the universe. It is so unnatural that we, in spite of all our advances in science, are still puzzled by it. The visible came from the invisible (80). In the language of the Copenhagen interpretation, God is the ever-present observer (81). He is also Aristotle's prime mover (82), if you will forgive a cavalier comparison. He creates reality, as He is aware of everything. This also explains why the wave of probability would collapse, if viewed by man. We are made in God's image. Clearly, this is not a reference to His likeness, but to His attributes. While we do not share all of God's attributes, we share those that He gave us authority to wield. Mankind was given mastery over creation, Psalms 8:6 (83). This explains how the universe is sustained by God, the all-seeing observer. But, within man's field of influence, creation responds to his 'observation'.

I know most of you realized that the concept of a two-step universal order fits perfectly with the rest of the book. We see duality in spacetime. We see a two-step matter-making process. Who can forget the two times that rule the universe: Newtonian, and Einsteinian time? In the paragraph above, we see that God, being ever-present, is the universe's observer. While man, being physical, is the Earth-bound observer. Just as with the dual time system, this local and universal observation sustains reality in the universe.

The wave we see in quantum physics is not a wave. It is all of the possibilities observed simultaneously from linear time. At any given time, in timeless time, there is a common reality in the universe. This means that there must be something that inhabits such a place. That would be everything that travels at light speed. Beyond this reality of time with no-time (figuratively), there must be an even slower time, or faster time, depending on how you view it. This next place would be eternity, the place where the physical emanated and emanates from (82). The difference between our time and a place with no-time is as great as the difference between no-time and eternity. All these realities are just as real. Eternity, however, is the first and the last. So this means that the most real and elementary reality is eternity (2). One thing I'm certain of, is that all three time frames have a clock. That being said, I do not believe that God is governed by time (84). His presence has, is, and will be (from our vantage point) present in all realities and times (85). "It is not that God is everywhere, it is that everywhere is in front of God", Pastor Conrad De La Torres.

All of the happenings within a physical world can be explained by the physical descriptions. For the most part, even a supernatural force acting upon the creation would follow the laws of physics. However, there are biblical accounts of things that have no physical explanation. For instance, the sun standing still, or the running back of the sundial (86). To any honest observer, it is easy to see God's hand in creation. The Biblical account places God on Earth, arranging this planet to sustain life (87). Our planet is teaming with life. Even under the Arctic Ocean, the abundance of life rivals that found at the Great Barrier Reef. We have a clear picture of the rest of the planets in the solar system. They are dead, inhospitable places. There is no reason to think that the rest of the universe is any different. Why did God not make the supernatural more evident? I don't think that it is an accident we have been shielded from the supernatural. We are given to superstition. A careful study of the Bible will reveal that God hid many items from us. I will name a few: The Ark of the Covenant;

Noah's ark; Moses' body; and the Holy Grail. All of these items would be things which man would revere, and even worship, if they were with us. God has specifically said that worship belongs to Him, and to Him alone (88).

God gave man dominion over Earth (37). He gave us the ability to control, create, or destroy. The evidence actually shows that we have the ability, not only to change our surroundings, but to change the reality of the quantum world itself. From what we can deduce, creation was ordered into existence by God, through the power of His word and the word of His power (89). It seems that He programmed that first Fountain of God to multiply and create everything we see. I don't think modern man should have a hard time with the concept of programmed energy. We, being made in His image, are doing something very similar. How many machines and electronic devices carry out your wish through programming, ranging from smart coffee pots to our computers and cell phones? Every time you ask your phone to perform an operation it is responding to programmed instructions to carry out that task. God, in His infinite power, has the power to order energy to execute an orderly program. The evidence of this fact is all around us. We call those instructions the Laws of Nature. We have discovered the more obvious ones. But I suggest to you that the program put into effect by God, ordering energy to replicate, is beyond our comprehension. There is no way that we can understand the complexity. Here is an idea to start your mind along the path of imagining what I'm proposing. The program encoding energy to reproduce itself would make our current computer operating codes look like a stick-drawing compared to the Mona Lisa.

I know that some of you, especially the unbeliever, has a hard time understanding how so much information can be encoded in something so small. Must I remind you that in the micro realm there is no time? How many books can you read in eternity? There is current scientific evidence for what I'm proposing. Do a net search, "DNA capacity to store data". A single ounce of DNA can store over

6 billion gigabytes of data. You may ask how much a modern, solid state drive would weigh, if it had that capacity. Well, the current weight per terabyte, in solid state drives, is about 33 grams per terabyte (1000 gigabytes). This means that to equal the storage capacity of one ounce of DNA, you need 3,047,625 2T SSD drives. Those drives would come in at 443,445 pounds in order to equal the storage capacity of one ounce of DNA. To put this in perspective, there is about 74 terabytes (74000 gigabytes) of digitized information available from the Library of Congress, available online. The entire digital content of the Library of Congress could be recorded 81,081 times in one ounce of DNA.

There are many lines of code of the program (the Laws of Nature) within life on Earth, which are hidden in plain sight. As a farmer, I have seen many of these firsthand. Allow me to share just two examples, one found in bees, and the other in trees. Firstly, I keep bees for their honey, and for pollinating my fruit trees. I notice many programmed behaviors within these bee-brain insects. Let me pick just one: swarming. Swarming is the way bees split and create new colonies. You might think it is a learned behavior, but you would be wrong. Bee's life span is very short. Individual bees that participate in one swarm event will most likely never participate in a second swarm event. Well, we could say that it is an instinct, and of course, we would be right. I contend, however, that instincts are programmed in each animal, just like Laws of Nature are programmed into energy. To a person who is not a beekeeper, the swarming of bees seems like a simple process. In reality, it is a complex choreographed event with logistics and preplanning that would make a Fortune Five Hundred company green with envy. I'm only just past my first decade of beekeeping, so I know more experienced beekeepers could add to this description of the chain of events. I was taught by a master beekeeper. He spent all of his life learning bee behavior, and yet he knew he still had much to learn. Secondly, most of our products at the farm come from fruit trees. Trees at a glance look like simple things. However, they are among the most beautiful and wondrous creations that God gifted man. Even without the use of a brain, they accomplish some of the most vital and complex feats in creation.

Let's dip our toes into the universe that is beekeeping. Let's talk about swarming. First, the bees cannot start the process once they have run out of room in the box. They must anticipate the need to swarm. They can only know it's time if they can calculate that the soon-to-be emerging brood will put them into a situation where they will be crowded. These new bees will also give enough numbers, so that both the swarm and the mother hive have enough population. They must come to a consensus, so that everyone is on board to carry out the swarm process. Once the decision is made, the workers build several large queen bee cells to make new queens. Starting from day one, these bees, designated to be queens, are fed royal jelly. As the new queens get close to emerging, the mother queen is put on a diet by her attendants. This is done so that she can fly. Before the first new queen emerges, the original queen flies away with 75% of the workers. She leaves behind the nest, with plenty of workers yet to emerge plus a small group of nurse bees and guards. When the new queen emerges, she performs a mating flight, where she mates with several drones, and stores their semen to fertilize all the fertile eggs she will lay in her lifetime. In the meantime, the swarm that emerged, lands on a tree nearby and sends scouts to search for a suitable permanent home. As the scouts return, they dance to communicate the location of the home they found, and entice the swarm to move there, permanently. When they reach a consensus, they all fly away and settle in their new home. All of this complex behavior is not a result of their intelligence, their ability to imitate, or of a learned behavior. After all, they only possess little bee brains.

The other example of programmed behavior I would like to tell you about is seen in trees. I have witnessed many sick trees that are about to die bear larger amounts of fruit than normal. Why would a tree that is trying to survive expend its remaining reserves in fruiting one last time? It is a last effort to propagate its kind. Knowing these built-in programs, we farmers take advantage of this. For instance, there is a chemical we use on Longan trees to induce flowering, both in and out of their normal flowering season. It stresses the tree, making it think it is about to die and causes it to flower and set fruit. You may also look up avocado girding as another example of this programming. In girding, it should be made clear that only the girded branch reacts to the stress and increases fruit production. This should prove to any astute observer that we are not dealing with a whole tree, or a trunk-based action. It seems all of the wood on the tree shares this line of code.

"Wait a minute, Mister Farmer, that is an outlandish claim. Ridiculous! Programmed energy? Instincts are really lines of code that are part of a master program? You are out of your mind!". Well, you had better tell the people who are working furiously on quantum computers. They are trying to encode energy to perform as a processor. Quantum computing is no longer theoretical. I agree, it is not yet practical (at least what is public knowledge), but there is no longer any doubt that our next computing revolution will be quantum computers. These new machines will not be comparable to what we are currently using. This machine is a completely new animal. From what I have read, they work best if a standard supercomputer interacts with them. They are so fast and complex that humans are not compatible with them. To set up a problem for them to solve, you must first set all the parameters, in a modern supercomputer, to then engage the quantum computer. As I understand it, even the answer must be processed by a supercomputer, so that it is understandable to us. I know most of you do not understand why I'm making such a big deal about quantum computers. Regular computers get faster all the time, right? Most of us remember the 286, and 386, and who could forget the Pentium? My first computing experience was a TI57 Texas Instruments programmable scientific calculator. From there I went to a Radio Shack color computer, then a 386, which was soon followed by a 486. These last two, I can honestly say, were the first useful computers I owned. The next one was really fast in comparison, a Pentium 200. But none of these new machines were a real improvement, of course, when compared to a quantum computer. If you upgrade and get a computer twice as fast, then most of us would be happy. So how much faster is a quantum computer? Would you be impressed if I told you one million time faster than the fastest supercomputer? Well, you impress easily. Quantum supercomputers are actually estimated to be 100 trillion times faster than our fastest supercomputer. Keep in mind that a supercomputer is already many thousands of times faster than your PC.

Why is a quantum computer so fast? First, I would say that calling a quantum system a computer is like calling a Saturn V rocket a bottle rocket. I really think we should come up with a fitting name for these quantum computing systems. But why are they so fast? After having read this book, I think most of you are capable of answering this question. This computational device does its computing in virtually a 'time with no-time'. As I told you before, our quest for miniaturizing computer components has to do foremost with the advantage in speed. Computers cycle through information, and information has a speed limit. It is light speed, the speed of the universe. It is the speed of replicating space, replicating spacetime. Any time you move information to another component, the movement takes time. Now you see why a quantum processor can achieve such speeds. It is of quantum size. I remind you that if it takes little to no space, then it takes little to no time. If it resides in no time, it can do things in virtually no time. After whetting your appetite with this new technology, do you still doubt that God, the Creator of all things, is not capable of programming energy? Do you think it is beyond His capacity to program animal life? You are free to believe as you wish. It is your God-given free will. As for me, I see no other possibility than that everything in the universe is following a complex program. This program is imbedded in the energy that makes everything within the universe.

We have come a long way with cameras. The first ones had such slow acting shutters and photographic plates, that subjects had to be very still. Today, we can take a picture of a single photon of light. That's right! We can photograph something at light speed. Have you seen a picture of a road at night where the cars' headlights seem like streams? That's done by increasing the exposure time. Does it mean that the picture shows a car in continual travel? Yes and no. It covers a given time in a single picture. When you see a photograph of a faraway galaxy do you think that is a single picture? Those pictures are composed of hundreds to thousands of exposures over many days to many months. Those exposures are assembled or combined by computers. A single exposure would produce such low resolution that it would be unrecognizable. The reason is simple. Light, from any source scatters, or dilutes with distance. If you are up close to a light source, it covers your entire field of view. The further you are from any light source, the less intense the light. Light travels with space in straight lines. Upon emerging from a light source, a slight change in the angle of emergence can result in a very large difference in trajectory over a long distance. This also explains the perceived drop in size with distance. The further away an item, the less percentage of your field of view is occupied by said item. This size difference also gives you less photons from those smaller, more distant items. This is why we need to combine so many exposures into a single picture.

The next two paragraphs would fit best in an earlier chapter, perhaps the one bringing to light the Rosetta stone, or the chapter on time. Maybe they should have gotten their own chapter. I have placed them here, because I think you are now versed enough on these concepts to understand. More importantly, you are now fully clear on what is essential for creation to exist. The most important and central need, of course, is a Creator. How does replicating space really function? Well, rev-up your mind to its highest setting, and let's see if we can really understand this WOW that we call the universe. In the beginning, God created the heavens and the Earth. This beginning, I believe, was started by God ordering energy to replicate. This first spec of energy was, for lack of a better word, ordered to replicate itself into everything we see around us. But our language is inadequate to convey the full scope of what this programmed energy can do, and what it has done. It is important to realize that the smaller an entity is, the less it interacts with time. Even in today's fully developed time-based universe, particles are not part of the macro world. Being part of the micro world, they are within the realm of quantum mechanics. This is why, at times, no connection is seen between time and space in this tiny of tiniest worlds. In a manner of speaking, the less space, the less time. There comes a point in the diminishing dimensions of these minute sizes, that we can no longer distinguish time. We even have instances where we perceive a time reversal. As a frame of reference, linear time is inadequate to observe a time with no-time. I would like to remind you, that in our experience with computers, we strive to miniaturize components. It is not merely to make computers cheaper and lighter. The biggest advantage of miniaturization is to gain speed. This is driving the current race to develop quantum computers. Is it any wonder that God would use the smallest entity, God's Fountain, to encode the programming needed to create an entire universe? Here you must understand that, prior to the beginning, nothing physical existed. This physical creation was not needed for anything that existed prior to the universe's physical beginning. I see no other reason for the existence of the universe, other than to house man.

Back to the beginning. This first Fountain Of God was programmed to self-replicate without limit of space or time. There is no limit to how old, or how big this universe can become. This first Fountain started replicating at a speed that can't be measured. Why can't we know how fast the universe is expanding? Because this rapid expansion is happening in the Creation Rim, where there is no-time.

This beginning that started at the center, very quickly became the outer rim. Meanwhile, the Fountains within the sphere of the universe are continually replicating. There came a time when the outward expansion could no longer increase its speed. The pressure created by this ever-present spatial pressure gave us time (covered in Chapter 2). Along with time came light. Now, the matter that had been created by the Creation Rim came together and formed stars, planets, galaxies and everything else we see. It is important you understand how this spatial pressure is created. Without it, the universe can't function. Spacetime replicates from every point in space, and moves out at light speed. If the speed was cumulative, this universe would have ripped apart early on. Instead, as spacetime replicates, it moves out in every direction, encountering more of itself traveling in the opposite direction. This interaction of spacetime colliding with itself, makes time. This is why traveling at high speed slows your clock. It relieves spacetime pressure. The rest of the story you already know.

I truly hope that the universe has come alive in front of your eyes as you read this book. I thank you for the opportunity to present these concepts.

If you are a son or daughter of the living God, make sure you do not stop congregating, as some have done (90). I believe time is short. Let's bring in as much of the harvest as possible, while there is time. May God bless you, and yours.

Do you know the peace and joy of knowing you will live forever in God's presence? If you do not, then pray the words below.

Prayer to Receive Christ.

Lord God, I believe Jesus, the Christ, is Your Son, He came to this Earth, and lived among men. He, who knew no sin, was crucified, died and paid for my sins, and three days later you raised Him from the dead. I accept Him as Lord and savior of my life. Amen.

Welcome to the family of God. Be assured that your sins are paid and forgotten. As far as East is from the West, the Bible says that He has removed your transgressions. Notice it does not say North to

South. The Earth has a North and a South Pole. But East to West has no measurable distance because it is a circular measurement (91). Now, find yourself a good Bible-believing Church, and be faithful.

I hope and pray that everyone reading to this point are sons and daughters of the one and only God, the God of Abraham, Isaac, and Jacob, and now of you and me.

I hope to meet you one day, here, there, or in the air.

God bless you all, Amen.

GLOSSARY

The Fountain Of God: an intersecting point in the energy fabric of spacetime. These tiny quanta particles, or more likely, self-replicating energy fountains, are doing today that which one single specimen began doing 13.8 billion years ago. It is duplicating itself, emerging from a place yet unknown to us, possibly emerging out of its predecessor. Once the first Fountain of God emerged, all the ingredients of the universe were present within it. It is responsible for all of the pivotal characteristics of space. Among these are gravity, orbits, the heavenly bodies and structures, including galaxies and black holes. It gives us the theme of the circle, the steady universal temperature, and a planet's counter-rotating cores. Buoyancy, atmospheric pressure and even atomic structure and cohesion would be impossible without God's Fountain. It is spacetime, the medium, the construct, the matrix and the first and most basic building block of creation. It is responsible for what we have called Quantum Fluctuations. The constant addition of energy keeps the temperature from plummeting throughout the entire universe. A constant and stable temperature prevents the universe from falling victim to The Big Freeze. The expansion caused by the growth of space furnishes a constant spatial pressure, keeping The Big Rip at bay. Likewise, the constant outward expansion provided by spatial growth prevents The Big Crunch. I believe, as unfathomable as it sounds, that this God

Particle has the ability to duplicate itself with no further energy input required. Being irreducible it cannot merely divide. It makes an exact copy of itself. The Fountain Of God is the only elementary particle. All that exists in this physical universe is made of this energy quanta. It is the one and only true God particle or quanta. Its elementary manifestation is spacetime. The emergence of spacetime is a direct result of the physical reality caused by the replication and movement of this entity. It is indivisible being composed of nothing but energy. It replicates in 3D, creating spacetime at the speed of light. The scale is so minuscule that it is impossible to detect the Fountain of God, a true God particle, an energy quanta, using present technology. To put it in perspective, it is like trying to see the furthest of galaxies, using reading glasses. I hope you will fully understand Replicating Space. With the understanding of this concept comes the ability to understand the mysteries of the universe.

Solid energy: a state of matter that I imagine, with no other characteristic than that of energy.

Impersonating thinking: I.T. for short. Imagining oneself as the thing or the process which one wishes to study, to gain a more accurate picture.

Spatial Hammer: named after the water hammer effect observed in plumbing, it is basically a shock or attempt to compress a substance by means of a clash or a sudden stop, as it encounters a barrier. In the case of space, the resulting compression of energy creates matter, be it basic gases, but matter just the same

Replicating Space Theory: (RST) The concept that space is not merely stretching, but that it is replicating. This spatial growth is pivotal to creating and sustaining a viable, functioning, universe.

Spatial pressure: this pressure is created by the emerging spacetime, as it pushes to expand the universe. It self-limits the growth of the universe. This pressure is also responsible for the inflationary epoch. Its absence created the rapid inflation. Its presence applied the brakes. It is produced when the emergence of spacetime applies pressure to expand existing spacetime. Spatial pressure is analogous to atmospheric pressure, but it refers to energy, not gasses. Remember, gasses are matter which, of course, is energy. We have 14psi of air pressure at sea level. This is because gravity pushes those gasses toward Earth's surface. As it replicates, the emerging spacetime creates a similar effect, but one of energy. It is responsible, among other things, for time and the visibility of light.

God of the gaps: a concept held by most Christians including prominent theologians. 'We should not credit God only for the unexplained, since He is the creator of all'. If God is only credited for the unexplained, then as science finds explanations, God's credit would diminish. Many atheists have misquoted this concept, not realizing its true meaning. The concept was coined by Christians as a warning to fellow believers, not to make that mistake. Its origins are from the 19th century, possibly older.

New concept: believed by the writer to be a new way of looking at existing information, or the interpretation of completely new information.

Time with no time: real time, Now-time, and a 'time with no-time' are descriptions of Newtonian time. They can be thought of as the time at any point in the universe, at this exact moment. In other words, ever-present time. This time is not visible, because it is the realm of the micro world. It is as vital to the existence of the universe as is relativity. This 'time with no-time' allows for entanglement. It supports universal cohesion by allowing the entire universe to share the same existence. This prevents a break in the spacetime continuum. It does not suffer from the effects of relativity.

Nothingness: a non-existing area that has, or will be, brought into existence through the action of God's Fountain.

Spatial time zone: A concept by which spacetime is divided by zones. These zones are defined by speed, not locality. It is a product of space and time. All objects moving at the same speed share the same spatial time zone. All items at a different speed have different clock speeds. Direction or vector of travel is irrelevant: it is only speed that is relevant.

Zigzagging spacetime: the result of spacetime regenerating, within a medium that prevents it from traveling straight through: most notable in stars and planets. This causes time dilation, which, in turn, causes gravity.

Redshift: as it refers to light, Redshift is a phenomenon where light from objects undergoes an increase in wavelength, shifting toward the red side of the spectrum. Extremely useful in finding distances in cosmology.

BIBLIOGRAPHY

1   Genesis 1:1 In the beginning God created the heaven and the earth. KJV

2   Romans 1:20 For the invisible things of him from the creation of the world are clearly seen, being understood by the things that are made, even his eternal power and Godhead; so that they are without excuse: KJV

3   Exodus 3:14 And God said unto Moses, I Am That I Am: and he said, Thus shalt thou say unto the children of Israel, I Am hath sent me unto you. KJV

4   Isaiah 45:5 I am the Lord, and there is none else, there is no God beside me: I girded thee, though thou hast not known me: KJV

5   Psalm 19:1 The heavens declare the glory of God; and the firmament sheweth his handywork. KJV

6   Hebrews 4:12 For the word of God is quick, and powerful, and sharper than any twoedged sword, piercing even to the dividing asunder of soul and spirit, and of the joints and marrow, and is a discerner of the thoughts and intents of the heart. KJV

7   John 3:3 Jesus answered and said unto him, Verily, verily, I say unto thee, Except a man be born again, he cannot see the kingdom of God. KJV

8   2 Timothy 3:16 All scripture is given by inspiration of God, and is profitable for doctrine, for reproof, for correction, for instruction in righteousness: KJV

9   Matthew 16:4 A wicked and adulterous generation seeketh after a sign; and there shall no sign be given unto it, but the sign of the prophet Jonas. And he left them, and departed. KJV

10 Psalm 115:16 The heaven, even the heavens, are the Lord's: but the earth hath he given to the children of men. KJV

11 Isaiah 45:12 I have made the earth, and created man upon it: I, even my hands, have stretched out the heavens, and all their host have I commanded. KJV

12 2 Corinthians 4:18 While we look not at the things which are seen, but at the things which are not seen: for the things which are seen are temporal; but the things which are not seen are eternal. KJV

13 Revelation 21:1 And I saw a new heaven and a new earth: for the first heaven and the first earth were passed away; and there was no more sea. KJV

14 Daniel 4:3 how great are his signs! and how mighty are his wonders! his kingdom is an everlasting kingdom, and his dominion is from generation to generation. KJV

15 Romans 8:11 But if the Spirit of him that raised up Jesus from the dead dwell in you, he that raised up Christ from the dead shall also quicken your mortal bodies by his Spirit that dwelleth in you. KJV

16 John 20:27 Then saith he to Thomas, Reach hither thy finger, and behold my hands; and reach hither thy hand, and thrust it into my side: and be not faithless, but believing. KJV

17 John 20:16 Jesus saith unto her, Mary. She turned herself, and saith unto him, Rabboni; which is to say, Master. KJV

18 Luke 24:15 And it came to pass, that, while they communed together and reasoned, Jesus himself drew near, and went with them. KJV

19 Luke 24:42-43 And they gave him a piece of a broiled fish, and of an honeycomb. 43 And he took it, and did eat before them. KJV

20 Luke 24:30 And it came to pass, as he sat at meat with them, he took bread, and blessed it, and brake, and gave to them. KJV

21 Luke 24:19 And he said unto them, What things? And they said unto him, Concerning Jesus of Nazareth, which was a prophet mighty in deed and word before God and all the people: KJV

22 Luke 24:27 And beginning at Moses and all the prophets, he expounded unto them in all the scriptures the things concerning himself. KJV

23 John 20:19 Then the same day at evening, being the first day of the week, when the doors were shut where the disciples were assembled for fear of the Jews, came Jesus and stood in the midst, and saith unto them, Peace be unto you. KJV

24 Luke 24:36 And as they thus spake, Jesus himself stood in the midst of them, and saith unto them, Peace be unto you. KJV

25 1 Corinthians 13:12 For now we see through a glass, darkly; but then face to face: now I know in part; but then shall I know even as also I am known. KJV

26 Revelation 22:13 I am Alpha and Omega, the beginning and the end, the first and the last. KJV

27 Psalm 147:4-5 He telleth the number of the stars; he calleth them all by their names. 5 Great is our Lord, and of great power: his understanding is infinite. KJV

28 Psalm 102:27 But thou art the same, and thy years shall have no end. KJV

29 1 John 4:8 He that loveth not knoweth not God; for God is love. KJV

30 Titus 2:11 For the grace of God that bringeth salvation hath appeared to all men KJV

31 Isaiah 6:3 And one cried unto another, and said, Holy, holy, holy, is the Lord of hosts: the whole earth is full of his glory. KJV

32 Isaiah 46:9-10 Remember the former things of old: for I am God, and there is none else; I am God, and there is none like me, 10 Declaring the end from the beginning, and from ancient times the things that are not yet done, saying, My counsel shall stand, and I will do all my pleasure KJV

33 Luke 1:37 For with God nothing shall be impossible KJV

34 Job 34:21 For his eyes are upon the ways of man, and he seeth all his goings. KJV

35 Joshua 10:12 Then spake Joshua to the Lord in the day when the Lord delivered up the Amorites before the children of Israel, and he said in the sight of Israel, Sun, stand thou still upon Gibeon; and thou, Moon, in the valley of Ajalon. KJV

36 Isaiah 38:8 Behold, I will bring again the shadow of the degrees, which is gone down in the sundial of Ahaz, ten degrees backward. So the sun returned ten degrees, by which degrees it was gone down. KJV

37 Genesis 1:26 And God said, Let us make man in our image, after our likeness: and let them have dominion over the fish of the sea, and over the fowl of the air, and over the cattle, and over all the earth, and over every creeping thing that creepeth upon the earth. KJV

38 1 Corinthians 8:6 But to us there is but one God, the Father, of whom are all things, and we in him; and one Lord Jesus Christ, by whom are all things, and we by him. KJV

39 Jeremiah 33:25 Thus saith the Lord; If my covenant be not with day and night, and if I have not appointed the ordinances of heaven and earth KJV

40 Psalm 14:1 The fool hath said in his heart, There is no God. They are corrupt, they have done abominable works, there is none that doeth good.

41 Revelation 1:8 I am Alpha and Omega, the beginning and the ending, saith the Lord, which is, and which was, and which is to come, the Almighty. KJV

42 2 Kings 6:17 And Elisha prayed, and said, Lord, I pray thee, open his eyes, that he may see. And the Lord opened the eyes of the young man; and he saw: and, behold, the mountain was full of horses and chariots of fire round about Elisha KJV

43 Genesis 1:3 And God said, Let there be light: and there was light KJV

44 Genesis 1:4 And God saw the light, that it was good: and God divided the light from the darkness KJV

45 Genesis 1:6 And God said, Let there be a firmament in the midst of the waters, and let it divide the waters from the waters KJV

46 Genesis 1:5 And God called the light Day, and the darkness he called Night. And the evening and the morning were the first day KJV

47 Genesis 2:2 And on the seventh day God ended his work which he had made; and he rested on the seventh day from all his work which he had made KJV

48 Psalm 44:1 We have heard with our ears, O God, our fathers have told us, what work thou didst in their days, in the times of old KJV

49 Genesis 1:2 And the earth was without form, and void; and darkness was upon the face of the deep. And the Spirit of God moved upon the face of the waters KJV

50 Genesis 3:19 In the sweat of thy face shalt thou eat bread, till thou return unto the ground; for out of it wast thou taken: for dust thou art, and unto dust shalt thou return KJV

51 Genesis 1:24 And God said, Let the earth bring forth the living creature after his kind, cattle, and creeping thing, and beast of the earth after his kind: and it was so KJV

52 Genesis 1:12 And the earth brought forth grass, and herb yielding seed after his kind, and the tree yielding fruit, whose seed was in itself, after his kind: and God saw that it was good KJV

53 Revelation 21:4 And God shall wipe away all tears from their eyes; and there shall be no more death, neither sorrow, nor crying, neither shall there be any more pain: for the former things are passed away KJV

54 2 Peter 3:8 But, beloved, be not ignorant of this one thing, that one day is with the Lord as a thousand years, and a thousand years as one day KJV

55 Revelation 6:10 And they cried with a loud voice, saying, How long, O Lord, holy and true, dost thou not judge and avenge our blood on them that dwell on the earth? KJV

56 Proverbs 15:3 The eyes of the Lord are in every place, beholding the evil and the good KJV

57 Psalm 33:11 The counsel of the Lord standeth for ever, the thoughts of his heart to all generations KJV

58 Hebrews 11:3 Through faith we understand that the worlds were framed by the word of God, so that things which are seen were not made of things which do appear. KJV

59 Job 1:12 And the Lord said unto Satan, Behold, all that he hath is in thy power; only upon himself put not forth thine hand. So Satan went forth from the presence of the Lord. KJV

60 John 3:16 For God so loved the world, that he gave his only begotten Son, that whosoever believeth in him should not perish, but have everlasting life. KJV

61 Genesis 1:28 And God blessed them, and God said unto them, Be fruitful, and multiply, and replenish the earth, and subdue it: and have dominion over the fish of the sea, and over the fowl of the air, and over every living thing that moveth upon the earth. KJV

62 John 10:10 The thief cometh not, but for to steal, and to kill, and to destroy: I am come that they might have life, and that they might have it more abundantly. KJV

63 Psalm 40:5 Many, O Lord my God, are thy wonderful works which thou hast done, and thy thoughts which are to us-ward: they cannot be reckoned up in order unto thee: if I would declare and speak of them, they are more than can be numbered. KJV

64 Genesis 1:31 And God saw every thing that he had made, and, behold, it was very good. And the evening and the morning were the sixth day. KJV

65 Psalm 139:14 I will praise thee; for I am fearfully and wonderfully made: marvellous are thy works; and that my soul knoweth right well. KJV

66 Matthew 19:4-5 4 And he answered and said unto them, Have ye not read, that he which made them at the beginning made them male and female, 5 And said, For this cause shall a man leave father and mother, and shall cleave to his wife: and they twain shall be one flesh? KJV

67 Genesis 2:24 Therefore shall a man leave his father and his mother, and shall cleave unto his wife: and they shall be one flesh. KJV

68 Matthew 19:4-6 And he answered and said unto them, Have ye not read, that he which made them at the beginning made them male and female, 5 And said, For this cause shall a man leave father and mother, and shall cleave to his wife: and they twain shall be one flesh? 6 Wherefore they are no more twain, but one flesh. What therefore God hath joined together, let not man put asunder. KJV

69 Psalm 19:7-11 7 The law of the Lord is perfect, converting the soul: the testimony of the Lord is sure, making wise the simple. 8 The statutes of the Lord are right, rejoicing the heart: the commandment of the Lord is pure, enlightening the eyes. 9 The fear of the Lord is clean, enduring for ever: the judgments of the Lord are true and righteous altogether. 10 More to be desired are they than gold, yea, than much fine gold: sweeter also than honey and the honeycomb. 11 Moreover by them is thy servant warned: and in keeping of them there is great reward.

70 John 5:39 Search the scriptures; for in them ye think ye have eternal life: and they are they which testify of me. KJV

71 Genesis 1:27 So God created man in his own image, in the image of God created he him; male and female created he them. KJV

72 Genesis 2:22 And the rib, which the LORD God had taken from man, made he a woman, and brought her unto the man. KJV

73 Genesis 5:2 Male and female created he them; and blessed them, and called their name Adam, in the day when they were created. KJV

74 Romans 5:12 Therefore, just as sin entered the world through one man, and death through sin, and in this way death came to all people, because all sinned—KJV

75 Isaiah 7:14 Therefore the Lord himself will give you a sign: The virgin will conceive and give birth to a son, and will call him Immanuel. KJV

76 Romans 6:23 For the wages of sin is death; but the gift of God is eternal life through Jesus Christ our Lord. KJV

77 Romans 5:17 For if by one man's offence death reigned by one; much more they which receive abundance of grace and of the gift of righteousness shall reign in life by one, Jesus Christ.) KJV

78 Psalm 19:1-4 1 The heavens declare the glory of God; and the firmament sheweth his handywork. 2 Day unto day uttereth speech, and night unto night sheweth knowledge. 3 There is no speech nor language, where their voice is not heard. 4 Their line is gone out through all the earth, and their words to the end of the world. In them hath he set a tabernacle for the sun, KJV

79 Psalm 102:25-26 25 Of old hast thou laid the foundation of the earth: and the heavens are the work of thy hands. 26 They shall perish, but thou shalt endure: yea, all of them shall wax old like a garment; as a vesture shalt thou change them,

80 Job 38:4-6 4 Where wast thou when I laid the foundations of the earth? declare, if thou hast understanding.5 Who hath laid the measures thereof, if thou knowest? or who hath stretched the line upon it?6 Whereupon are the foundations thereof fastened? or who laid the corner stone thereof; KJV

81 Colossians 1:17 And he is before all things, and by him all things consist. KJV

82 Colossians 1:16 For by him were all things created, that are in heaven, and that are in earth, visible and invisible, whether they be thrones, or dominions, or principalities, or powers: all things were created by him, and for him: KJV

83 Psalm 8:6 Thou madest him to have dominion over the works of thy hands; thou hast put all things under his feet: KJV

84 Isaiah 57:15 For thus saith the high and lofty One that inhabiteth eternity, whose name is Holy; I dwell in the high and holy place, with him also that is of a contrite and humble spirit, to revive the spirit of the humble, and to revive the heart of the contrite ones. KJV

85 Jeremiah 23:24 Can any hide himself in secret places that I shall not see him? saith the Lord. Do not I fill heaven and earth? saith the Lord. KJV

86 Joshua 10:12 Then spake Joshua to the Lord in the day when the Lord delivered up the Amorites before the children of Israel, and he said in the sight of Israel, Sun, stand thou still upon Gibeon; and thou, Moon, in the valley of Ajalon. Isaiah 38:8 I will make the shadow cast by the sun go back the ten steps it has gone down on the stairway of Ahaz."' So the sunlight went back the ten steps it had gone down. KJV

87 Genesis 1:9 And God said, Let the waters under the heaven be gathered together unto one place, and let the dry land appear: and it was so. KJV

88 Luke 4:4 And Jesus answered and said unto him, Get thee behind me, Satan: for it is written, Thou shalt worship the Lord thy God, and him only shalt thou serve. KJV

89 Isaiah 55:11 So shall my word be that goeth forth out of my mouth: it shall not return unto me void, but it shall accomplish that which I please, and it shall prosper in the thing whereto I sent it. KJV

90 Hebrews 10:25 Not forsaking the assembling of ourselves together, as the manner of some is; but exhorting one another: and so much the more, as ye see the day approaching. KJV

91 Psalm 103:12 As far as the east is from the west, so far hath he removed our transgressions from us. KJV